Be Full of Yourself!

The Journey from
Self-Criticism to Self-Celebration

PATRICIA LYNN REILLY

OPEN WINDOW CREATIONS

CALIFORNIA

I dedicate this book to my grandmother,
Catherine Smith Reilly (1902-1963),
Daughter of Anna Tyndale Smith,
Granddaughter of Anna Neville Tyndale,
Great-granddaughter of Catherine Kelly Neville,
In gratitude for her ongoing inspiration.

Blessed are you among women, dear Grandma.
When the challenges of life loom large, I imagine sitting on your lap.
While there, I am comforted by your unconditional love.
While out in the world doing what I'm called to do,
You remind me that home is always waiting.
That I can always return home again, to your lap.
I honor your spunky loving spirit in every word of this book.

Published by Open Window Creations
P. O. Box 493, Gualala, California 95445

Text design by Emily Douglas
Cover concept by Patricia Lynn Reilly
Cover design by Emily Douglas and Ann Kelly
Cover photograph by Jon Michelle Addor

ISBN 0-9661642-0-2
Library of Congress Catalog Card Number: 98-91322

How To Order: Copies may be ordered from Open Window Creations, P.O. Box 493, Gualala, California 95445, fax/telephone:
707-785-1902, e-mail: openwin.mcn.org. Quantity discounts are
available. See appendix for companion resources.

PRINTED IN THE UNITED STATES OF AMERICA

CONTENTS

LIST OF EXERCISES, MEDITATIONS, AND RITUALS

LIST OF CONTRIBUTORS

Acknowledgments

I acknowledge with gratitude the friends, colleagues, and sisters-on-the-journey who contributed their poetry, prose, and self-celebrations to Be Full of Yourself! *Thank-you for sharing your stories and lives with me. Many readers will be blessed by your words. Thanks, too, for your practical support along the way—meals on my doorstep, rituals to encourage me in challenging moments, careful readings of the manuscript, and wise feedback at every stage of the book's evolution.*

And special thanks to Nick Molinari who read the manuscript from a man's perspective. In Chapter 7, I have included an example of his courage to speak the truth challenging inequality.

Carroll Begley, Jennifer Biehn, Gretchen Blais, Mary Bolling, Valerie Bowman, Mimi Carlson, Joanne Coleman, Karla Crescenta, Carla De Sola, Carolyn Edwards, Mani Feniger, Amy Fishbach, Cristina Goulart, Isie Hanson, Karen Heide, Katie Hendricks, Elizabeth Jensen, Emily Krahn, Annette LaPorte, Olivia Lara, Ginny Logan, Joan Lohman, Robbie Lottero, Mary Ellen McNelly, Carol Marshall, Patricia Meadows, Irene Nicol, Marcelline Niemann, Cody Douglas Oreck, Debby Ostlund, Maria Ramos, Ferrel Rao, Rita Reed, Freda Rhodes, Elena Richmond, Elizabeth River, Beverly Roach, Karen Schnietz, Erin Louise Stewart, Susan Scott, Sophia Serrena, Nancy Smith, Maria Elena Springsted, Jane Sterrett , Donna Strachan-Ledbetter, Amy Weintraub, Kris Welch, Colleen West, Kate Wolf-Pizor, Patrice Wynne, Kris, Carlene, and Becky.

I acknowledge with gratitude the "Circle of One Hundred and Sixty Good Folks" who helped Open Window Creations raise the money to get Be Full of Yourself! *to the printers. Thank-you for your belief in the project and your willingness to support it before you could hold the actual book in your hands. Thank-you for imagining the book into being with your monetary support.*

Cody Douglas Oreck, Karla Crescenta, Elena Richmond, Erin Louise Stewart, Claire Dixson, Jean Hauser, Mary Bo Gassman, Donna Strachan-Ledbetter, Nancy Ahern, Kathy Hainsworth, Mary Ann Christian, Yvette Rudnitski, Carroll Begley, Nancy Smith, Amy Fishbach, Madeline Steeg, Emily Douglas, Kate Wolf-Pizor, Suzanne Alterman, Theresa Draught, Sharon Vandegrift, Sue Brinton, Marie & Nick Molinari, Carol Marshall, Allyson Rickart, Susan Scott, Karen Schnietz, Ferrel Rao, Jane Sterrett, Irene Nicol, Carla DeSola, Charlotte Monte, Maria Ramos, Jennifer Biehn & Joan Lohman, Elizabeth Jensen, Geraldine Stone, Beverly Roach, Mani Feniger, Valerie Bowman, Toby Berlin, Becky Teel, Lin Carleen, Robbie Lottero & Jean Ledoux, Anna Page Lucas, Teresa Lampton, Mary Lynch, Ray Reiss, Linda Sylvestri, Patricia Meadows, Nancy Smith, Margaret Rose, Sharyn Peterson, Carol Stockwell, Cheryl Marshall, Olivia Lara, Lloyd & Lynn Fickett, Rosemary Howes, Esther Lorance, Carol Rand, Claire Robbat, Sally Yeomans, Colleen West, Kris Morton, Elizabeth River, Bellavia, Robert Carroll, Yvette Rudnitski, Kathy Rampton, Gina Zeller, Arlene Hagoski, Barbara Lyon, Sarah Herbold, Jess Blackstone, Elaine Lee, Cynthia Kimball, Jennifer Eshelman, Susan Branscome, Mary Hazlet, Sarah Speaker, Patricia Schwartz, Linda Lundborg, Rebecca Simon, Grethchen Blais, Amy Weintraub, G. C. Mc Cool, Chuck Henry, Sheri Orne, Elizabeth Jensen, Jodie Hollinger-Lant, Marcelle Moran, Brenda Hilger, Lee Ann Schlaf, Jill Becker, Susan Auglis, Joayn Milazzo, Jocelyn & Robbie Dunbar, Connie Hewlett, Diane Gornell, Anna Griffin, Nancy Hood, Lucy Bonacquist, Anne Borregine, Virginia Costich, Elizabeth Weiss, Linda Allen, Rita J. Wolf, Jo Ann Smith, Mary Becker, Julie Keefer, Becky Stover, Phyllis Meyer, Julie Vinson-Clarke, Ardis Westwood & Rod Aurada, Wendy Barry & Richard Owens, Cristina Goulart, Priscilla Hine, Lacy Gargan, Mary Ann Christian, Barbara Rogers, Gloria Bisaccia, Leslie Perkins, Annette LaPorte, Jennifer Louden, Ginger Kaneshiro, Isie Hanson, Karen Cabral, Karen Clark, Marcelline Niemann, Michelle Massey, Barbara Jean, Lacy Gargan, Carol Dovi, MeShelle Charles, Wanda Kelley, J.S. Bulau, and Evelyn Eads.

Introduction: An Overview of the Journey

*The long work of turning their lives
into a celebration is not easy . . .*

—MARY OLIVER, *"The Sunflowers"*

Sitting in a Twelve Step meeting several years ago, I listened as a woman spoke about learning to trust the God of her understanding: "When I let Higher Power take charge, everything works out fine. When I'm in the driver's seat, I blow it every time." Inspired by her talk, several other women acknowledged that they were fundamentally ill-equipped to deal with life. Based on their sense of inadequacy, each one found it necessary to "surrender" to a power greater than themselves. Later that week I sat in a women's support circle as a woman complained about the unavailability of her therapist who was on vacation: "I have to see her every week or things begin to fall apart around me. I don't seem to have what it takes to live my life without the assistance of a trained professional."

While on the book tour supporting my first book's presence in the world, I was interviewed on a religious radio show. During the call-in part of the program, the inevitable question about sin and salvation was asked, "Do you believe we are sinners and in need of the salvation God offers?" I told the caller that my own inner wisdom was trustworthy and that it was communicated to me through my natural impulses, instincts, and intuition. I no longer needed the salvation offered by gods, higher powers, therapists, or gurus. The caller was appalled. "We can't trust ourselves," she exclaimed, "we are sinful and left to our own devices, we will mess things up every time. God is the only trustworthy one."

"You may not be able to trust yourself," I responded, "but I have learned to trust myself and so have the women with whom I sit in circle. We no longer choose to expend our precious life energy scrutinizing every facet of our beings to figure out what is wrong with us. Instead, we celebrate ourselves as gifted and powerful children of life."

Yes, today I experience the trustworthiness of my natural impulses, instincts, and intuition. Trusted, they do not lead me to commit horrible acts of sin, to make self-destructive choices, or to fall into psychological waywardness. Rather, they blossom into life-affirming behaviors that bring creativity, satisfaction, and joy to me and to my friends, colleagues, and chosen family. Today at 47 I celebrate myself as a child of life. It has been a long journey from self-criticism to self-celebration.

A MINISTRY AMONG WOMEN

While at Princeton Theological Seminary, I looked at my life through a wide angle lens to consider the historical, religious, and familial contexts within which my attitudes toward myself had been shaped. On a personal level, I took responsibility for my healing journey by exploring the nature and impact of alcoholism on family systems. Over time, I realized that I didn't cause the craziness in my family of origin—alcoholism has a life of its own within the family. Simultaneously, I sought to unravel the "veil of shame" that had been my constant companion since childhood. In rare moments, I experienced the veil lift, allowing me freedom of expression and a sense of deep satisfaction with myself. I longed for those momentary feelings to be my ongoing experience. Acknowledging childhood's influence on my adult life, I chose to walk through my past to heal into the present.

Studying at the Women's Theological Center in Cambridge, Massachusetts, I explored the systemic dimensions of my seemingly personal journey. The roots of my self-critical attitudes were traced to the influential doctrines of Western civilization, the idolatry of the Judeo-Christian male God, the establishment of a hierarchical paradigm that assumes my inferiority, and the historical linkage of women's inferiority with "the veil of shame." Along the way, I assumed intellectual and theological equality with the gods of traditional religion and Western civilization and their sacred text, the Bible. The dethronement of the male God was a crucial task on my journey. My imagination, intellect, and vision were freed of the shackles of a lifetime as his words and images were exorcised from my mind, heart, and body.

When I entered into ministry among women, working in churches, hospitals, and women's shelters, and then eventually developing my own community ministry in Northern California, I noticed that the self-critical question "what's wrong with me" found its way into every women's circle and that its pervasiveness cut across racial, ethnic, economic, religious, and generational boundaries. The question was asked in women's tendency to belittle themselves; to second-guess their impulses; to pathologize their decisions; to theorize about their feelings; to process every detail of their relationships; and to attribute any positive achievement to an external force of one sort or another, ranging from a transcendent god, goddess, or higher power to a particular guru or self-improvement regimen.

In an attempt to address women's self-critical attitudes, I designed a series of workshops entitled, "The Journey from Self-Criticism to Self-Celebration." The structure of the book parallels the three paths we explore while on the journey. Acknowledging the past's influence on the present, each path includes two essential movements: a walk through the past and a choice to heal into the present, full of ourselves.

Part One: *Dismantling The Question "What's Wrong With Me?"*
We walk through our communal/historical past, actively engaging the words and ideas of the architects of Western civilization that shaped the question "what's wrong with me" and provided legitimacy to our self-critical attitudes. (Chapter 1) We heal into the present as we assume *intellectual equality* with their systems of thought and dismantle the question "what's wrong with me." We are supported by courageous women who have challenged the traditional "doctrines" of biology, history, psychology, and philosophy from a woman's perspective.(Chapter 2)

Part Two: *Exorcising The Question "What's Wrong With Me?"*
We walk through our religious past, actively engaging the sin-based words, images, experiences, expectations that shaped the question "what's wrong with me" and gave authority to our self-critical attitudes.(Chapter 3) We heal into the present as we assume *theological equality* with the traditional doctrines of religion and exorcise the question. We are supported by Eve who commits the forbidden act of breaking out of traditional religious interpretation and telling her own story, and by her defenders throughout religious history. (Chapter 4)

Part III: *Reversing The Question "What's Wrong With Me?"*
We walk through our personal past, actively engaging the "reversals of value" embedded within our family experience, reversals that shaped the question "what's wrong with me" and that taught us the language of self-criticism. (Chapter 5) We heal into the present as we assume *personal responsibility* for our transformative journey and reverse the question by reclaiming our inner wisdom and natural capacities. We are supported by our deep commitment to the health and sanity of our daughters, grand-daughters, and nieces who in the very beginning of their lives are full of themselves! (Chapter 6)

Throughout Parts One, Two, and Three, you will read the stories of women who have walked through their communal, religious, and personal pasts to heal into the present, full of themselves. Some of the women have sat in circle with me for years. Together we have traveled these paths and supported each other toward self-celebration. Others read my first book *A God Who Looks Like Me: Discovering a Woman-Affirming Spirituality* and sent me their stories, poems, and reflections. They are part of our extended circle and we send them strong, tender support daily. They too are on the journey from self-criticism to self-celebration, employing their rich creativity to sustain them along the way. These stories are presented as whole creative pieces. I have not censored their poetry, prose, or stories in the editing process, nor do I interpret them in the text. Much as we do in our support groups, each contributor will acknowledge her walk through the past and her choice to heal into the present.

"BE FULL OF YOURSELF!" GROUPS

In conjunction with "The Journey from Self-Criticism to Self-Celebration" workshops, I developed "Be Full of Yourself!" support groups as an alternative to recovery-oriented ones. Although I have received many gifts of support and insight from the Twelve Step community during my years of attendance, its emphasis on ego-deflation, a concept designed by men based on their experience of themselves, concerns me.[1] Perhaps ego-deflation is an appropriate remedy for men who consider pride to be their beset-ting sin. Self-acceptance and self-celebration are more appropriate reme-dies for women whose besetting "sins" are self-loathing and self-criticism.

My critique of the ego-deflation model was confirmed by the initial reac-tions of women to the words "be full of yourself." Held within their reac-tions are a lifetime of warnings and expectations designed to keep women in their place as inferior and secondary:

"Throughout my childhood, I was told 'don't be full of yourself' so those words are a reversal of everything expected of me."

"I feel uncomfortable hearing 'be full of yourself.' Women are supposed to be quiet about themselves."

"The words sound like an exhortation to be proud and boastful. I was taught to be quiet about my accomplishments so others won't feel uncomfortable."

"I was taught that people like you better when you don't have it all together. If I become 'full of myself,' I won't have any friends."

"The words 'pride goeth before a fall' rise up from my past to counter those words as if to attend this workshop is a prideful act. I'm waiting for a calamity to drop from heaven as retribution for my audacity to even consider being full of myself."

"Men are full of themselves and I find them obnoxious. I don't want to be like men so I stay small and within a controlled and manageable sphere of living. Coming here is my first step out."

"The words confuse me. They contradict a whole other set of words shouted at me in childhood: egotistical, narcissistic, conceited, too big for your britches."

"Full of what? I'm empty inside—that's why I'm always filling myself up with other people's ideas, words, advice, and validation. The inner void is petrifying to me."

In spite of the self-critical voices, women come to the "Be Full of Yourself!" groups prompted by a longing to sit among women who have stepped out of chronic self-criticism. Groups are springing up all over the country, and women are remembering the time in the very beginning of life when they were full of themselves. They are practicing self-celebration. Instead of asking "what's wrong with me," they are celebrating their rich inner resources and their life-affirming behaviors.

In Part Four the concept, language, and practice of self-celebration will be introduced. In Chapter 7, we will explore the language of self-celebration, rewrite our inner dialogs to reflect the movement from self-criticism to self-celebration, and incorporate self-celebration into our conversations and relationships, and into our daily meditation practice. In chapter 8, you will sit in a self-celebration circle of twenty-six women who are full of themselves. I invited my friends, colleagues, mentors, and sisters-on-the-journey to celebrate themselves in poetry, prose, and collage. They will celebrate their bodies, their capacity to feel, their rich creativity, their self-defined spiritualities and lives, the lessons of their ordinary lives, and their willful presence in the world. Chapter 8 may inspire you to begin a "Be Full of Yourself!" group for your friends and colleagues, and your daughters, granddaughters, and nieces. A sample format and an agenda for the first year of meetings are included.

AN INVITATION

The journey from self-criticism to self-celebration is a warrior's journey through the critical words, images, experiences, and expectations cluttering our historical and personal landscapes. The journey calls for nothing less than a transformation of our inner worlds, a complete reversal of everything we were taught to believe about ourselves. A mere rearrangement of our outer lives will not do. The journey will lead us home to ourselves and to our rich inner capacities and resources.

The journey from self-criticism to self-celebration is a shared journey. We join women from every age who have committed the forbidden act of stepping outside systems of thought and belief that denied their very existence. Intellectually, spiritually, and emotionally arrogant women who trust themselves and their own experience. Women who refuse to ask "what's wrong with me." Women who make a powerful statement with every thought they share, every feeling they express, and every action they take on their own behalf.

The journey from self-criticism to self-celebration is an essential journey. Our beloved planet is in desperate need of women full of themselves. Women who use their personal and communal resources to address the challenges confronting humankind as it enters the 21st century. Women who give birth to images of inclusion, poems of truth, rituals of healing, experiences of transformation, relationships of equality, and households of compassion. Women full of themselves!

Come, let us begin the journey from self-criticism to self-celebration!

PART ONE

DISMANTLING THE QUESTION "WHAT'S WRONG WITH ME?"

1

THE HISTORICAL ORIGINS OF THE QUESTION

*As girls study Western civilization, they
become increasingly aware that history is the history of men.
History is His Story, the story of Mankind.*

—MARY PIPHER, *Reviving Ophelia:
Saving the Selves of Adolescent Girls*

I have two very special seven year old friends—Moizeé Simone Stewart and Carson Fox Young. They are my teachers. They remind me of a time in the very beginning of my life when I was full of myself. As we talk, sing, play, and adventure together, snapshots of that earlier time pass through my mind's eye. Inspired by their fullness and remembering my own, I wrote the following word-collage of fragments, fragments of a forgotten time.

In the very beginning the girl-child is full of herself. She moves through each day with an exuberant strength, a remarkable energy, and a contagious liveliness. Her days are meaningful and unfold according to a deep wisdom that resides within her. It faithfully orchestrates her movements from crawling to walking to running, her sounds from garbles to single words to sentences, and her knowing of the world through her sensual connection to it.

Her purpose is clear: to live fully in the abundance of her life. With courage, she explores her world. Her ordinary life is interesting enough. Every experience is filled with wonder and awe. It is enough to gaze at the redness of an apple, to watch the water flow over the rocks in a stream, to listen to the rain dance, to count the peas on her plate. Ordinary life is her teacher, her challenge, and her delight.

She says a big YES to Life as it pulsates through her body. With excitement, she explores her body. She is unafraid of channeling strong feelings through her. She feels her joy, her sadness, her anger, and her fear. She is pregnant with her own life. She is content to be alone. She touches the depths of her uniqueness. She loves her mind. She expresses her feelings. She likes herself when she looks in the mirror.

She trusts her vision of the world and expresses it. With wonder and delight, she paints a picture, creates a dance, and makes up a song. To give expression to what she sees is as natural as her breathing. And when challenged, she is not lost for words. She has a vocabulary to speak about her experience. She speaks from her heart. She voices her truth. She has no fear, no sense that to do it her way is wrong or dangerous.

She is a warrior. It takes no effort for her to summon up her courage, to arouse her spirit. With her courage, she solves problems. She is capable of carrying out any task that confronts her. She has everything she needs within the grasp of her mind and her imagination. She accomplishes great things in her mind, in her room, and in the neighborhood. With her spirit, she changes what doesn't work for her. She says "I don't like that person" when she doesn't, and "I like that person" when she does. She says no when she doesn't want to be hugged. She takes care of herself.

WHAT'S WRONG WITH ME?

As I celebrate the remarkable capacities of Moizeé and Carson, I am aware of critical words from my childhood and adolescence, echoing across the decades to challenge their fullness, and my own. These deeply imprinted words recount what happened to the precious being I once was, we once were in the very beginning of our lives. Over time, the inner voice that led us into wonder-filled explorations was replaced by critical voices. As a result, the girl-child's original vision is narrowed; she sees the world as everyone else sees it. She loses her ability to act spontaneously; she acts as expected. Her original trust in herself is shattered; she waits to be told how to live. Her original spunk is exiled; she learns that it is dangerous to venture outside the lines. Her original goodness is twisted and labeled unnatural-unfeminine-too intense-evil by the adults in her life.

She will grow up asking "what's wrong with me." This question regularly punctuates women's lives as they search far and wide for someone to give them an answer, for someone to offer them a magical insight, treatment, or cure. We have learned a criticism-based way of perceiving ourselves and relating to the world. As a result, our automatic tendency is to feel inadequate, that we're never quite good enough no matter what we do.

VARIATIONS ON A THEME

The question "what's wrong with me" is spoken regularly by women and appears over and over again in their writings and stories. Sometimes it is asked in a straightforward manner. A woman came to me for spiritual direction. Her first words were, "What's wrong with me? Everyone loves my husband, so why am I having trouble in our marriage?" A woman raised her hand after a presentation and asked, "Everyone enjoyed the presentation but me—what's wrong with me?" At a weekly support group, a woman wondered aloud, "The group gets along so well. I am the only one who voices disagreement with the agenda. What's wrong with me?" In desperation, a woman asked, "What's wrong with me? I've spent a fortune attending the workshops of Bradshaw, Chopra, and Williamson and nothing I try seems to work for me."

In our "Telling the Untold Stories" groups, the question reaches to painful depths. A young woman asks, "My father told me it was my fault that he was attracted to his own daughter. What's wrong with my body that it can have such a horrible effect on men?" Another woman remembers looking into the mirror as a child and wondering, "What's wrong with my face?" The white children turned away from her at school. They told her she was dirty. She believed that one day the dirt would wash off and she would look like them. "I'm not married—no man has ever wanted me. That's what's wrong with me . . ." offered a young woman who had already figured out her problem and was engaging in extreme measures of self-mutilation to remedy her undesirability. A thirty-something group member laments, "We've tried everything and have used up all our savings and I still can't get pregnant. I wake up every morning beating myself up. A woman who can't get pregnant is a freak of nature—that's what's wrong with me."

Sometimes the question is asked indirectly—in the form of a related question directed toward an expert of one sort or another:

"What did I do wrong . . . am I crazy?" asked a powerful woman who had just ended an unhealthy work relationship.

"Do I make sense?" asked an articulate business woman after a brilliant presentation.

"Did I sound stupid?" asked a successful lawyer after an impressive opening argument.

"Do I look ugly?" asks a lovely-to-behold adolescent daughter as she leaves for school each day.

"Did I make a fool of myself?" asks a gifted dancer after each of her stunning performances.

A question, waiting for a response . . . a reassurance that the flawed part of us doesn't show through our competent facade.

Sometimes the question is expressed in the form of an apology—the ever-present litany of "I'm sorry" that seasons women's writings and conversations. Women are much more experienced at using the words "I'm sorry" than men are. These words are not a mere perfunctory bow to politeness when uttered by most women. They contain a self-deprecating quality as if we are apologizing for our very existence—as if the answer to "what's wrong with me" is embedded within our femaleness.

On the plane to Portland, the stewardess carried a tray of beverages, ably distributing them to the passengers. She said "I'm sorry," to a young man who desired to walk up the aisle. What was she sorry for—that she was doing her job? She wasn't in his way. He walked right by her with relative ease. As he did, she repeated the apology, "I'm sorry."

On the same plane, a woman noticed a man fumbling with her coat in the overhead compartment as he was locating his own luggage. She said "I'm sorry. Could you hand me that coat it's mine. I'm sorry." What was she sorry for, that she had made a request? It was an effective request that saved her time and required very little energy of the man who handed the coat to her.

Sitting beside a woman in church, we shared a hymnbook. She began to locate the page for the next hymn. Self consciously, she hurried to complete the task and muttered "I'm so slow. I'm sorry." What was she sorry for, that it took time to turn the pages? The page was found long before the congregation rose to sing the hymn.

The coordinator of a successful Irish dance troupe was asked to share the history of the folk dance tradition before the group performed. "I don't know very much about it," she began and then proceeded to deliver an excellent historical overview, ending with the words "I'm sorry." What was she sorry for, that she actually knew a lot about a subject important to her? She was the most articulate presenter of the evening.

A young woman is obsessed with receiving the forgiveness of her father who raped her throughout childhood. She repeats the words "I'm sorry, Daddy" over and over again, hoping that he'll hear her and respond from his grave with the longed-for words of forgiveness. What is she sorry for, that she was born with a female body? It was her father's "sin" and yet she carries it within her body and life.

A woman has given birth to five daughters, each an attempt to satisfy her husband's desire for a son to "carry on the family name." After each birth, her first words to him have been "I'm sorry," words spoken in her very posture and bearing throughout each pregnancy. What is she sorry for, the fruit of her womb? Is not the conception of a child a partnership of sperm and egg, a dance of X and Y chromosomes, a co-creative adventure between male and female?

And finally, the question has taken on disturbing overtones for those 90s women schooled in the "women can do anything and everything—women can have it all" atmosphere of feminist America. The zeal of the women's movement of the 1960s and 1970s to transcend the perceived weaknesses of womankind and to reverse "biological destiny" sent many of its daughters to graduate schools and then into briefcased professions in corporate America. Exhausted, a lawyer asked the question in whispers lest she be branded a traitor by her comrades: "What's wrong with me? I am drawn to strong men. I want a baby. Working in a hard-core law firm just doesn't appeal to me anymore. I want the life my mother had: loving her kids, baking cookies, the whole nine yards of motherhood. To admit these things to myself has been terrifying. I feel like a wimp who's unable to sustain my hard earned independence."

The search for an answer to the question "what's wrong with me" consumes our valuable time, depletes our precious life energy, exhausts our limited resources, and distracts us from taking responsibility for our lives:

> We frequent the therapist's office, hoping the past holds an answer within it. We fill the churches, maybe God knows the answer. We attend self-help meetings, assured there is an answer encoded within the Twelve Steps. We write Ann Landers and every other expert, certain that they must know the answer. We sit at the feet of spirituality gurus, believing they will show us the way to an answer. We buy every self-help book that hits the market, confident that a new self-improvement project will quiet the question. We consent to outrageous measures to guarantee our fertility or our attractability, convinced that the presence of a child or a lover in our arms will dissolve the question. We sign up for diet clubs and plans and spas, convinced that our bodies are at the core of the answer, whatever it turns out to be. We spend hundreds of dollars on new outfits to hide the question and on new body parts to eradicate the question.

And then at night after the day's search is over,
we binge on a quart of ice cream or a bottle of wine,
or we spend hours on the internet or telephone
in tormented conversations trying to figure out
why the current relationship isn't working,

hoping that when we reach the bottom of the quart or bottle,
or the far reaches of the net or conversation,
things will have shifted deep within us
and once and for all we will know the answer
and what to do about it.

Yet no matter what we do
in search of an answer:
no matter how much we lose or how slimming the dress,
no matter how expensive or authoritative the expert,
no matter how many babies, relationships, possessions
we have or don't have,
no matter how spiritual, therapeutic, or recovered we become
we are left with the same question over and over again
as we look into the mirror horrified
that the restructuring of our relationship, our womb, or our breasts
did not quiet the question
there it is in the morning whispering from the mirror
"What's wrong with me? What's wrong with me?"
A mantra that accompanies us the length of our days.

Pause for a moment to acknowledge the direct and indirect ways you've asked, "What's wrong with me?" Tally the resources of time, energy, attention, and money you have expended in your quest to find out the answer.

A HISTORICAL PERSPECTIVE

The question "what's wrong with me" does not develop within us naturally. My young friends Carson and Moizeé do not expend one ounce of their precious life energy trying to figure out what is wrong with their bodies, feelings, and thoughts. They just live. They make a statement with every thought they share, every feeling they express, and every action they take on their own behalf.

On a personal level, the question is shaped over time by the critical words, images, experiences, and expectations of childhood. We become convinced that something is fundamentally wrong with us and that our life-task is to find out what it is. The roots of the question reach beneath our personal histories, however, they reach into the ground of Western civilization and the formation of its intellectual, theological, and psychological thought and practice.

An examination of the question reveals the critical words, images, experiences, and expectations of many lifetimes of women convinced through theology and psychology; through intellectual and social history; and through societal scripts and family customs that something is wrong with them. Clearly, the question's presence within us is not an arbitrary occurrence. The belief that something is fundamentally wrong with women is woven into the fabric of Western civilization.

Many American women did not reap the intellectual and psychological benefits of the women's consciousness-raising movement of the 1960s and 1970s. And many more women have not had access to the insights of feminist scholarship into the systemic nature of women's seemingly personal challenges and concerns. The women attending my 1987-1997 workshops and retreats assumed that their quest to discover what's wrong with them was particular and unique. Caught in the swirls of everyday living with its demands and challenges, they had no time to wonder about the larger dimensions of the question: perhaps the design of society did not sanction their full satisfaction and contentment. Perhaps it required them "to fit in" at the expense of their sanity, health, and pride. Perhaps fitting in required them to become alienated from themselves, from all that is naturally and organically theirs as children of life. Perhaps the question is much larger and more encompassing than they could have imagined: What's wrong with us? What's wrong with women? A mantra passed down from generation to generation . . . a mantra formulated by others.

Dissatisfied with the temporary relief offered by self-improvement regimens, consisting of pep-talks and reassurances, mantras and affirmations, positive thinking and self-talk, these women became willing to explore the origins of their self-critical attitudes. Our first step on the transformative journey from self-criticism to self-celebration was an acknowledgment of the past's influence on the present. We began by walking through our communal past to expose the historical/intellectual roots of our self-criticism.

THE GREATEST MINDS OF WESTERN THOUGHT

Remember the compulsory Western civilization class in high school or college? I still have my college notes. Searching for the roots of the question "what's wrong with me," I perused them 25 years later. I was reminded of the architects of Western civilization, the so-called "greatest minds of Western thought." They were all men: Aristotle, Tertullian, Augustine, Aquinas, Luther—to name a few.[2] As I reread their words, this many years later, from my perspective as a woman, I asked new questions: What was their perspective about women? Were women included in their world and life view? As my questions were answered, I became outraged. Outraged at their self-serving dissection of the nature of women. Outraged at the influence of their words. Words, echoing across the centuries in authoritative philosophical, theological, and psychological theories and practices. Words, trickling down and touching my life, our lives, in the homes, churches, and schools of our childhoods. And yes, words that touch our daughters' and granddaughters' lives today.

Our free-thinking foremothers recognized that the rearrangement of society to allow women full political, social, and economic participation would not be sustainable unless women addressed their own internalized "oppression" and became willing to dismantle all remnants of it from their lives. They understood that five centuries of "trickle down" had taken its toll on womankind, that the ideas, theories, and theologies of these influential men had become embedded within us, monopolizing our attitudes toward ourselves until we become willing to step outside of them and wrestle with them across a critical distance.

Imagine with me a one day symposium, featuring the architects of Western civilization. They will consider the topic, "On the Nature of Woman: A Historical Perspective." Aristotle, Philo, Paul, Tertullian, Augustine, Aquinas, Luther, Kramer and Sprenger, Rousseau, Freud, and Barth address a subject which, in Freud's words, "has a claim on our interest second almost to no other. Throughout history people have knocked their heads against the riddle of the nature of femininity." [3] I invite women to eavesdrop on the symposium, to grapple with the ideas of these influential men just as free thinking women have done throughout history. As they engage the symposium with their minds, bodies, and hearts, with all of their intelligences, they have a variety of reactions:

Intimidation. Many women believe they are incapable of grappling with ideas. In the presence of men and their ideas, these women feel intimidated and assume a one-down position. At a loss for how to meaningfully participate, they become quiet and dissolve into a familiar invisibility. A participant reflected on the gifts of the symposium for her, "Without the support of women, I couldn't have engaged the words of the symposium participants. Like God, they have always seemed untouchable. To disagree with them would be irreverent and arrogant, I thought. They are the first men whose ideas and opinions I have taken on."

Fear. Women have been taught not to question the ideas of the "fathers." As we critically distance from their ideas and consider this material together, it is not unusual for women to have dreams of our meeting space being vandalized, of God the father ranting and raving from the heavens, and of witch-burnings and lynchings. In addition, women are afraid of the intensity of feeling that may surface as their eyes are opened to the wider reality of a woman's life. A woman's intensity makes everyone uncomfortable, including herself. We were taught to be nice, not angry, even when our own lives and sanity are at stake.

Anger. To explore their communal past touches a deep rage within some women—the accumulated rage of generations of women who believed the lies they were told about themselves and then passed on those lies to their daughters and granddaughters. One woman wrote, "As I read, rage moves through my body. I am in shock that the fathers of history wrote this stuff and that we were exposed to their writings either directly or indirectly. Their notions are so insidious and damaging. I love/hate the symposium. It feels necessary, a wake-up call." Another woman became consumed with a need to shout "Shut-up!" as she engaged the ideas of the symposium and recognized their presence within her, a need she addressed by writing, drawing, and dancing the "Shut-up!" until it was fully expressed. As women make the connections between their internalization of these ideas and their own self-criticism, their anger energizes them to assume intellectual equality and to dismantle the question "what's wrong with me" for the sake of their children.

Longing for Women's Voices. Women read the daily newspaper and wonder: "What about the interests, concerns, and perspectives of women?" We sit at the feet of male preachers and teachers and wonder why their words don't resonate with our experience. We are bombarded with the ever-present male pronoun in reference to God and "mankind" and our longing for the inclusion of women's experience deepens. We notice the photos of men on Time and Newsweek covers and the achievements of men lauded in their feature stories and we wonder, "What about the women world-changers and thinkers?" We hear men's argumentative voices on radio interview programs and long to hear the voices of women debating topics of interest to us. We attend a philosophy class to study the greatest minds of Western thought and while flipping through the all-male text, wonder where the women are. As women work through the symposium, this deep longing is triggered—a longing for women's voices to alleviate once and for all the persistent imbalance of voices that trickle down to us in the newspapers and magazines, the sermons and lectures, the opinions and perspectives we are bombarded with daily.

A SYMPOSIUM ON THE NATURE OF WOMAN

As you read through the symposium, notice the depth of your breath and the sensations in your body. Notice if there is intimidation, fear, anger, a longing for women's voices. Take note of the phrases of particular significance to you: the ones that touch your body, cause your heart to tremble or to rage, or trigger a memory of how their ideas trickled down to you in the home, church, and school of your childhood. Some women have found it helpful to note these phrases with a highlighter. Others jot them down in their journals.

Lest we think the attitudes represented at "The Symposium" are relics of a distant past, I have included the responses of women who kept track of the words and phrases, childhood messages, and current experiences that were triggered as they engaged the ideas of the architects of Western civilization. Add your words to theirs at the end of each section. In addition, I have included excerpts from the bestseller *The Rules,* providing evidence that the attitudes represented at "The Symposium" are alive and well, and being marketed among our daughters and granddaughters.

Invite your daughters to take this journey with you. "It's important for girls to explore the culture's impact on their growth and development," writes Mary Pipher. "They all benefit from, to use an old-fashioned term, consciousness raising. Once girls understand the effects of the culture on their lives, they can fight back. They learn that they have conscious choices to make and ultimate responsibility for those choices. Intelligent resistance keeps the true self alive."[4]

ARISTOTLE (384-323 B.C.E.)

Aristotle is introduced as the honored speaker in recognition of the far-reaching influence of his theories about the biological differences between men and women. They provided the framework for many of the theologies and philosophies represented at the symposium.

Aristotle begins by setting forth his theory that all living things have souls and that a woman's soul differs from a man's in all three of its components. He then outlines those differences and their consequences in terms of the function, role, and place of men and women in the family and society: "A woman's *nutritive* soul requires less nourishment than the man's. Her *sensitive* soul is devoid of sexual desire therefore she assumes the passive role in copulation. And her *rational* soul does not include the capacity to govern her own life and manage her own actions. Consequently, the husband, who is superior in reason, rules in the home. The wife is to obey. One of the functions of a village, as a conglomerate of households, is to supervise the activities of women."[5] Aristotle then reads from two of his "seminal"[6] manuscripts:

From *Historia Animalism*
For nature has made the one sex stronger, the other weaker, that the latter through fear may be the more cautious, while the former by its courage is better able to ward off attacks, and that the one may acquire possessions outside the house, the other preserve those within.[7]

From *Economics*
The fact is, the nature of man is more rounded off and complete . . . Hence woman is more compassionate than man, more easily moved to tears, at

the same time is more jealous, more querulous, more apt to scold and to strike . . . more prone to despondency and less hopeful than the man . . . more false of speech, more deceptive, and of more retentive memory. She is also more wakeful, more shrinking, more difficult to rouse to action, and requires a smaller amount of nourishment.[8]

Aristotle's Trickle Down Effect: *Women's Responses*

"I can't leave my husband. I wouldn't know how to manage without him."

"Women are jealous creatures."

"A woman's place is in the home, safe and protected."

"I feel uncomfortable initiating sexual activity."

"I am embarrassed by my big appetite. I always eat more than any other woman at a party or gathering. It's not a compulsive thing. I need lots of food to maintain my energy. Sometimes I deny my body what it needs to fit into the stereotype that women don't need as much to eat as men."

"My daughter, Sara, read Aristotle in her philosophy class. One night she read a section aloud to me and said, "This guy doesn't respect women." I wondered what it means to her that one of the wisest men of the ages is misogynistic." (Mary Pipher, Reviving Ophelia, *page 42)*

PHILO OF ALEXANDRIA (20-50 C.E.)

After the applause quiets down, the Jewish philosopher, Philo is invited to read from his own writings. He acknowledges the great debt that Western civilization owes to the Hebrew tradition. Many of its stories, symbols, and mythologies are woven into the understandings of gender and morality that have defined cultural history throughout the ages. He reminds his distinguished audience of the success of the Jewish patriarchs—over six centuries—in replacing the worship of the Goddess with the worship of Yahweh. This success, he continues, provided his colleagues with two powerful notions which have supported their ongoing investigations into the nature of women's inferiority: the idea of life originating entirely from the male rather than a female source, and the idea of woman as the instigator of evil.[9] Philo reinforces these ideas by reading from his *Questions and Answers on Genesis, Book I*:

Question 27: (Genesis 2:21) Why was not woman (like other animals and man also) formed from earth instead of the side of the man?

Answer: First because woman is not equal in honour with the man. Second, because she is not equal in age but younger. Wherefore those who take wives who have passed their prime are to be criticized for destroying the laws of nature. Third, he wishes that a man should take care of the woman as a necessary part of him; but the woman, in return should serve him as a whole. Fourth, he counsels man figuratively to take care of the woman as of a daughter, and woman to honour the man as a father . . .[10]

Question 33: (Genesis 3:1) Why does the serpent speak to the woman and not to the man?

Answer: In order that they may be potentially mortal, he deceives by trickery and artfulness. And woman is more accustomed to be deceived than the man. For his judgment, like his body, is masculine and is capable of dissolving or destroying the designs of deception; but the judgment of the woman is more feminine and because of softness she easily gives way and is taken in by plausible falsehoods which resemble the truth.[11]

Question 37: (Genesis 3:6) Why does the woman first touch the tree and eat of its fruit, and afterward the man also takes of it?

Answer: . . . the priority of the woman is mentioned with emphasis. For it was fitting that man should rule over immortality and everything good, but woman over death and everything vile.[12]

Philo's Trickle Down Effect: *Women's Responses*

"My husband treats me like a child."

"My boss talks down to me. His condescending manner reminds me of my father."

"My dad always said women are more gullible than men."

"Men think their lives run smoothly until a woman comes along. Then all hell breaks loose."

PAUL THE APOSTLE (5?-67? C.E.)

Paul was invited to the symposium to represent the early Christian perspective. He begins his remarks by reminding Philo that Christianity articulated the theological seriousness of Eve's responsibility for the fall of Adam. The Genesis story was not used to elucidate the origins of evil in Rabbinical writings nor was it taken seriously in the Hebrew Scriptures. Christianity elevated the Genesis account to the level of divine inspiration, rescuing it from its peripheral status as mere folk tale or myth. Christianity elevated Adam and Eve to archetype-status. In them, the whole history of humankind was foreshadowed and determined. The superiority of men and the inferiority of women are set forth unequivocally in the sequence of creation, and the subjection of women to men's authority is cast in stone as a result of Eve's disobedience. Having set the record straight, Paul reads from his writings, and Timothy's, to point out the practical ramifications of the sequence of creation and the disobedience of Eve.[13]

From *I Corinthians 14: 34-35*
Let your women keep silence in the church: for it is not permitted unto them to speak; but they are commanded to be under obedience, as also saith the law. And if they will learn anything, let them ask their husbands at home: for it is a shame for women to speak in the church.

From *Ephesians 5: 22-33*
Wives, submit yourselves unto your own husbands, as unto the Lord. For the husband is the head of the wife, even as Christ is the head of the church; and he is the savior of the body. Therefore as the church is subject unto Christ, so let wives be subject to their own husbands in everything.

From *I Timothy 2:9*
Let the woman learn in silence with all subjection. But I suffer not a woman to teach, not to usurp authority over the man, but to be in silence. For Adam was formed first, then Eve. And Adam was not deceived, but the women being deceived was in transgression. Notwithstanding she will be saved in child-bearing, if they continue in faith, charity, and holiness with sobriety.

Paul's Trickle Down Effect: *Women's Responses*

"Around men I get quiet."

"I feel uncomfortable chairing meetings with men present—as if I'm stepping outside acceptable bounds."

"My parents made it very clear that they wouldn't come to my wedding if a woman officiated. A woman minister is going against the natural order of things."

TERTULLIAN (160-230)

Tertullian and Augustine represent the church fathers of the second through fifth centuries. Tertullian reiterates how important it is that women's clothing and appearance reflect their status as Eve's daughters.

He reads a series of passages, exhorting women to dress in a manner commensurate with their shameful condition:

From *"On the Apparel of Women"*
. . . no one of you, from the time she had first learned the truth concerning woman's condition, would have desired too gladsome a style of dress; so as rather to go about in humble garb, and rather to affect meanness of appearance, while walking about as an Eve mourning and repentant in order that by every garb of penitence she might the more fully expiate that which she derives from Eve—the ignominy, I mean, of the first sin, and the odium of human perdition.[14]

From *"The Veiling of Virgins, An Appeal to the Virgins Themselves"*
Veil your head: if a mother, for your sons' sakes; if a sister, for your brethren's sakes; if a daughter for your fathers' sakes. All ages are periled in your person. Put on the panoply of modesty; surround yourself with the stockard of bashfulness; rear a rampart for your sex, which must neither allow your eyes egress or ingress to other people's. Wear the full garb of women, to preserve the standing of virgin.[15]

From *"On the Veiling of Virgins, An Appeal to Married Women"*
The whole head constitutes the woman. Its limits and boundaries reach as far as where the robe begins. The region of the veil is co-extensive with the space covered by the hair when unbounded; in order that the necks too may be encircled. For it is they which must be subjected: the veil is their yoke. Arabia's heathen females will be your judges, who cover not only the head, but the face also, so entirely that they are content, with only one eye free, to enjoy rather half the light than to prostitute the whole face.[16]

Tertullian's Trickle Down Effect: *Women's Responses*

"I always feel like I'm wearing a veil—covering aspects of myself so others will not be intimidated."

"I feel responsible when men gawk at me when I walk down the street. They are the ones gawking and I feel responsible. There's something twisted in that way of seeing myself."

"I feel weird about my body and go through tremendous conflict over what to wear. I can't wear something really tight because then I have to deal with men looking at me as if I'm a sexual object, not an intelligent woman."

AUGUSTINE (354-430)

Augustine, African Bishop of Hippo, begins his remarks by emphasizing the hierarchic principle laid out in Genesis: "We do not possess equality of standing but each of us is subordinated to the one above. Based on the sequence of creation, the headship and dominion of men are divinely ordained. Eve was created because the man needed a help-mate." He reads from *The Confessions:*

> From *The Confessions*
> There is one power which rules by directing, another made subject that it might obey, so also for the man a woman was corporeally made, who, in the mind of her rational understanding should also have a like nature, in the sex, however of her body should be subject to the sex of her husband, as the appetite of action is subjected by reason of the mind, to conceive the skill of acting rightly . . .[17]

Augustine concludes by acknowledging that he considers it unconscionable to deny women participation in the image of God. Yet a distinction must always be kept in mind: a woman's possession of the image of God is secondary and derivative based on her relationship to her husband.[18] To clarify this point he reads from *De Trinitate:*

> From *De Trinitate*
> . . . the woman together with her own husband is in the image of God . . . but when she is referred to separately in her quality as help-mate, which regards the woman herself alone, then she is not the image of God; but as regards the man alone, he is in the image of God as fully and completely . . .[19]

Augustine's Trickle Down Effect: *Women's Responses*

"Feminist rhetoric aside, I still feel a woman is incomplete without a man, that there's something wrong with me because I'm single at 40."

"The society is set up to reward women who are connected to men. Without one, you're considered pitiful at best and a freak of some sort at worst."

THOMAS AQUINAS (1225-1274)

Thomas Aquinas, the Dominican friar who was an influential participant in the development of Catholic theology, is introduced. He acknowledges his great debt to Aristotle whose biological understandings of male and female provided the foundational support for much of the development of

Catholic theology: "Your words did not go to the grave with you, Aristotle. Your insights have become part of the theological and philosophical heritage we continue to disseminate through our writings in the Catholic Church. By means of the ongoing interchange of our thoughts and words across the centuries, the position and status of women in the church, as well as in the society at large, will continue to reflect the biological reality of their inferiority to men." [20]

From *Summa Theologica*
As regards the individual nature, woman is defective and misbegotten, for the active force in the male seed tends to the production of a perfect likeness in the masculine sex; while the production of the female comes from defect in the active force or from some material indisposition, or even from some external influence, like the south wind, for example which is damp, as we are told by Aristotle . . .

Subjection is two-fold. One is servile, by virtue of which the superior makes use of a subject for his own benefit; and this kind of subjection came after sin. There is another kind of subjection, which is called economic or civil, whereby the superior makes use of his subjects for their own benefit and good. And this kind of subjection existed even before sin. For good order would have been wanting in the human family if some were not governed by others wiser than themselves. So by such a kind of subjection woman is by nature subject to man, because in man the discretion of reason predominates. [21]

Aquinas' Trickle Down Effect: *Women's Responses*

"I was taught that feelings weren't as important as thoughts. And because boys think and girls feel, girls are not as important as boys."

"Women were not trusted in our family because their feelings kept them from getting the job done. They were fickle. Men were in charge because they mastered their feelings and completed the task at hand. They were rational."

"I overheard the guys at work say that women are too emotional and good for nothing especially 'at that time of the month.' Men, they said, could be counted on all the time. These same attitudes were expressed by my father 30 years ago. Not much has change."

MARTIN LUTHER (1483-1546)

Martin Luther, Wittenberg professor and founder of Protestantism, admits his amazement at the proceedings: "Although we represent different traditions and disagree heartily about many theological issues, I am astonished at the level of agreement among us about the nature of women as supported by natural law and theological reflection. Clearly Eve is to blame. *We can hardly speak of her without shame."* [22]

Woman Unexcelled - if She Stays in Her Sphere
Men are commanded to rule and to reign over their wives and families. But if a woman forsaking her position, presumes to rule over her husband, she then and there engages in a work for which she was not created, a work which stems from her own failing and is evil. For God did not create this sex to rule. For this reason domination by women is never a happy one. The history of the Amazons, celebrated by Greek writers, might be advanced against this view. They are reported to have held the rule and to have conducted wars. But I believe what is told of them to be a fable.

To be sure, the Ethiopians choose women to be both queens and princesses, in accordance with their customs, as the Ethiopian Queen Candace is mentioned in Acts 9:27; but this is stupid of them. There is no divine permission for ruling by a woman. It may of course happen that she is placed in the position of a king and is given the rule; but she always has a senate of prominent men according to whose counsel all is administered. Therefore even though a woman may be put in the place of a king, this does not confirm the rule of woman; for the text is clear: "Thy desire shall be to thy husband, and he shall rule over thee." (*Genesis 3:16*).[23]

Luther's Trickle Down Effect: *Women's Responses*

"When I speak my mind in the marriage, there's always conflict. My mother says this is because I'm going against natural law by not being submissive. When I stay in my place, everything works fine."

"On my wedding night my mother told me not to refuse my husband's sexual advances—ever. According to her, it's a woman's duty to meet her husband's needs no matter how uncomfortable or painful the experience."

"In a relationship, the man must take charge. He must propose. We are not making this up—biologically, he's the aggressor." (The Rules, *page 9*)

HEINRICH KRAMER & JAMES SPRENGER (15TH CENTURY)

The Dominican monks Heinrich Kramer and James Sprenger are introduced next. They were appointed by Pope Innocent VIII in 1484 to ferret out the heresy of witchcraft, and authored *The Malleus Maleficarum*, a handbook outlining the official methodology for persecuting witches. Their

presence at the symposium is an acknowledgment of the church's successful attack on Mother Goddess worship and its successful restriction of
women's power in the church and society.

Kramer thanks Martin Luther for his support in their monumental task
of destroying every last vestige of witchcraft: "Thanks to you and all good
men everywhere we are making strides in our God-given task." Sprenger
expresses his gratitude for the theological work of the men invited to the
symposium: "We are often asked *why a greater number of witches is
found in the fragile feminine sex than among men. This is a fact that it
were idle to contradict.* Our answer, as outlined in *The Malleus Maleficarum*, draws upon many of the biological and theological insights we have
heard here today. There is an undeniable link between women's suscepti-
bility to witchcraft and her inferior nature."[24]

> From *The Malleus Maleficarum*
> Since women are feebler both in mind and body, it is not surprising that
> they should come under the spell of witch craft. For as regards intellect or
> the understanding of spiritual things, they seem to be of a different nature
> from men . . . But the natural reason is that she is more carnal than man,
> as is clear from her many carnal abominations. And it should be noted that
> there was a defect in the formation of the first woman, since she was
> formed from a bent rib, that is, a rib of the breast which is bent as it were
> in a contrary direction to a man. And since through this defect she is an
> imperfect animal, she always deceives . . . And all this is indicated by the
> etymology of the word, for Femina comes from Fe and Minus, since she is
> ever weaker to hold and preserve the faith. Therefore a wicked woman is
> by nature quicker to waver in her faith and consequently quicker to adjure
> the faith, which is the root of witchcraft.[25]

Kramer and Sprenger's Trickle Down Effect: *Women's Responses*

*"I was taught to fear witches and to remember how they ended up. My
secret fascination with their power frightened me."*

*"Independent women were always put down in my family. We were
warned against being strong and independent through jokes, sarcasm,
and innuendo."*

JEAN-JACQUE ROUSSEAU (1712-1778)

The moderator reads an opening statement and portions of the writings of
Jean-Jacque Rousseau who was not able to be present due to pressing family concerns. "It is essential that our educational system reflect our under-

standing of the nature of women. The sexual energies of young girls must be repressed in order to encourage the most essential virtue of chastity. The autonomous energies of girls must be redirected into obedience and fidelity in service to the man. We must encourage the development of only those qualities which will guarantee right order and patrilineal inheritance."[26]

From *Emile*
In the union of the sexes . . . it is necessary the one should have both the power and the will, and that the other should make little resistance. The principle being here established, it follows, that woman is expressly formed to please man. If the obligation be reciprocal, also, and the man ought to please her in turn, it is not so immediately necessary: his great merit lies in his power, and he pleases merely because he is strong.

Woman and man were made for each other; but their mutual dependence is not the same. The man depends on the woman, only on account of their desires; the woman on the man, both on account of their desires and their necessities: we could subsist better without them than they without us. Their very subsistence and rank in life depend upon us, and the estimation in which we hold them, their charms and their merit.

By the law of nature itself, both women and children lie at the mercy of men; it is not enough they should be actually estimable, it is requisite they should be actually esteemed; it is not enough they should be beautiful, it is requisite their charms should please; it is not enough they should be sensible and prudent, it is necessary they should be acknowledged as such: their glory lies not only in their conduct, but in their reputation; and it is impossible for any, who consents to be accounted infamous, to be ever virtuous.[27]

Rousseau's Trickle Down Effect: *Women's Responses*

"My partner seems less attached to us than we are to him. We are not as necessary to him as he is to us."

"I was afraid of being branded a "whore" even though I didn't know what that word meant. To step outside of the lines, a girl was marked for life."

"I was taught that a girl's reputation was her most valuable asset. If I squandered it by exploring my sexuality, I would become damaged goods and undesirable to any man."

SIGMUND FREUD (1856-1939)

Sigmund Freud is introduced and launches right into his presentation: "My esteemed colleagues, my ideas may seem far-fetched to some of you. Your belief, influenced by Aristotle, that women are devoid of sexual desire severely limited your understanding of the nature of woman and led you to ignore an important and fascinating area of exploration, women's sexuality. Because of your neglect of this area of exploration, I have been privileged to lay the groundwork for a radical redefinition of female sexuality, influencing all Western societies. I will begin by reading an appropriate section from "On the Sexual Theories of Children" to clarify for my distinguished colleagues the nature of the clitoris, an unheard of anatomical reference for most of you.[28] I will conclude with selections from "Femininity" which will further elucidate the nature of women.

From *"On the Sexual Theories of Children"*
Anatomy has recognized the clitoris within the female pudenda as being an organ that is homologous to the penis; and the physiology of the sexual processes has been able to add that this small penis which does not grow any bigger behaves in childhood like a real and genuine penis that it becomes the seat of excitations which lead to it being touched, that its excitability gives the little girl's sexual activity a masculine character and that a wave of repression in the years of puberty is needed in order for this masculine sexuality to be discarded and for the women to emerge.[29]

From *"Femininity"*
The castration complex of little girls is started by the sight of the genitals of the other sex. They at once notice the difference and, it must be admitted, its significance too. They feel seriously wronged, often declare that they want "to have something like it too," and fall victim to "envy for the penis," which will leave ineradicable traces on their development and the formation of their character and which will not be surmounted in even the most favorable cases without a severe expenditure of psychical energy . . . The wish to get the long-for penis eventually in spite of everything may contribute to the motives that drive a mature woman to analysis, and what she may reasonably expect from analysis—a capacity, for instance, to carry on an intellectual profession—may often be recognized as a sublimated modification of this repressed wish . . .[30]

Freud's Trickle Down Effect: *Women's Responses*

"Any woman who wanted to pursue a career was called a "dyke" by my father—meaning a masculinized and unacceptable woman."

"I was told that if I masturbated I would ruin my chances for a good sexual relationship with a man by using up my limited sexual energy on myself."

"In this age when women are expected to be liberated and know their own bodies, I feel ashamed because I have never touched my clitoris or explored my own vagina. My husband knows my body better than I do."

"Biologically, the man must pursue the woman. If you bring up sex all the time, you will emasculate him." (The Rules, *page 127*)

KARL BARTH (1886-1968)

The distinguished 20th-century theologian Karl Barth is the final speaker of the day. After being introduced, he reads from his highly regarded *Church Dogmatics.*

From *"The Ordering of Male and Female"*
(Man and woman) stand in sequence. It is in this that man has his allotted place and the woman hers. It is in this that they are oriented on each other. It is in this that they are individually and together the human creature as created by God. Man and woman are not an A and a second A whose being and relationship can be described like the two halves of an hour glass, which are obviously two, but absolutely equal and therefore interchangeable. Man and woman are an A and a B, and cannot, therefore be equated.

Every word is dangerous and liable to be misunderstood when we try to characterize this order. But it exists. And everything else is null and void if its existence is ignored, if we refuse to recognize it as an element in the divine command, if it is left to chance. If order does not prevail in the being and fellowship of man and woman . . . the only alternative is disorder . . . A precedes B, and B follows A. Order means succession. It means preceding and following. It means super- and sub-ordination . . . Properly speaking, the business of woman, her task and function, is to actualize the fellowship in which man can only precede her, stimulating, leading and inspiring.[31]

Barth's Trickle Down Effect: *Women's Responses*

"I've been looking for an "A" all my life. What is the purpose of a "B" without an "A" to precede it. Barth's words gave voice to my life-long quest."

"The men in my life have always been taller, smarter, and wealthier than I am. It seems that the only possible relationship is one in which the man is dominant and I am subordinate."

"Men's interests, careers, and decisions are much more important than mine. I've expanded my life to include their interests. I've set aside jobs to support their careers. I've deferred to their decisions. They've never shown an interest in something of importance to me."

" . . . the premise of The Rules is that we never make anything happen, that we trust in the natural order of things - namely, that man pursues woman." (The Rules, *page 26*)

A TRICKLE DOWN THEORY: EVE'S DAUGHTERS

A s I imagine the good old boys hanging around after the symposium, to pat each other on the back, to network across the centuries, to applaud their successful dissection of the nature of woman, to celebrate their impressive unanimity spanning 2,250 years, I become nauseated. In a moment I realize all that I have absorbed—their words like the steady drip of an IV inserted at birth. Their words trickling down to me by way of history lessons in elementary and high school; philosophy and theology lectures in college and graduate school; countless homilies in the Catholic church and sermons in the Protestant church; daily Bible readings; advertisements and television programs; and societal expectations, family customs, and parental mantras.

The history, philosophy, and theology we were taught was written by men, based on men's experience, and celebrated men's superiority in thought, body, spirit, achievement, and value.
While brushing up on the details of the development of Western civilization, I discovered a book with an intriguing title, *A World Made By Men: Cognition and Society.* In the prelude the author writes, "The title of this book—which of course does not exclude women as the makers of the world—points to the theme. . . the relationship between cognition and the creation of society. Human intelligence actively created the social world."[32] The author's disclaimer to the contrary, his title says it all. It has been men, limited by their psycho-social projections; their sexual anxiety, discomfort, and insecurity; and their ignorance and dismissal of the female experience, who have shaped the intellectual, philosophical, theological, and mythic traditions passed on to us. All claims to objectivity dissolve. These men were writing from their perspective as men, subject to the distortions inherent within a male-centered world view.

Preparing for a women's retreat in an East coast Unitarian church, I took a break to look around the unfamiliar room. On the far wall were photographs of nine men, the fathers of the church. There were no women among them. The participants arrived and we spent a meaningful day together occasionally turning toward the good old boys hanging on the wall. We wondered about the stories of the women in their lives. We imagined these supportive women propping up the public life of their men: women who researched, typed, and provided invaluable feedback for their dissertations, sermons, and books; women who cleaned, cooked, and maintained the private world of the home; women who met their emotional, sexual, and practical needs day in and day out. Ironically, these supportive tasks were assigned to women by the men on the wall and their historical counterparts who constructed self-serving definitions of the nature of women, maintaining a hierarchy of role and position to the advantage of boys and men and the disadvantage of girls and women.

The history, philosophy, and theology we were taught excluded women's thoughts, experience, and achievements. Women served as specimens to be observed, scrutinized, and defined based on the projection-prone viewpoint of male theologians, philosophers, and historians.

Sitting in traffic school just last week, I listened to a policeman describe his world inhabited by male drivers, pedestrians, and accident victims; male police officers, judges, and insurance carriers. I wondered whether I existed at all after six hours of traffic school:

"You come up behind some *guy* and pass *him* on the right."

"*He's* down to about 15 mph and you pass *him* on the left."

"The doctor hasn't returned from *his* golf game so you put an extra dime in the meter."

"A police*man* is your friend if your house is robbed. *He's* your adversary if *he* gives you a traffic ticket."

"When *he* goes into court and says you made an unsafe lane change, the judge, if *he* is awake, will give you a ticket."

On and on, descriptions of a world in which I don't exist, in 1997.

Listening to each participant at the imaginary symposium, viewing the good old boys on the wall, sitting in traffic school, I realize that every use of "man" and "male," every image of world-changer, church father, or God excludes me, excludes all women. The ever-present male pronoun reinforces our exclusion from full participation in creating the worlds we inhabit and contributes to the question "what's wrong with me." Male and female were definitely separate categories in the world view of the architects of Western civilization, the good old boys on the wall, and the officer who taught traffic school. They were writing and speaking about men unless otherwise indicated. "Woman" is not and never has been included in man. The use of exclusive language hints at the essence of what's wrong with us and contributes to the spirit of exclusion influencing our daughters' lives today. Mary Pipher acknowledges the tenacity of these attitudes in her book, *Reviving Ophelia:*

"Girls come of age in a misogynistic culture in which men have most political and economic power. Girls read a history of Western civilization that is essentially a record of men's lives . . ."[33]

"By junior high girls sense their lack of power, but usually cannot say what they sense. They see mostly men are congressmen, principals, bankers, and corporate executives. They notice that famous writers, musicians, and artists are mostly men. But they don't focus on the political - their complaints are personal."[34]

The history, philosophy, and theology we were taught set forth women's inferiority in thought, body, spirit, achievement, and value as an undisputed article of faith supported by natural and divine law.

According to the symposium participants and their devoted followers, the crux of our problem is that we are the daughters of Eve. Eve was given a pivotal role in men's developing mythology. First of all, "Adam was formed first, then Eve" (I Timothy 4:9). She was created from the man. The mythmakers' reversal of biological process established Adam as the first "A" and Eve as the first "B." This influential notion has effectively supported the inferiority of women throughout the ages.

Our inferiority is all encompassing. As misbegotten males, we are biologically inferior. Taken from the male's body, we are derivative and incomplete. As "other" than God, we are spiritually inferior; we do not look like the male God of the fathers. As irrational, we are intellectually inferior; our minds are subject to the baser passions of the body and cannot be trusted. As castrated males, we are sexually inferior; our bodies are devoid of sexual desires. As second in the divine order of things, we are socially inferior and to be ruled by men.

Secondly, "Adam was not deceived, but the woman being deceived was in transgression." (I Timothy 2:9) Eve is the instigator of evil. Out of feminine weakness she ate the fruit and then seduced Adam to do the same, setting in motion a series of events that resulted in our exile from the garden and the release of misery and death into the world. Eve has been demeaned throughout Christian history as the Mother of Evil, who was disobedient and sinful. Humanity's fall from grace was instigated by the loss of her innocence. Through the disobedience of this one woman, sin entered the world. Eve is the Fallen Woman.

Thirdly, God cursed Eve for her disobedience with these words, "Thy desire shall be to thy husband, and he shall rule over thee." (Genesis 3:6) Theologians from Paul onward have used this verse for their own purposes to the detriment of women. "The text is clear . . .," wrote Luther in the fifteenth century, "Woman was created for the benefit of the man, that is, for the prudent and sensible training of children. Everyone does best when he does that for which he was created. Therefore let everyone stick to the work to which God has called him and for which he was created."[35] The same verse is woven into the underside of Barth's warning in the twentieth century: "The task and function of woman is to submit to her "B" status allowing the man to precede her, as stimulator, leader, and inspirer. How could she submit to her divinely ordained "B" status without the precedence of the man? How could she envy or reject his precedence? To wish to replace him in status or to assume equality with him, would be to wish not to be a woman."[36]

The history, philosophy, and theology we were taught assumed that shame is an essential female characteristic. The historical linkage of women's constitutional inferiority with shame has been used to keep women in line for centuries.

Throughout the development of Western civilization, women were expected to wear shame like a garment, covering, or veil to remind them of their inferiority and their proper place in the hierarchic scheme of things, and to protect others from the peril and temptation of their unveiled presence. Shame was considered an essential female characteristic.[37] Shame kept women in line.

Shame was to be demonstrated in a woman's behavior: A virtuous woman was silent, chaste, obedient, discreet, shy, restrained, timid, and passive. It was to be displayed in a woman's appearance: A virtuous woman lowered her head and her eyes to avoid direct eye contact with men, blushed to acknowledge the embarrassment of being female, covered her head to indicate her subordination to her husband's authority, and covered her body to protect men from the peril of her natural seductiveness.

Shame was to be illustrated in the amount of space a woman occupied. A virtuous woman made herself small to fit into the scheme of things. Her feelings remained quiet and acceptable; her thoughts, tame and unthreatening; her needs, silent and non-existent; her appetites, manageable. A virtuous woman took up very little space with her body. She was and still is in danger of disappearing.

Shameless women refused to stay in line. They were condemned for their audacity to refuse "B" status and their arrogance to step into "A" status beside men. They were damned for exhibiting the unbecoming qualities of immodesty and personal ambition, and upsetting the divine order of things. In second century Rome, the humiliation of an unfaithful wife was made into a public spectacle. She was paraded nude on a donkey into the town center, vulnerable to the glaring crowd's insults and mockery. A sexually autonomous woman was without shame and could not be tolerated. In the third century the church father Epiphanius railed against the "heretical" Montanist sect because the women among them claimed Eve as their champion and assumed leadership roles, ignoring "the differences of nature:"

They bring with them many useless testimonies, attributing a special grace to Eve because she first ate of the tree of knowledge . . . Women among them are bishops, presbyters, and the rest, as if there were no difference of nature . . . even if the women among them were ordained to the episcopacy and presbyterate because of Eve, they hear the Lord saying: "Your orientation will be toward your husband and he shall rule over you." The apostolic saying escaped their notice, namely that: "Man is not from woman but woman from the man;" and "Adam was not deceived, but Eve was first deceived into transgression." Oh, the multifaceted error of this world![38]

A literal and figurative veil of shame has been passed from one generation of women to another, reminding us to always bear in mind, heart, and body our proper place in the hierarchic scheme of things. The veiling is for our own good, our mothers told us in word and action. They know what happens to women who step outside the lines, to shameless women who refuse to hide their creativity, intelligence, physical strength, ambition, and sexuality. Be careful, dear, the world doesn't like uppity women. They are called names: witch, ball-buster, bitch, man-hater, bra-burner, old maid, whore, spinster, selfish, ambitious. They are ostracized, remember Eve. They are burned, remember the witches. They are stoned, remember the woman caught in adultery. They are exiled, remember the rebellious first woman, Lilith. They are locked up, remember poor Grandma. They grow old alone, remember old maid Aunt Matilda. Women who are full of themselves meet with an awful end.

The world view of the architects of Western civilization is held firmly in place by monotheism's central belief in a male God who presides over a hierarchic reality.

To fully understand our communal history we must explore religion's pivotal role in the development of Western civilization's historical, philosophical, theological, and psychological viewpoints. Origen, an Alexandrian Church Father wrote these words in the third century: "What is seen with the eyes of the Creator is masculine, and not feminine, for God does not stoop to look upon what is feminine and of the flesh." [39] Clearly, the architects of Western civilization attributed the male gender to the divine, supporting their notions of the superiority of the male—he looks like God and is looked at by God, and the inferiority of the female—she does not look like God and he does not stoop so low as to look at her.

"What's the big deal about the gender of God" is a question I have considered with audiences all over the country in bookstores, churches, and women's centers, and on radio and television interview and call-in programs. We consider the question in response and reaction to a performance piece-reading entitled "Imagine" based on my first book. The piece invites audiences to imagine how their lives might have been different surrounded by images of the divine feminine in the churches, synagogues, and homes of childhood. Through performances and presentations, and through my ministry, writing, and life, I challenge the human community to confront its idolatry of God the father.

The responses I have received illustrate the pervasive influence of the male god-image and the dangers of stepping outside the lines to question, to reject, and to redesign religion from our perspective as women—even in 1990s! In Salt Lake City, Mormon men expressed outrage that women would even consider naming and imagining their own gods; "a blasphemous enterprise" was one caller's response. A Utah Sunday School teacher and his class became concerned about me after reading an interview in a local paper. They sent me a stack of letters, inviting me to "come back to father God." The teacher rebuked me for encouraging women to create gods in their own image and likeness. "Lay down your pride and leave God alone" was his message to me.

In Albuquerque, conservative Christian women and men called with similar outrage, name-calling, and concern that I find my way back to the one true God. In Hayward, California, the callers criticized the station for allowing such a blasphemous discussion to be aired. An Oakland caller assured me that her church would pray for my wayward soul. In response to a Boulder magazine interview, a flurry of letters attacked anyone who would question the male God of traditional religion. A Colorado man labeled our search for a God who looks like us "narcissistic feminism;" an interesting comment given the tenacity with which men have safeguarded the image of a God who looks like they do for the past 4,000 years.

"God is male and that's a fact" sums up the response of many women and men in this country. There is a BIG DEAL about the gender of God. "His" image and likeness have been woven into the history, philosophy, religion, and psychology that trickle down to us through the ages, a legacy passed on from generation to generation in the unexamined beliefs, customs, and preferences of a society that worships a male God and offers particular privileges to those who look like "him." God the father has remained an undisturbed idol for too long.

WOMEN'S STORIES
A WALK THROUGH THEIR COMMUNAL PAST

INTIMIDATION AND AWE   *Erin Louise Stewart*

Working my way through the symposium brought up an old sense of intimidation with ideas and concepts. I am an intelligent woman and yet the experiences in my family and in school convinced me that there was something wrong with me intellectually. How does a child so full of enthusiasm and potential become an adult who questions her capacity to engage ideas?

As I look back, all of my childhood energy and intelligence were used for survival in an alcoholic home so there was little left to use in school. I was sleep deprived because the violence happened at night. I went to school very tired and consumed by what was going on at home. Even at school, most of my energy was used to make sure that I followed all the rules. I always befriended the adults in my world. Because most of my energy was used for survival, conformity, and people-pleasing, I wasn't able to hold academic information. And the lessons were not presented to me in a way that held my interest or supported me to understand them so I felt very inadequate.

As an adult, I feel like I'm always trying to catch-up. It is a challenge for me to let go of the old vision of myself as intellectually flawed and to take the manageable steps to learn the basics. I feel vulnerable and embarrassed when I ask questions—ashamed of not having the information other people seem to possess.

I brought this background with me as I worked through the symposium. Their words tapped the old sense of intellectual inadequacy. I was most aware of my body's reactions as I read their words. My body knows and understands and it is from my body-knowing that I take on these men and their ideas. I felt nauseous, angry, and appalled at their blatant ignorance of women. I was shocked by the power they assumed and how out of line they were to use that power to define women—what nerve and audacity!

I wondered about the women who lived with these men. A dank and musty feeling swept through my body. I felt small, tight, claustrophobic, and trapped. It was hard to keep reading—and not because I didn't understand their words. I realize now that there are some words I no longer accept into my being. There is a healthy part of me that shuts down and refuses to listen to words that deny my existence.

I wondered why they used so many words and so much energy to convince themselves of our inferiority. My awe of women's power grew as I read their words because those men were threatened by us: by our power, by our bodies, by our influence over them. And respect for my own intelligence grew as I listened to my intuitive evaluation of their unacceptable words.

LONGING FOR WOMEN'S VOICES   *Susan Scott*

All the way through the symposium I wanted to hear women's voices challenging the men's cold and clinical assertions. Women were being dissected and disposed of and I wanted an intelligent and wise woman to repudiate their assertions. I hungered to hear a rebuttal to their words. Someone to tell me that we're neither defective nor misbegotten.

Accepting the challenge to assume intellectual equality, I refuted their assertions myself with the assistance of female philosophers of antiquity. I found one source book about women philosophers at my college library among the 496 texts about male philosophers. Through that one book, I discovered new friends who introduced themselves across the centuries:

Cleobulina of Rhodes (ca 570 BCE) was a Greek philosopher and rhetorician. She wrote riddles in hexameter verse, one of which Aristotle quotes in his *Poetics* and in his *Rhetoric*.

Aspasia (ca. 470-410 BCE) was an Athenian courtesan and rhetorician. In Plato's dialog the Menenenus, Socrates acknowledges that she taught him rhetoric and influenced the so-called Socratic method.

Arete of Cyrene (ca 370-340 BCE) was a teacher in the schools and academies of Attica. She was a pupil and friend of Socrates and founded the hedonistic Cyrenaic school of philosophy. She taught philosophy for thirty-five years and wrote forty books.

Catherine of Alexandria (?-305 CE) was an Egyptian philosopher, ordered by Emperor Maxentius to dispute fifty pagan philosophers. She was martyred and eventually canonized.

Hypatia (ca 370-415 CE) was a Greek philosopher, scientist, and mathematician. She taught and at 25 was appointed director of the Neoplatonic school in Alexandria.

Asclepigenia (ca 375 CE) was a Greek Neoplatonic philosopher. She taught and later directed Plutarch's school.

Elizabeth of Bohemia (1618 - 1680 CE) was the German disciple of Descartes. He recognized that she understood his writings more thoroughly than anyone he had encountered.

These are only a few of the many learned women I came to know in my exploration. I had to work hard to find them. They were overshadowed by their lovers, fathers, and brothers. Their ideas clamor in obscurity until we resurrect them in our minds and hearts. Though I grieve the loss of their voices, I rejoice that with effort I can rescue them from their silent oblivion. I now know that I am not alone—I just have to work harder to find evidence of my truth and to discover intellectual mentors.

BUT I WANTED TO WRITE ABOUT ANGER
Women are "the devil's gateway," etc.
Isie Hanson

I read and tasted
your unkind
ignorant words,
so, so old
like rust in my mouth.
My tongue burned fiercely,
my mind shrieked "No!"
my heart cramped,
my spirit held its breath.
And the bile of other betrayals
flooded me.
My body bowl held it all
and listened
to know.
Then I remembered
and spit it out
and breathed.
Remembered my womanness.
Which chooses not to be snared
by twisted hooks of misguided power.
Which desires instead
to swim past
such ludicrous bait,
onward, upstream,
where clear, roaring
waters spawn
a far more rewarding
adventure
than hating
you.

A WALK THROUGH THE PAST
ENGAGING ALL OF YOUR INTELLIGENCES

1. Give voice to the whole range of human emotion provoked by the Symposium. Acknowledge your own anger, intimidation, fear, and longing for women's voices in poetry or prose.

2. Find a movement, image, or sound to express each of the phrases you marked. Draw your outrage. Write down your memory. Dance your body's response.

3. Assume intellectual equality with these men by writing a sermon of outrage in response to the participant's ideas or a rebuttal of their arguments from your own experience as a woman. For example:

Refute Aristotle's definitions of the inferiority of the woman's soul from your own experience as a woman:

    1. Her nutritive soul requires less nourishment than the man's.

    2. Her sensitive soul is devoid of sexual desire therefore she assumes the passive role in copulation.

    3. Her rational soul does not include the capacity to govern her own life and manage her own actions.

Develop alternative answers to Philo's questions 27, 33, and 37.

Refute Freud's statement: "It seems that women have made few contributions to the discoveries and inventions in the history of civilization." (Refer to end note #37)

4. Reread the words and phrases, childhood messages, and current experiences triggered by the symposium. Add your words and develop your own "trickle down theory."

5. Spend an afternoon at the library, finding out about the wives, sisters, daughters, and women-colleagues of the men featured in the symposium. Gather the fragments of women's stories, ideas, and accomplishments from the margins of history and religion.

2

OUTRAGE-OUS WORDS: ASSUMING INTELLECTUAL EQUALITY

To step outside of patriarchal thought means: . . .
overcoming the deep-seated resistance within ourselves
toward accepting ourselves and our knowledge as valid.
It means getting rid of the great men in our heads and substituting
for them ourselves, our sisters, our anonymous foremothers.

—GERDA LERNER, *The Creation of Patriarchy*

You are not alone in your search to find out and to remedy what's wrong with you. Eve's daughters have been trying to get it right for centuries. Some women worship the gods, learn the language and ways, and take the names of men. They step into the place prescribed for them as a "B" convinced that there isn't any reason for living without an "A" in their lives to stimulate, lead, and inspire. They indwell their biological destiny and stay in the private world of home and family where they are expected to anticipate and then meet the emotional and physical needs of others. Preoccupied with servicing others with their energy, attention, and creativity, they lose touch with their own needs and wants. Assuming inappropriate responsibility for the cause, modification, and outcome of the choices, behaviors, and actions of family members, they lose touch with their own lives and well-being.

These women become over-achievers within the private sphere. Always striving to please others, they develop a crippling over-sensitivity to and dependence on the opinions of others and lose touch with their own feelings and thoughts. And they pass on to their daughters the gods, language, and subversive manipulations allowed of women in a society that prefers men. Their intention is to make our way easier. They know what happens to those who do not stay in their place, those who refuse inferiority and subordination.

And yet even these quintessential females are never quite good enough as mothers, chauffeurs, hostesses, servers, caterers, and sexual providers. They are labeled lazy or selfish if they stop for even a moment to consider if they are truly satisfied. Echoes of another time rise up from within them along with a profound sense of disappointment—immediately eradicated by a glass of wine, a tranquilizer, a pint of ice cream, or another redecoration project. They are never quite good enough no matter what they do.

Describe your quest to become the quintessential female. Once you acquired the husband to legitimize you, the children to validate you, the perfect home to distract you, did the self-critical voice quiet down, did the question "what's wrong with me" dissolve?

BECOMING MALE

Other women have attempted to transcend the weakness of being female by "becoming male." This strategy has its historical and theological roots in the concept of progress, defined by Philo: "Progress is nothing else than the giving up of the female gender by changing into the male since the female gender is material, passive, corporeal, and sense-perceptible, while the male is active, rational, incorporeal, and more akin to mind and thought."[40] In the Gnostic Gospel of Thomas, a woman's salvation is linked to her willingness "to make herself male:"

> *"Simon Peter said to the disciples 'Let Mary leave us, for women are not worthy of life.' But Jesus said, 'I myself shall lead her, in order to make her male, so that she too may become a living spirit, resembling you males. For every woman who will make herself male will enter the kingdom of heaven."[41]*

Historically, "becoming male" was accomplished through virginity, martyrdom, or severe asceticism. By rejecting both their sexual and reproductive capacities, women virgins, martyrs, and ascetics transcended the weakness of being female, a weakness clearly located in the female body. They were acknowledged for taking on a manly mentality, for being a man in everything but body. They were praised for surpassing the limitations of their sex and for performing manly deeds like a man.[42]

These women have contemporary counterparts. Many of us watched our quintessentially female mothers ignore their own creativity and vocational interests, set aside their own projects and dreams, and postpone completing their own degrees in order to finance the dreams of others with their blood, sweat, and tears. As we observed our mothers' lives, we went to any lengths to do it differently. We left home, following our fathers. Creating a home, and bearing and nurturing a child, were not considered compelling tasks. Making our mark in the fathers' world was.

Encouraged by the women's movement, we postponed or eliminated family as an option. We pursued our careers and wouldn't allow anything to stop us. We felt it necessary to cut off access to our dreams, intuition, feelings, and tenderness. We considered our so-called feminine qualities an obstacle to our success, so we worked hard to eradicate them. We adopted "male characteristics" to make it in a man's world. We became relentless in our pursuit of perfection, doers and overachievers always on the move.

And yet we are never quite good enough as men. We hit the glass ceiling. We long for a child. And our female body just keeps reminding us that we are other than the men we work with. Its sensations distract us; its cycles and rhythms are relentless; and its power to attract—no matter how carefully neuterized or disguised—makes us vulnerable in a way our male colleagues are not. We try so hard to hang with the boys, to do it all—yet we're never quite good enough no matter what we do.

Describe your attempts to transcend the "weakness" of being female. Once you acquired the job or degree to legitimize you and achieved mastery of your emotions and your body's rhythms and cycles to prove you were as competent as a man, did the question "what's wrong with me" dissolve?

ADDICTION

Some of Eve's daughters choose to hide in food, work, alcohol, drugs, or relationships. Our addictions function as a veil of shame separating us from the human community. At times we long for reconnection. We search for a magical insight or treatment that will exorcise the flawed part of us. At other times our addiction feels like a warm protective covering, behind which we hide essential parts of themselves in response to and in avoidance of the exposure, scrutiny, and judgment of others.

Isolation from others and alienation from ourselves culminate in the contraction of our lives. Fearful of exposure, depleted of our life energy, our lives become smaller. We are available for superficial relationships—the ones that don't require access to the hidden parts of ourselves. Addiction becomes our gatekeeper, circumscribing our lives. We live within a very small circle, fearful of moving out to explore, to experiment, to risk exposure. If we venture out too far, the critical voices begin and we return to the safety of our contracted existence. Numbness (no feeling), boredom (predictable activity), and habit (controlled regularity) become our companions.

Describe your attempts to quiet the critical voices by "hiding out" in an addictive relationship to work, food, drugs, alcohol or another person. Was your addiction an effective gatekeeper? Was it successful at keeping the question "what's wrong with me" from disturbing your contracted existence?

SUICIDE

The final recourse is suicide
successfully attempted
by many women throughout the ages.
The ultimate choice to transcend
the weakness
the responsibility
the harassment
of being female.

The way out of it all, the final relinquishment,
to die in one dramatic moment of courage and willfulness
or to slowly disappear
under layers of fat,
in a drug-induced stupor,
or in the vagueness of an unformed life.

Palladius traveled through Egypt in the fourth century
to gather anecdotal tales of holy women and men.
He records the story of Alexandra.

"A maidservant named Alexandra left the city and immured herself in a tomb. She received the necessities of life through a window and for ten years never looked a woman or man in the face. In the tenth year she fell asleep after she had arranged herself. The woman who used to go to her received no answer and announced this to us. Breaking open the door, we entered and found her dead.

Melania also told us about her: 'I never beheld her face to face, but I stood near the window and asked her to tell why she had immured herself in a tomb.' She then told me: 'A man was distracted in mind because of me, and rather than scandalize a soul made in the image of God, I betook myself alive to a tomb, lest I seem to cause him suffering or reject him.'

When I asked, 'How do you persevere, never seeing anyone, but battling against weariness?' she said: 'From early dawn to the ninth hour I pray from hour to hour while spinning flax. The rest of the time I go over in my mind the holy patriarchs, prophets, apostles, and martyrs. Then I eat my crusts and wait patiently the other hours for my end with good hope.'"[43]

Some women are murdered
by the words absorbed into their life-stream.
Like the steady drip of an IV inserted at birth
the words of the holy patriarchs, prophets, apostles, and martyrs
are responsible for Alexandra's death.
Their words held her body
responsible for the distraction of men.
Their words slowly poisoned her
as they praised her virtue
for successfully surpassing the weakness of being female.
May she rest in peace.

Acknowledge the women in your family and in your circle of friends and colleagues who have committed suicide by naming them in the quietness of your heart or aloud into the space. Acknowledge in words, images, or movements the times you've wanted to die because you couldn't figure out what was wrong and how to remedy it.

OUTSIDE THE SYMPOSIUM: WOMEN'S VOICES

There have always been women who remember the old ways.
Women who hold within them
the memory of a time
in the very beginning
when women were honored.

Women who refuse
to worship the gods,
to learn the language,
to take the names
of the fathers.

Women who refuse to twist
their female bodies out of shape
to fit into definitions,
to transcend limitations.
Women who love their bodies. Regardless.

Women who refuse to please others
by becoming smaller than they are.
Women who take space
with their thoughts and feelings,
their needs and desires,
their anger and their dreams.

I imagine them
outside the symposium
loud and strong
women from every age
wild women
spinster women
wise women
rebellious women
women who love women
midwives
witches
healers
activists.

Banners and placards aloft . . .
Eve, the Mother of All Living
    Take and eat of the good fruit of life. Take a big bite!
Sappho
    She Who Gives Birth Has Power Over Life And Death
Mary Wollstonecraft
    Break The Silken Fetters
Sojourner Truth
    Ain't I A Woman!?!
Margaret Sanger
    Speak And Act In Defiance Of Convention
Elizabeth Cady Stanton
    Whatever the Bible may be made to do in Hebrew and Greek
    in plain English it does not exalt and dignify women.
Karen Horney
    Womb Envy Is More Like It

Audre Lorde
The Master's Tools Will Never Dismantle the Master's House

Women's speeches and songs
questions and answers
suspicion and anger
greeting the men
as they emerge from the symposium.

One by one the women step up
and speak the truth of a woman's life
they commit the forbidden act
of biting into patriarchal thought
refuting it, smashing it,
discarding it and beginning again
in the very beginning when women
loved their bodies
named their gods
authored their lives
when women refused to surrender
except to life as it pulsated through them.

Women full of themselves
their ideas
their stories
their anger
their passion.

Women reminding us
there is nothing wrong
there never has been anything wrong
there never will be anything wrong
with woman
that's why nothing ever works.
Stop asking the question!

OUTRAGEOUS WORDS

Biting into Rousseau's educational philosophy, Mary Wollstonecraft (1759–1797), philosopher, social theorist, champion of women, and mother of two daughters reads from her *Vindication of the Rights of Woman.* A product of the Enlightenment, she considered lack of education to be the primary cause of women's social challenges. She championed equal educational opportunities for girls and in the process challenged Rousseau's misogyny.

> Rousseau declares that a woman should never, for a moment, feel herself independent, that she should be governed by fear to exercise her natural cunning, and made a coquettish slave in order to render her a more alluring object of desire, a sweeter companion to man, whenever he chooses to relax himself. He carries the arguments, which he pretends to draw from the indications of nature, still further, and insinuates that truth and fortitude, the corner stones of all human virtue, should be cultivated with certain restrictions, because, with respect to the female character, obedience is the grand lesson which ought to be impressed with unrelenting rigour. What nonsense! When will a great man arise with sufficient strength of mind to puff away the fumes which pride and sensuality have thus spread over the subject![44]

> Probably the prevailing opinion, that woman was created for man, may have taken its rise from Moses's poetical story; yet, as very few, it is presumed, who have bestowed any serious thought on the subject, ever supposed that Eve was, literally speaking, one of Adam's ribs, the deduction must be allowed to fall to the ground; or only be so far admitted as it proves that man, from the remotest antiquity, found it convenient to exert his strength to subjugate his companion, and his invention to show that she ought to have her neck bent under the yoke, because the whole creation was only created for his convenience or pleasure . . .[45]

Biting into Biblical theology and exposing its fallibility, Elizabeth Cady Stanton (1815–1902), founder of equal rights and suffrage associations, organizer of annual conventions, editor of the *History of Women's Suffrage,* and mother of seven children reads from her introduction to *The Woman's Bible.* Its publication was a courageous act. In it, Stanton and her revising committee dismantled the question "what's wrong with woman" by challenging the powers that be: divine authority in the heavens, centuries of male biblical interpretation, and ingrained church custom.

> From the inauguration of the movement for woman's emancipation the Bible has been used to hold her in the "divinely ordained sphere," prescribed in the Old and New Testaments. The canon and civil law; church and state; priests and legislators; all political parties and religious denominations have alike taught that woman was made after man, of man, and for man, an inferior being, subject to man.
>
>   These familiar texts are quoted by clergymen in their pulpits, by statesmen in the halls of legislation, by lawyers in the courts, and are echoed by the press of all civilized nations, and accepted by woman herself as "The Word of God." So perverted is the religious element in her nature, that

with faith and works she is the chief support of the church and clergy; the very powers that make her emancipation impossible . . .

The canon law, the Scriptures, the creeds and codes and church discipline of the leading religions bear the impress of fallible man, and not of our ideal great first cause, "the Spirit of all Good," that set the universe of matter and mind in motion, and by immutable law holds the land, the sea, the planets, revolving round the great center of light and heat, each in its own elliptic, with millions of stars in harmony all singing together, the glory of creation forever and ever.[46]

Biting into Freud's psychoanalytic musings about women, Simone de Beauvoir (1908–1986), writer, philosopher, and feminist, reads from *The Second Sex.* Although current feminist scholarship debates the merits of her work, thousands of American women experienced a profound awakening while reading *A Second Sex* during feminism's resurgence in the 1960s and 1970s. De Beauvoir dismantles the question "what's wrong with woman" by exposing the inferiority-based socialization of the girl-child and by offering a girl-affirming vision of parenting as relevant today as it was in 1949.

If the little girl were brought up from the first with the same demands and rewards, the same severity and the same freedom, as her brothers, taking part in the same studies, the same games, promised the same future, surrounded with women and men who seemed to her undoubted equals, the meanings of the castration complex and of the Oedipus complex would be profoundly modified.

Assuming on the same basis as the father the material and moral responsibility of the couple, the mother would enjoy the same lasting prestige; the child would perceive around her an androgynous world and not a masculine world. Were she emotionally more attracted to her father—which is not even sure—her love for him would be tinged with a will to emulation and not a feeling of powerlessness; she would not be oriented toward passivity.

Authorized to test her powers in work and sports, she would not find the absence of the penis—compensated by the promise of a child—enough to give rise to an inferiority complex; correlatively, the boy would not have a superiority complex if it were not instilled into him and if he looked up to women with as much respect as to men. The little girl would not seek sterile compensation in narcissism and dreaming, she would not take her fate for granted; she would be interested in what she was doing, she would throw herself without reserve into undertakings.[47]

Biting into recorded history's inherent bias, Gerda Lerner, a founding member of National Organization for Women, professor of history, and one of the founders of the academic discipline of Women's History, reads from two of her pivotal books: *The Majority Finds Its Past* and *The Creation of Patriarchy*. She dismantles the question "what's wrong with woman" by challenging women and men to think themselves out of patriarchy's social organization and to imagine into being "a world that is truly human."

> Women's history asks for a paradigm shift. It demands a fundamental re-evaluation of the assumptions and methodology of traditional history and traditional thought. It challenges the traditional assumption that man is the measure of all that is significant, and that the activities pursued by men are by definition significant, while those pursued by women are sub-ordinate in importance. It challenges the notion that civilization is that which men have created, defended, and advanced while women had babies and serviced families and to which they, occasionally and in a marginal way, "contributed."[48]

> As long as both men and women regard the subordination of half the human race to the other as "natural," it is impossible to envision a society in which differences do not connote either dominance or subordination. The feminist critique of the patriarchal edifice of knowledge is laying the groundwork for a correct analysis of reality, one which at the very least can distinguish the whole from a part. Women's History, the essential tool in creating feminist consciousness in women, is providing the body of experience against which new theory can be tested and the ground on which women of vision can stand.

> A feminist world-view will enable women and men to free their minds from patriarchal thought and practice and at last to build a world free of dominance and hierarchy, a world that is truly human.[49]

Biting into the inherent bias of Aristotelian biology, Maryanne Cline Horowitz historian and professor reads from her essay "Aristotle and Women." She represents the arrogance of feminist scholarship, challenging the heretofore inalienable doctrine of "natural law" in every arena of male thought and dismantling it one idea, one theory, and one distortion at time.

> It is time for us to recognize that infiltrating Aristotle's erudition was a very common prejudice: an unquestioned belief that the female sex is inferior to the male sex. Further proof comes from the fact that he very cleverly argued to explain away apparent female superiorities . . . His observations led him to conclude that females develop more slowly in the womb, but that after birth they pass more quickly through the stages of puberty, prime, and old age. Slowness in the womb, resulting from coldness, is interpreted as a defect, despite his recognition that colder embryos are less damaged. Quickness out of the womb is also interpreted as a defect resulting from female weakness: " . . . for all inferior things come sooner to their

perfection or end, and as this is true of works of art so it is of what is formed by Nature." Women can't win with the supposed "empiricist;" all apparent differences between male and female are attributed to the "natural deficiencies" of the female sex.

The complexity and accomplishment of Aristotle indicate his overriding concern for scientific and philosophical truth. What we must recognize is that the truth discovered was not neutral, but value-ridden. The inferiority of the female sex was not in Aristotle's works an explicit end-point, a doctrine to be proved or justified, but rather a value-ridden premise underlying his logical arguments on other topics.

It is not enough that Aristotle gets his due from womankind, womankind must also get her due.[50]

Biting into women's self-negation and exposing its origins, Audre Lorde (1934–1992), lesbian, poet, and feminist theorist reads excerpts from her essay "Uses of the Erotic: The Erotic as Power." Her life and writing inspire twentieth century women to expose and extricate every remnant of oppression from within them as well as around them, and to view every personal choice they make for health, inclusivity, and freedom as a political act.

There are many kinds of power, used and unused, acknowledged or otherwise. The erotic is a resource within each of us that lies in a deeply female and spiritual plane, firmly rooted in the power of our unexpressed or unrecognized feeling . . . As women, we have come to distrust that power which rises from our deepest and non-rational knowledge. We have been warned against it all our lives by the male world, which values this depth of feeling enough to keep women around in order to exercise it in service of men, but which fears this same depth too much to examine the possibilities of it within themselves . . .

But the erotic offers a well of replenishing and provocative force to the woman who does not fear its revelation, nor succumb to the belief that sensation is enough . . . When we begin to live from within outward, in touch with the power of the erotic within ourselves, and allowing that power to inform and illuminate our actions upon the world around us, then we begin to take responsibility to ourselves in the deepest sense. For as we begin to recognize our deepest feelings, we begin to give up, of necessity, being satisfied with suffering and self-negation, and the numbness which so often seems like the only alternative in our society. Our acts against oppression become integral with self, motivated and empowered from within.[51]

Biting into God, Elinor Gadon, art historian and professor reads from *The Once and Future Goddess.* She challenges women and men of the late twentieth century to dismantle the idolatry of God the father and to reclaim ancient female images of the divine.

Merlin Stone began her ground-breaking book with the revelation that in the beginning God was a woman. And so she was. Accumulating archaeological evidence affirms overwhelmingly that prehistoric peoples worshipped a female deity. This evidence and the earliest writings document the persistence of Goddess religion for nearly 30,000 years, beginning in the Late Paleolithic, the Ice Age. With the coming of agriculture, in the Neolithic Age that followed, the religion of the Goddess flowered.

Goddess religion was earth-centered, not heaven-centered, of this world not other worldly, body affirming not body-denying, holistic not dualistic. The Goddess was immanent, within every human being, not transcendent, and humanity was viewed as part of nature, death as a part of life. Her worship was sensual, celebrating the erotic, embracing all that was alive. The religious quest was above all for renewal, for the regeneration of life, and the Goddess was the life force.

It is useful to put the ascendancy of the male God, of patriarchy, into perspective. The concept of monotheism is a relatively recent one, first expressed by the ancient Hebrews less than 4,000 years ago. The exclusive authority of one universal male God in Western culture goes back to less than 1,700 years to the conversion of the Roman Emperor Constantine in 320 C.E. and his imposition of Christianity as the state religion. Since that time Christianity has actively attempted to convert the rest of the world to the one "true" faith.[52]

WOMEN AWAKENING

One by one they step up and speak the truth
the truth of a woman's life
told with heart, mind, and body
refusing dissection
they are women and poets and theorists
who gather our brokenness
into their words
an impulse toward wholeness
awakens within us
and we become again
as we once were
whole.

The outrageous words of Mary Wollstonecraft, Elizabeth Cady Stanton, Simone de Beauvoir, Gerda Lerner, Maryann Horowitz, Audre Lorde, and Elinor Gadon, and the poetry of Susan Griffin, Virginia Wolf, Marge Piercy, Alicia Ostriker, and Ntozake Shange escorted me through my historical past to dismantle the question "what's wrong with me."[53] These women supported me to assume intellectual equality with the traditions I had been taught to revere as untouchable and God-ordained. My awakening came late in time. Some of us missed the second wave of feminism in the late sixties-early seventies. We were immersed in fundamentalistic traditions that kept us isolated from the political movements in the wider culture. We were dealing with the aftermath of growing up in severely dysfunctional homes—the kind of home situations no one wanted to hear about because they were so "depressing." We were struggling with our addictions to food, drugs, alcohol, and relationships. Addictions that kept us comatose, numbed out until we were ready to walk through our personal pasts. Or we were immersed in the isolation of being Mrs. Somebody, as fearful of those angry feminist "bra-burners" as our husbands were.

Our "consciousness raising" came much later than our feminist sisters. The "knight in shining armor" mythology shattered as we found ourselves divorced and the sole financial and emotional provider for our children. We sought support at a local women's center and began to listen to women's stories, shedding the competitive attitudes of a lifetime. We stumbled into a self-help meeting and a woman said "Goddess" instead of the compulsory "God" in the Twelve Steps, and we wondered how she got the courage to commit such a heretical act. Our therapist suggested we read *The Second Sex* or *The Creation of Patriarchy* and we were stunned that women were writing such powerful treatises and that we knew nothing about them. We showed up at seminary to major in religious education, the appropriate focus for young women, only to discover most of our classmates were "radical" women going into the ordained ministry. We relocated and found ourselves drawn to the local Unitarian church. We sat with tears in our eyes every Sunday listening to the preacher. *Her* words resonated with our deepest experience in a way that the words of male ministers had never been able to do.

WOMEN, FULL OF THEMSELVES

It is always in the company of women that we are reminded of our common heritage as women. A heritage that reaches beyond "the beginning" defined by men to the "very beginning" when the divine was imagined as woman. We discover that we are surrounded by a courageous cloud of witnesses—their experience and stories, their ideas and images, their creativity and outrage become healing resources for us. No longer asking the question what's wrong with me, we are freed from our obsession with the works, words, and lives of men. Self-possessed, we step outside of patriarchal thought and immerse ourselves in women's history, philosophy, theology, creativity, and spirituality. Receive Gerda Lerner's strong challenge:

> *To step outside of patriarchal thought means: . . . Being skeptical toward every known system of thought; being critical of all assumptions, ordering values and definitions . . . Being critical toward our own thought, which is, after all, thought trained in the patriarchal tradition. Finally, it means developing intellectual courage, the courage to stand alone, the courage to reach farther than our grasp, the courage to risk failure.*
>
> *Perhaps the greatest challenge to thinking women is the challenge to move from the desire for safety and approval to the most "unfeminine" quality of all—that of intellectual arrogance, the supreme hubris which asserts to itself the right to reorder the world. The hubris of the godmakers, the hubris of the male system-builders.*[54]

Women have been warned against exhibiting hubris ("arrogant pride") all of their lives. Our feminist sisters support us to be arrogantly full of ourselves for the salvation of a planet out of balance and in danger of annihilating itself. In their every word, we hear the powerful affirmation, "It is right and good that you are woman. Be full of yourself!"

WOMEN'S STORIES
ASSUMING INTELLECTUAL EQUALITY

THE ABSENCE OF WOMEN   *Irene Nicol*

Except for Elizabeth Cady Stanton, I had never learned about the women who spoke "outside the symposium." If I had only known about them when I was younger and hungered so to hear about women's accomplishments. I remember going to the library with my dad on Saturday mornings. I searched the biography shelves for females important enough to have whole books written about them. Even though there were many rows of books about men, I could only find two about women—Joan of Arc and Amelia Earhart. Poor Joan was burned at the stake for her beliefs and Amelia vanished into mystery.

During my college years I was overwhelmed with the pressures of life and the shame of having been raped. I was unaware of the feminist movement as I plunged into substance abuse to numb the memories and to avoid a life I didn't know how to live. When my daughter was born I gained the strength to crawl out of my victim hole. I discovered a new facet of my being—a fierce protective woman willing to face any challenge on my daughter's behalf. Inspired by her, I tackled my own dysfunction and found my way into recovery.

I have not become the perfect mother of my childhood fantasies—the one who walks through fields of flowers with cherubic children tagging behind gently pulling at my skirt. Being a parent is challenging. There have been many tears, much laughter, long days, and sleepless nights. Yet I will always be grateful that the experience of parenting led me home to myself as a woman. It was not in consciousness raising groups that I discovered feminism. My brand of feminism was forged by my choice to give birth and by my fierce desire that my daughter's visits to the library and her discoveries along the pathways of life fill her with a sense of pride and confidence in being a woman.

AN ALTERED COSMOLOGY   *Ferrel Rao*

The feminist movement of the 1960s and 1970s left my perceptions of myself and my possibilities pretty much unaltered. Feminists ("they") had nothing to do with me. At the heart of my experience of myself was a belief that I was unalterably damaged. This belief isolated me from feminists as effectively as it isolated me from every other group. I spent the 1960s through the 1980's just barely managing to stay alive emotionally and spiritually. My incest history left me addicted to relationships with low functioning men just like me.

My healing journey began through a spiritual connection with the divine feminine. This "spiritual awakening" was instigated one evening in 1990 when I showed up at an Al-Anon meeting expecting to encounter the man of my latest obsession, and instead encountered that night's speaker. She spoke about her understanding of recovery and spirituality from a woman's perspective. She challenged the prevailing norms of recovery which were based on a masculine understanding of the divine. Before she finished speaking, I knew that I needed to work with this woman on my recovery.

She introduced me to the non-shaming, feminist approach she had developed to support women to work through the Twelve Steps. As I sat in women's circles with her, a deepening relationship with the divine feminine altered my entire cosmology including how I viewed myself, other women, the world I live in, the options available to me, and even my awareness and understanding of my own personal history. After years of what felt like fruitless effort, my vision and experience of life's possibilities expanded. I am grateful feminism came into my life one evening seven years ago when I was searching for yet another man to "save" me. Instead, I found the way home to myself in the company of women.

THE DEATH OF AN ILLUSION   *Elizabeth Hughes*

I have had a huge resentment against myself, to the extent that I nearly took my own life a few years ago. I resent the ways I have betrayed myself over the past forty years by turning my will and my life over to men, a male-centered deity, and a male-worshipping society. For four decades I have been killing myself off by pretending to be less than I am. I have pretended to be less intelligent, creative, refined, hungry, sexual, joyful, depressed, angry, competent, fun, spiritual, clear, graceful than I really am. I did this to make others feel better about themselves, to win their love and acceptance by posing no threat to them, to keep them from deserting me because I was "too much," and to appear not to be a "show-off."

I have finally and painfully come to realize that I made all of my choices to ignore my own truth in favor of men, out of fear. Fear of being unloved, unprotected, uncared for, and left alone. Fear of powerlessness, helplessness, and hopelessness. Fear of ostracism, criticism, and sarcasm. And underlying them all was the fear of losing myself. That's the reason I have wanted to take my own life. The choice for suicide would have been a simple closure on the body housing the soul I had already destroyed.

I am reclaiming my soul, my truth, and my choice for life as I stop asking, "What's wrong with me?" The running commentary of judgment has been the background noise (like "Talk Radio" in the head!) going on all the time, and rarely pausing even when in the forefront of my mind something else is going on. I am changing this station on my talk radio channel. I want to start living in "What's right with me," in my own present, in this fine moment. I want to see, feel, and know myself as whole and loving even as I am human, making mistakes, causing others pain, and feeling my own. I want to honor, respect, and love the outrageous woman I am. I want to put my own loving arms around myself—today and everyday.

HEALING INTO THE PRESENT
REPLACING THE MEN IN OUR HEADS

Begin a four month immersion in the works of women with your daughter, co-worker, or friend. Surround yourselves with women's ideas, history, stories, books, films, art, music, and spirituality. Reflect on how these woman-affirming resources make you feel about your life, body, relationships, dreams, and goals.

Judy Chicago's art project *The Dinner Party* celebrates the contributions and achievements of 1038 women. The project is described and illustrated in an inspiring book you will find in your local library or women's center. Throughout the four months, read ten entries at the start of each day to become acquainted with your heritage.

Month 1   Women's History
Gather more of the fragments of women's stories from the margins of history and religion. These books will inspire your quest for a heritage, a history, a noble lineage, reaching back to the very beginning. *The Creation of Patriarchy* and *The Creation of Feminist Consciousness*, Gerda Lerner; *When God Was a Woman*, Merlin Stone; *The Once and Future Goddess*, Elinor Gadon; *The Dinner Party*, Judy Chicago.

Month 2   Women's Ideas
Women experience the world differently than men do. Reclaim your unique woman-intelligence and bring its gifts into the world. Allow the works of these creative thinkers to inspire you: *Vindication of the Rights of Women*, Mary Wollstonecraft; *The Second Sex*, Simone de Beavoir; *Women's Reality*, Anne Wilson Schaef; *Of Woman Born*, Adrienne Rich; *Sister Outsider*, Audre Lorde; *Blood, Bread, and Roses: How Menstruation Created The World*, Judy Grahn.

Month 3   Women Writers and Poets
Allow the brilliance of women's words to inspire your own writing. Be full of yourself! Write a novel. Compose a poem: *A Room of One's Own*, Virginia Woolf; *Made From This Earth*, Susan Griffin; *Circling the Waters*, Marge Piercy; *A Daughter's Geography*, Ntozake Shange; *Getting Home Alive*, Aurora and Rosario Morales; *Cries of The Spirit*, Marilyn Sewell; *The Temple of My Familiar*, Alice Walker.

Month 4   Women Artists, Dancers, and Musicians
Surround yourself with women's music, images, and movements this month. In response, allow the creative fruit of your womb to thrust forth. *The Dinner Party* and *The Birth Project*, Judy Chicago; "Shadows On The Dime," Ferron; "A Circle is Cast," Libana; "City Down," Castleberry & Dupree; *The Spirit Moves*, Carla De Sola.

PART TWO

EXORCISING THE QUESTION "WHAT'S WRONG WITH ME?"

3

The Religious Origins of the Question

For those feminists concerned with the religious dimensions of life,
the absence of any spiritual tradition which resonates
with their experience and which grounds women in the religious cosmos
is one of the most insidious aspects of Western culture.

—PAULA FREDRIKSEN LANDES
Signs: A Journal of Women in Culture and Society

Religion powerfully affects every aspect of a woman's unfolding life whether it was an *active participant* in her development as it was in my life and the lives of the women whose stories you will read in this chapter or a *silent partner,* providing the underpinnings for her development as it may have been in yours. It's impossible to fully understand our personal past if we don't explore the religious reality that shaped all of us. Many of the life patterns, gender attitudes, family customs, and child-rearing practices that our families took for granted have their roots in religious myths, dogmas, and stories. There was no way to escape religion's pervasive influence in our childhoods and in the formation of the question "what's wrong with me."

Religion pursues us into adulthood as well. Although Sophia grew up in an atheistic home, she was not able to escape the influence of religion. As an adult she married a Catholic and agreed to raise their children within the church. Sophia was led to my first book by her concern about the effect of religion on her children, particularly her daughter. I remind women, even the most irreligious among us, that religious issues, questions, dilemmas, and concerns come up all the time:

Awaiting word about the fate of a dying friend, we wonder if God will hear our prayers even though we haven't prayed to "him" for years;

Deciding whether to be married or to "just live together;" whether to be married in the church or in a garden; or whether to baptize and confirm, to circumcise or bar/bas mitzvah the children in order to please the extended family;

Sitting in a Twelve Step meeting desperately wanting serenity and/or sobriety yet ambivalent if surrender to a higher power a lot like the God of our childhood is the prerequisite;

Describing our emerging spirituality to a friend, we notice our inability to articulate its depth and meaning without using the antiquated language of our religious past.

We've all been immersed in the ideas of Western civilization and the Judeo-Christian tradition. Just as Aristotle, Paul, Tertullian, and Freud poisoned the well for all of us, so too the vilification of Eve, the dominance of the Genesis creation myth, and the idolatry of male images of divine are not the exclusive concern of religious women. It is essential for all of us to explore the religious origins of our self-critical attitudes. Along the way, we are challenged to assume theological equality with religious "truths" accepted as inalienable and to exorcise them from our personal attitudes and our parenting customs for the sake of our children, and ourselves.

RELIGION'S CRITICAL INFLUENCE

The criticism-based socialization, indoctrination, and parenting of girl-children within the larger society, the church, and the home are linked to four pervasive religious attitudes conveyed through the words, images, experiences, and expectations of childhood. The girl-child becomes convinced of *her defectness* as Eve's daughter through the sin-inspired vocabulary of childhood; of *her inferiority* as "other than God" through the idolatry of exclusively male images of divine; of *her exclusion* from full participation in the human community through her experience of the absence of women's reality in the rituals of childhood; and of her *"divinely ordained" subordinate role* through the expectation of humility.

As we travel the second path on our journey, imagine walking through your religious past to actively engage the religious words, images, experiences, expectations that shaped your self-critical attitudes and continue to nourish them today. Write them in your journal or draw them in your sketchpad as we continue our journey from self-criticism to self-celebration. Take note of the phrases of particular significance to you, especially the ones that trigger a connection between your religious past and your challenges in the present. Some women find it helpful to note these phrases with a magic marker. Others jot them down in their journals.

If you sorted through your religious past while reading A God Who Looks Like Me, *celebrate the steps you have taken as you read this chapter. Perhaps you will discover new insights and deepen your self-understanding along the way. Perhaps the chapter will sharpen your ability to articulate religion's critical influence on the girl-child's development or provide the outline for a parenting presentation at your next women's circle or church forum.*

If you are tempted to disregard Chapter 3's exploration because you "didn't have such an intense experience of religion," or your "family was only nominally religious," or you "left all that religious stuff behind," read beneath the specific details of each story and reflect on the ways religious words, images, and expectations influence your life and family today. Perhaps the chapter will illuminate the origin of disturbing religious images and expressions that float through your mind and heart without your consent, making no sense given your irreligious past. Perhaps you will examine more deeply the question "what's the big deal about the gender of God" and come to understand why the task of dismantling the idolatry of God the father is the one of the most significant personal and political challenges facing the human community as it enters the 21st century.

RELIGIOUS WORDS

In my workshops, I invite women to list the religious words and phrases that they remember from childhood. The lists are impressive, representing hymns, bible verses, childhood prayers, and particular family or denominational peculiarities. The word "sin" in one of its many variations tops the list every time: sinner, sinful, original sin, mortal sin, unforgivable sin. The two hymns acknowledged most often are "Onward Christian Soldiers" and "Amazing grace how sweet the sound that saved a wretch like me." Four Bible verses are often repeated: "For God so loved the world that he sent his only begotten son . . . ," "Spare the rod and spoil the child," "Pride goeth before a fall," and "In the beginning was the word." Eve is remembered in the phrases: "It was Eve's fault," "All because of Eve," and "It all goes back to Eve." "Impure thoughts" is regularly acknowledged by Catholics and "the woman caught in adultery," by Protestants. Catechism responses and confessional protocol linger in the memories of Catholic women: "Bless me, Father for I have sinned" topping the list. "Bible," "Word of God," "Thus saith the Lord," "Thou shalt not . . . " and portions of the 10 commandments are called out regularly. "Honor thy father and mother" is the commandment most often remembered.

Clearly, religious language exerts a long-lasting influence on our lives. And sadly it is most often the words of unworthiness, judgment, and punishment that pursue us into adulthood. Religious words convinced many of us that we were born sinful. In most churches, humankind's sin-based beginning requires baptism to cleanse the infant of the pollution of parental intercourse, of passing through the female body, and of inheriting original sin. And clearly, it was the first woman Eve who bears the primary responsibility for humankind's fall into sin. She became the scapegoat for all of humanity and her daughters carry her shame within their bodies, lives, and destinies.

The concept of original sin as universal and hereditary sinfulness and the portrayal of Eve as the instigator of evil provide the cornerstones of a criticism-based childhood. It *does* matter what a community believes about its personal, historic, and mythic beginnings. The belief in original sin and the vilification of Eve trickled down and influenced the theological, educational, and developmental theory and practice that touched our bodies, minds, and spirits in childhood. It affected the attitudes, behaviors, and disciplinary tactics of our parents, teachers, and religious leaders. It affects *our* treatment and expectations of our daughters and sons, and of ourselves. The belief that children are born naturally evil, sinful, willful, and wayward has had grievous consequences in the personal lives of many of us and tragic consequences for the human community.

The contemplation of sin fills theological volumes. Sin has been dissected, defined, and catalogued: Original sin. Universal sin. Hereditary sin. Actual sin. Venial sin. Mortal sin. Unpardonable sin. Four sins crying to heaven for vengeance. Six sins against the Holy Spirit. Seven capital or deadly sins. Nine ways of being accessory to another's sin. Degrees of punishment have been measured out appropriate to the gravity of the sin. Various remedies, rituals, and prayers have been developed to deal with the consequences of sin.

Even more profound than the elaborate intellectual spinnings of theologians are the definitions of sin women picked up in their childhoods through catechisms, hymns, and repetitive admonitions and warnings. Two variations on the sin-theme recur in women's writings. First of all, many churches introduced the Communion service with elaborate warnings about not taking communion "unworthily." It was serious business to partake of the body and blood of Christ! This warning was never explained clearly so we were constantly scrutinizing our hearts and minds for what might be considered "unworthy." In Irene Nicol's Lutheran church, she experienced a weekly conflict: "Before communion we were to reflect on our sins so we would not take communion unto our own damnation. We were to examine ourselves and see if we had an unclean heart. I was never quite sure what that vague reference referred to. For many years I did not take communion for fear my heart wasn't clean enough."

In the Bible Belt, Susan Scott was going through an identical inner conflict in the Church of Christ: "There were strict guidelines in my church about taking communion. If you missed church without a very good reason such as death or sickness, then you couldn't partake without making a public confession first. Behaviors you intended to keep doing, like adultery or stealing from your job, made you ineligible to partake. For "smaller" sins like telling a lie or being disobedient to your parents, you had to pray for forgiveness before partaking. It became too confusing for me. I wanted to avoid communion altogether because I believed I wasn't a worthy person anyway."

The second confusing sin-reference is the often repeated warning not to commit the unpardonable sin, sometimes referred to as "blasphemy against the Holy Spirit." This was the ultimate sin. The very mention of the words brought fear to Susan's heart, "This phrase scared me more than any other thing in my religion. I was truly afraid I would do something I wouldn't be forgiven for." Irene writes, "No one ever defined 'blasphemy against the holy spirit.' There was a lingering fear that anything I did could be the unpardonable sin which meant that there was no forgiveness and I would most certainly go to hell. Was it masturbation? Disrespect for my parents? Was it that time I stole a piece of candy? Or the time I told my best friend I didn't like my mother? I was constantly looking over my shoulder waiting for the ax to fall and not knowing what to do to prevent it."

The cosmic put-down of original sinfulness echoed from the heavens and was heard in our homes by way of the admonitions of our parents. Most of them were immersed in the unexamined religious belief that children are naturally sinful and that it was their God-given duty to bring us into line. In Robin's words, "There were no positive affirmations in my childhood just admonitions to get better grades, to lose weight, and to be a perfect little girl. My family reflected what the church taught: I was born in original sin and not good enough as is. I was taught that I had to rise above all that it meant to be human. Through prayer and doing good acts, I could atone for Eve's sin and for being evil to my core."

The sin-inspired words of childhood contributed to the internalization of the question "what's wrong with me." The emphasis on sin required constant vigilance as we scrutinized the minutest details of our every thought, motive, and action to expose the horrible monster, SIN. Our growing personal concern about sinning crushed the free spiritedness of the very beginning. Our natural spontaneity was replaced by a self-conscious monitoring of speech and action. Our natural life-energy was depleted by an all-consuming observation of the self.

List the religious words you remember from childhood. How would you have described "sin" when you were five, ten, fifteen, today? As a child would it have been easier to answer "What's wrong/bad about me?" or "What's right/good about me?"

Consider the recovery synonyms for sin and add your own: shortcomings, character defects, pride, "self-will run riot." Has it been easier for you to share what's wrong with you at meetings than what's right and good about you and your life?

Consider the new age synonyms for sin and add your own: negative thinking, fear, separation, darkness, ego, illusion. Is it more acceptable for you to pretend all is positive and light-filled at gatherings than to acknowledge the totality of your human experience?

Consider the psychological synonyms for sin and add your own: denial, avoidance, pathology, narcissism, egocentrism, personality disorder. Has your therapeutic experience been focused on the questions "what's wrong with me?" and "who will save me?"

Have you brought a criticism-based perspective into your adult pursuits, using "new and enlightened" dogmas to scrutinize and batter yourself?

RELIGIOUS IMAGES

Scanning my religious memory, there are three sets of images that drift through my mind. The first are Protestant images of bible stories told in Sunday School accompanied by flannel graph visuals or read to us by my mother from a bible story book with lots of pictures: images of a bearded God with his arms outstretched, ordering the world into being; of the woman Eve emerging from the sleeping Adam's side; of the baby Moses in a reed basket being placed in the flowing river; of the bright red burning bush that spoke to Moses; of the cracked-down-the-middle tablet on which the ten commandments were written; of the Red Sea parting for the Hebrews and then closing again, swallowing the Egyptians and their chariots; of Abraham holding a knife above his son's body poised to kill him; of tiny David readying the sling shot that eventually topples the giant Goliath; of Jesus in the manger surrounded by his parents and gentle animals; of three kings of different colors dressed up in robes and crowns, holding sparkling gifts in their hands; of Jesus, the good shepherd, holding his long staff while searching for the one lost sheep; of Jesus in a boat during a turbulent storm; of Jesus carrying the cross to Calvary; of Jesus dead on the cross; of Jesus' tomb, a rock covering the opening.

There are also Catholic images influenced by stained glass and statues, and pictures in my missal and prayer books: of Jesus with an open chest, displaying his most sacred heart; of Jesus on the cross with his head lowered, his body uncovered except for the cloth around his waist; of Jesus on the cross wearing the crown of thorns on his head, blood dripping from his brow; of Jesus ascending into heaven surrounded by light and angels; of Mary wearing long robes, covering her entire body including her head; of Mary holding the infant Jesus; of Mary high and lifted up with stars encircling her head; of Mary with her hands folded in prayer; of Mary with her arms outstretched, an ever expanding halo emanating from her head; of the flames of hell burning people who are crying and pleading; of light-filled heaven with angels and a big throne for God.

Images surface that are more like snapshots formed from childhood memories: of my mother held by the minister as he dipped her into a pool of water and then raised her up again-to my relief; of the priest with his back toward the congregation, lifting up the Sacred Host and saying, "For this is My Body;" of the nuns in their long black robes and black shoes with not even a hint of flesh or a strand of hair showing beneath their flowing veils; of the shiny black shoes lined up in priest's closet; of a white dress, veil, and shoes worn on the day of my first holy communion; of the minister pounding the pulpit to make a point; of crowds of women and men "going forward" to invite Jesus into their hearts at a Billy Graham Crusade.

Religious images filled my childhood and adolescence. Although I saw many more images of Mary and Jesus than I did God, his image was the most influential in my life. He was the unseen power behind the scenes. He was at the top—in the highest heavens. Every other image pointed to him, bowed to him, and owed its very existence to him. He was everywhere, they said, even in your mind, heart, and body. He could see your every thought and feeling, wish and dream. He knew your every move. It felt scary to have a big stranger always there, always watching. After they told me about the all-seeing God, nothing was all mine, private and untouchable. There was no safe and quiet place that was my own.

The image of an ever-present God is a shaming image that embodies the three essential ingredients of a shaming event: *exposure*—God sees everything even the most private thought or feeling; *scrutiny*—God searches the depth of our being to find sin; and *judgment*—God is the judge. His verdict is final. There is no arguing with God. The evening prayer I was encouraged to say in childhood clearly expresses these aspects as they trickled down to us in the churches of our childhoods:

Prayer before Examination of Conscience: O ALL-WISE and All-seeing God! Thou who dost always look upon my actions and count my steps, from whom no thought is hidden, enlighten my understanding that I may clearly see what evil I have done this day and what good I have left undone; move my heart that I may sincerely repent of all evil actions and that hereafter, I may dread nothing so much as ever to commit them again.[55]

Although I was taught that God was loving, he seemed harsh, unlike Jesus who was gentle and kind and loved little children. Yet Jesus' love could not erase the punitive nature of father God who sentenced his only begotten son to die on the cross. A sacrifice was essential in both Judaism and Christianity to atone for human sin. According to Christianity, Jesus was the final sacrifice. His blood was shed for the remission of our sins. Hopeless and hell-bound, we were to turn to him for our salvation.

Not only were there catastrophic consequences on a cosmic level for the sin of humankind, there were severe consequences for "walking away from God" after becoming a Christian. God punishes any deviation from his will. The pastor at Calvary told stories of families ruined by accident, fire, and death as a result of deviance from the straight and narrow. I "walked away from God" my sophomore year of high school. To walk away from God took a lot of courage because you were stepping outside of God's protection and anything could happen to you. I didn't stay away from God for very long that time. The warnings, admonitions, and threats were effective. They kept me in line for years, in a constant battle with my natural sensations, needs, desires, and capacities. It was my "natural self" that got me into trouble. It was to be "crucified with Christ." Driven to please God, an ever increasing chasm existed between my natural-essential self and the artificially constructed Christian self necessary for acceptance within the church.

And finally, the most influential aspect of the image of God for women is "his" maleness. No images in the churches or synagogues of our childhood acknowledged the divine as feminine. The use of exclusively male imagery convinces women that they are other than God therefore deficient, flawed, and inferior. We are never quite good enough because we will never be God. There will always be something out of our reach. The boy-child looks like God and his resemblance to the divine affords him power and privilege. The girl-child is a "misbegotten male" and the shame of her otherness accompanies her throughout life.

No matter how far we may have traveled from the religion of our childhoods, this image lingers within us. It was the image of a male God who exposed, scrutinized, and judged us. A male God who is "ALL-WISE and All-seeing, who dost always look upon our actions and count our steps, from whom no thought is hidden." An invasive male God whose image overshadowed even our most private moments. His image must be exorcised.

List the religious images you remember from childhood. What did God look like when you were five . . . ten . . . fifteen . . . today? In childhood, did someone accompany you into your most private thoughts and feelings, dreams and fantasies? Who was it?

Consider the recovery synonyms for God and add your own: Higher Power, "God as we understand him," "Our Father." Who accompanies you into your heart of hearts? What will be the consequences if you walk away from recovery's straight and narrow? What warnings keep you coming back?

Has the male god of traditional religion found "his" way into New Age circles? Is there a "New Age Monitor" who accompanies you into your most private thoughts and feelings? What will be the consequences for walking away from New Age beliefs and practices? What warnings keep you in line?

Is there a "Therapeutic Judge" who accompanies you into your most private thoughts and feelings, dreams and fantasies? What fears/warnings keep you from leaving therapy?

Have you brought a male-centered perspective into your adult pursuits, finding yourself drawn to male higher powers, gurus, teachers, and therapists? Do they seem more authoritative and effective than women?

Through whose eyes do you look at yourself in the mirror? According to whose perspective do you evaluate your decisions? Based on whose expectations do you design your life?

RELIGIOUS EXPERIENCES

The girl-child's sense of otherness and exclusion were intensified each time she sat in a religious service. Religion's dual-belief in her original sinfulness and in Eve's instigation of humankind's fall from grace, and religion's central image of an exclusively male God were woven into each ritual of the church. It was a deeply belittling experience to sit in services week after week that excluded us from the language and imagery used in the liturgy, hymns, and sermons; and that marginalized or ignored the contributions, concerns, and realities of a woman's life.

The Absence of the Mother

There were no religious images in the churches or synagogues of our childhood that celebrated the birthing powers of women. According to religion's myths, the world was brought into being by a male God, and woman was created from man. This reversal of biological process went unchallenged. Most of us didn't even notice the absence of the mother. Although we may not have been consciously aware of her absence in bible stories and sermons, her absence was absorbed into our being. And its painful influence was intensified as we observed the design of our parents' relationship and the treatment of our mothers by our fathers and brothers. Our families mirrored the hierarchical reality of the heavens. In a society that worships a male God, the father's life is more valuable than the mother's. The activities of a man's life are more vital and necessary than the mother's intimate connections with the origins of life. The father is God.

The Inferiority of The Girl-Child's Birth

There were no religious rituals in the churches or synagogues of our childhood that celebrated the birth of the girl-child. According to religion's myths and customs, the birth of the boy child was honored: Cain and Abel, Moses, John the Baptist, and Jesus, come readily to mind. There were no girl-children whose births were announced and celebrated by angels, whose comings merited regal visitors and precious gifts, and in whose honor the peoples of the world gathered for a yearly exchange of generosity. Psalm 127: 3-5 sums up the blatant exclusion of the daughter from the Scriptural record: "Sons are a heritage from the Lord, children a reward from him. Like arrows in the hands of a warrior are sons born in one's youth. Blessed is the man whose quiver is full of them." Daughters, like their mothers, were seldom mentioned. The exclusion of the girl-child from religious consideration was intensified in our family experience. In a family that worships a male God, sons are more important than daughters. Boys are groomed to administer the world. Girls are groomed to attract and take care of men.

For some girl-children, the question "what's wrong with me" begins in the womb as her parents pray for a boy. I met a woman at a book event in the South. She told me the sad story of her father's preference for sons. He was the head coach in their little town and all the townsfolk hoped, wished, and prayed along with the family that he would be blest with a son. To no avail, however. His wife had a series of daughters and the whole town participated in each of his disappointments. Finally after four daughters, the long-awaited son arrived and then tragically died in early childhood. The son's death catapulted her father into a severe depression that lasted until the day he died. He rarely spoke to his daughters.

Harriet didn't know she was a girl until she was twelve. Her father wanted a son and groomed her to be athletic. She dressed like the boys and hung out with her dad. While sledding one day, a friend asked her if she had cut herself because there was blood on her pants. There was no cut. She returned home to tell her mother that she was bleeding. Her mother proceeded to inform her about the "curse" of being a woman, a revelation they had kept from her as long as possible. From that point until she sat in my workshop as a seventy-something woman, everything associated with being a woman appalled her. She had been able to transcend the weakness of being female until her bleeding time began. And then she ignored her body as much as possible. She wasn't acknowledged as a strong, powerful, and fast girl-child. She had been misnamed "tomboy." That day we celebrated her as woman.

The Curse of the Girl-Child's Body and Natural Processes

There were no religious rituals in the churches or synagogues of our childhood that celebrated the girl-child's body and her natural processes. According to religion's myths and customs, the blood of sacrificed animals was ceremonialized and the body and blood of a male savior were honored. In a society that worships a male God, the blood of competition, revenge, and warfare are valued. The girl-child's blood, holding within it both life and death is messy and inconvenient. Her body and natural processes are "other" than God, a curse to be borne in silence. The girl-child learns to hide the realties of her life in a paper bag as she scurries from the office to the bathroom, hoping no one will notice that it is "her time of the month." The realities of a woman's life are to be hidden from view in the church . . . and in the home.

Two stories come to mind—stories of women I met on a retreat tour. Poignant stories that outrage me. An Albuquerque woman told me of her great aunt who wasn't allowed to dust the altar in the local Catholic church while she was menstruating. Her blood would pollute the altar, the priest told her. This monthly experience was witnessed by the niece, reminding her of the curse of being female and assaulting her developing woman-body. A Denver woman told me her mother's story, a story repeated by others throughout the country with startling congruity. During the forty years her parents have been married, her mother has never uttered a word to her father about menarche or about the changes that came with menopause. They have an unspoken agreement that her mother will keep "all that stuff" to herself. He doesn't want to hear about any of it. He shuns his wife during her bleeding time. They sleep separately. The taboo is deeply ingrained.

The Veiling of the Girl-Child's Sexuality

None of the religious rituals in the churches or synagogues of our childhood celebrated sexually autonomous women. They were exiled from the religious history we were taught. Chaste and submissive women were raised up as the ideals to emulate. In the beginning, as defined by men, Eve elevated sexuality. She committed the sexual act. Her body seduced Adam to join her in sin. As a result, she was exiled from heaven as Whore and

Temptress. In the beginning of Christian history, Mary the Queen of Heaven was shaped by men to eliminate the woman's body and its troublesome sexuality. The Sacred Woman elevates virginity; she abstains forever from the sexual act. Her body is eternally covered and beyond desire. The Virgin Mary was robbed of her body and stripped of her sexuality. She is allowed in the heavens only as Madonna and Virgin of all Virgins.

At every point in religious history, women's bodies have been assaulted by male priests, ministers, rabbis, theologians, and religious writers. Men have always feared women's bodies. Religious males in particular have had a powerful obsession with them. They have written volumes on the subject. Instead of dealing with their own attitudes toward sexuality and women, they have twisted us out of shape through their teachings and theologies. Our bodies bear the brunt of their deeply embedded fear of the feminine. In a society that worships a male God, the boy-child's body is subject to uncontrollable sexual urges. The girl-child's body is responsible for and vulnerable to these urges from birth. In a society that prefers men, "boys will be boys" even when they grow-up and marry. Girls are expected to be virgins with clean hearts who grow up to be faithful wives.

The necessity of a "clean heart" unblemished by "impure thoughts" lingers in women's consciences long after they discard the religion of their childhoods. "Impure thoughts" is another nebulous phrase we were expected to define for ourselves. In the confessional booth, we pretended to know what it meant to please the priest who inevitably asked, "Did you have any impure thoughts this week?" And then the expected answer: "Bless me father for I have sinned. I had four impure thoughts this week." We hoped he didn't pursue the issue by asking what they were since we'd made the whole thing up. We were to go to any lengths, including deception, to expose and wipe them out. In time, we figured out that "impure thoughts" had something to do with boys and girls doing forbidden things. Religion's words concerning sexuality, masturbation, and pre-marital sex trespassed even our most private moments. Over time, we developed a confused relationship to our bodies, natural desires, and sexual inclinations.

What religious experiences contributed to your sense of otherness and exclusion, to your sense of the unimportance of your mother and the inferiority of your body and its natural processes?

Where does a woman's body and natural processes fit into recovery principles and practices? Would it be acceptable for you to acknowledge the changing relationship to your body through each season of life and its effect on your recovery?

Where does a woman's body and natural processes fit into New Age principles and practices? Is New Age spirituality defined as an ascent out of all that is bodily and particular or as a descent into one's own body and life?

Are the contributions, concerns, and realities of a woman's life marginalized or celebrated?

Has your therapeutic experience been body- or word-centered? Do you feel more at home in your body and more aware of its rich resources as you leave therapy sessions?

RELIGIOUS EXPECTATIONS: HUMILITY, DENIAL, AND SURRENDER

Images of strong, self-contained women were exiled from the religious history we were taught. Images of passive women were elevated as the ideals to emulate. Mary was shaped and molded by male theologians to eliminate her capacity for choice and independent action. Without any resistance, she allowed her body and reputation to be disrupted. She allowed others to shape her life, destiny, and choices. She was the willing vessel and container for the birth of Christ. She surrendered to God's will.

Eve, on the other hand, refused to obey God and ate the fruit. She wanted to be God and the desire to be God, we were told, was the most blatant form of pride. Eve was punished for her prideful act and her punishment was used to remind us of the truth of Proverbs 16: 18: "Pride goeth before destruction. And a haughty spirit before stumbling." When Eve bit into the apple, she committed the forbidden act of stepping outside of the lines drawn by God. Whenever I noticed a good thought about myself, I waited for the ax to fall, proving that I had become too big for my britches, that I was stepping out of line. Any step out of line was an attempt to be God and any attempt to be God was pride, the first of the seven deadly sins.

The manual of Catholic devotions I was given in grade school includes a series of questions to consider as we prepared for confession and communion. The questions concerning pride included: "Have you vainly esteemed yourself on account of your fine appearance, your riches, your talents, or your birth? Have you blushed at the condition of your parents; spoken vainly of yourself, and taken pride, even in your faults; taken delight in the esteem and applause of others; been ruled by human respect in your exercises of piety?"[56]

We were not to vainly esteem or speak of ourselves, to take pride in ourselves, or to delight in human esteem, applause, and respect. We were to be humble, lowly, and unassuming. God deserved all the credit for our talents and accomplishments. A workshop participant shared the story of a nun who loved working with young people. She was very happy and satisfied in her ministry. Yet the senior priest transferred her to another job that didn't suit her so she wouldn't be prone to pride. Although she accepted the assignment with humility, she harbored a secret sadness because she wasn't doing what she wanted to do and what she was most gifted to do. Humility always had a tinge of "suffering and martyrdom" attached to it.

The girl-child's healthy narcissism and self-centeredness becomes crushed under the weight of religious expectations. Susan's mother once said to her, "Why can't you be more like your friend Cathy? She is quiet and nice and helps her mother in the house." Unlike Cathy, Susan was loud, opinionated, tomboyish, and full of herself. Her mother recognized early on that Susan did not possess the qualities of a humble woman as defined by their religion. She thought her daughter's haughtiness was ungodly. "She secretly wished for something to bring me down," Susan wrote as she sought to exorcise her mother's expectations and warnings and to reclaim her healthy narcissism and self-centeredness.

Along with pain and suffering, humility involved the "denial of self" and the surrender to "God's will." We were expected to deny our natural wants and desires, gifts and talents, thoughts and feelings, dreams and goals because anything spontaneous and natural could not be trusted. We were expected to surrender our natural selves and our willfulness to the will of God. God's will was imposed from outside of us and often had nothing to do with our natural capacities and gifts. We were encouraged to see all of life in terms of right decisions in line with God's will and wrong decisions out of God's will. There was one right college, life partner, and vocation. If we chose the wrong one based on our own desires and instincts, we were "out of God's will." We expected a divine "zapping" of some sort (divorce, disaster, disease . . .) to prompt a speedy capitulation to God's will.

Jean was gifted at mathematics. She won the prestigious math awards in high school. Without any consideration of her natural talents and their development, her parents considered it to be "God's will" that she attend a Christian college. Relinquishing her interest in math and surrendering to God's will, Jean attended a small college in New England without a substantial math department. Unchallenged, she eventually dropped out of college and began working for an insurance company. Ironically, the "secular" insurance company recognized her natural abilities. She was promoted year after year in recognition of her outstanding achievement. Jean's parents were more interested in requiring her surrender to God's will than in supporting her natural abilities to flourish.

List the religious expectations you remember from childhood. Who was your role model: Mary or Eve? With your non-dominant hand, write each of their stories as you remember it. Did religion encourage you to be full of yourself or to be quiet about yourself?

How have you understood the surrender called for in Step 3: "We made a decision to turn our will and life over to the care of God as we understand him." Are you encouraged to surrender to a power outside of you or to a wisdom resident within *you? Are you supported to be full of yourself or to be quiet about yourself? Do the requirements of humility and anonymity keep you in line?*

How is God's will defined by the New Age movement? Is it imposed from outside of your life or does it unfold from within your life? Is willfulness celebrated or demeaned? Are you supported to be full of yourself or to deny yourself?

Is therapeutic health defined and orchestrated by your therapist or does it occur organically as you turn loving attention toward your own life? Are you supported to be full of yourself or dependent on the therapeutic process?

AN EXORCISM

While studying at Princeton Seminary, I reread the Bible from my perspective as a woman free of the fundamentalistic trappings of adolescence. No longer fearful that I would be damned for tampering with "God's Word," I began to assume equality with this very human book. I gathered the fragments of women's stories from my religious memory and from the margins of the text itself. I invited the women of old to visit my dreams and to tell me their names. I also re-wrote some of the stories I identified with during adolescence, changing the gender of the characters if necessary, inserting the specifics of my story into the text. I imagined Jesus as a Woman-Rabbi and Healer.

I found myself drawn again to the story of the man possessed by demons in Chapter 5 of the book of Mark. At that point in my life, I felt possessed by alien energies in the form of childhood's critical words, images, experiences, and expectations. They had taken on a life of their own, pursuing me into adulthood and dictating the terms of my existence— without my consent. Raging within me, their force could no longer be contained. I was in need of an exorcism. I rewrote the Mark 5 story and continued to interact with it over the years as I journeyed toward self-possession in the company of women from every age.

The story is actually three stories woven together over time: the universal story of women of every age possessed of alien energies, deposited within them by intellectual, philosophical, theological, and mythic traditions we explored in Chapters 1 and 2 (**bold font**); the personal story of the child, who was criticized for her body, her expressiveness, and her truth (*italic font*); and the story of the adult who internalizes the critical messages, resulting in her isolation from others, her alienation from herself, and the contraction of her life (plain font). Three voices telling one story, the story of women who acknowledge the past's influence on the present, women who walk through the past and heal into the present, self-possessed and full of themselves!

A woman possessed by alien spirits had her dwelling among the tombs.
I see them in the distance. I watch them live out their days.
They visit each other's homes. They converse in public places.
They eat, live, and play together. They touch.
It has been many years. I long to draw near.
My eyes are weary from watching them at a distance . . . longing.

She had often been fettered and chained up, but she had snapped her chains and broken the fetters. She could no longer be controlled; even chains were useless. No one was strong enough to master her. And so, unceasingly, night and day, she would cry aloud among the tombs and on the hill-sides and cut herself with stones.
A scream lived in a little girl's heart.
Just say good morning and good night, no other exchanges are acceptable.
Be sure the image is protected, kept securely in its place. Don't assault it with your feelings. Don't challenge it with your needs. Don't question it with your individuality. Stay quiet, except as appropriate. Maintain the image-at the expense of truth. No loud noises, no strange movements, no bright colors, no humming. Wipe the water off before you come out. Don't rub your leg. Don't chew your food in front of me. Watch out who your friends are. There's a string on your shoulder. There's blood on your sheet. It's your fault. It's your body's fault. It's your mother's fault. Just say acceptable things about us. A press release, carefully prepared to protect our image. Just say good morning and good night.
The scream grew bigger as they twisted her goodness into evil.
It grew louder as they twisted her strength into weakness.
It grew stronger as they twisted her truth into lies.

When she saw the Healer in the distance, she came out from among the tombs and ran and flung herself down before the Healer shouting loudly, "What do you want with me, Healer? Do not torment me."
Hiding from a painful touch of long ago.
The distance keeps me safe. It has become my friend.
I cover my body. I watch it grow beneath the layers.
No touch will penetrate the uncleanness of my being.
My hands are tired of concealing my shame . . . hiding.

The Healer asked her, "What is your name?"
"My name is Legion,' she said, 'there are so many of us."
"Speak their names one by one and be healed."
Requires less nourishment. Devoid of sexual desire. Incapable of governing her life. Passionate not rational. Bodily not soul-full. Weaker and colder. Deformity of nature. False of speech. Not equal in honor. Not equal in age. Easily

deceived. Ruler of death and everything vile. Imperfect and ignoble. The beginning of transgression. Prone to vanity. The devil's gateway. The unsealer of the forbidden tree. Deserter of divine law. Destroyer of God's image. Responsible for Jesus' death. Perillous to all ages. Defective and misbegotten. Feeble in mind and body. Carnal. Imperfect animal. Foe to friendship. Necessary evil. Natural temptation. Desirable calamity. Domestic danger. Delectable detriment. Evil of nature. Genitally deficient. A 'B' and not an A.

The Healer addressed Legion, "Out, alien spirits, come out of this woman!" The Healer gave them leave; and the alien spirits came out-one by one.
One day, Gentle Love—in the shape of a blue chair with a big lap just like her grandma's—approached the little girl. Her body shook. Her life twisted. Her heart ached. Gentle Love came close enough to hear the scream in her shaking, her twisting, and her aching. "I will not hurt you," Gentle Love said. "Please do not twist me into the shapes of the past. Allow me to live freely. Allow me to grow within you. Sit down and rest, and your scream is welcome too." Gentle Love set free the scream.

It erupted in blood and darkness. It circled the planets, shouting in the open spaces of the universe. It splashed across the sky as sparkling fireworks brightening the darkness. The little girl rode on the back of the scream as it danced, circled, and splashed.

Exhausted the woman fell to the ground. In the fullness of time, she awakened and the Healer asked her again, "What is your name?"
"I am Daughter of Woman," she answered.
"Rise up and go into the dark of the night," said the Healer.
"Go to the women. They will tell you more of the truth."
I rise up and go into the night. In its darkness, my eyes and hands rest. The moon calls to me. She tells me of a time when a woman's life was sacred. When there were no shameful separations. She tells me of a time when a woman's body was honored. When there were no painful touches.

My eyes closed, I find myself in a clearing of light with women from every age. Their song calls to me: "You who stand apart, come close. You who are out of touch, come near." They do not throw stones, instead they offer me flowers and they touch me with healing and light. They sing to me: "It is right and good that you are woman." And they tell me stories of a time that once was:

Of ancient beliefs in a Great Mother who gave birth to the cosmos and its inhabitants, both human and divine; of ancient times when it was from the mother, the giver of life, that the line of the generations was traced; of ancient women who did not apologize for their fertile wombs, pregnant bellies, and full breasts, women who did not apologize for their girl-children.

Of ancient times when women were honored for both their capacity to nurture and to accomplish great things, when virginity meant "woman, complete in herself," owned by no man, creator of her own destiny; of ancient women who did not apologize for their sexuality and who refused to surrender except to their truest self, their wisest voice, and to the natural rhythms of life.

Of ancient ways that held a woman's blood to be magic, flowing in harmony with the moon, that celebrated the accumulation of a woman's years; of ancient women who did not apologize for their bleeding time, women who did not apologize for the fullness of their years and their wisdom.

Women from all ages, dancing and telling stories in the light of the moon.
In their stories, I hear my truth.
In the dance, I shed my veil of shame.
It is right and good that I am woman, that I am mad woman.

So the little girl, holding her tired scream, rested in the clearing.
As she drank of the golden green blue stream surrounding the clearing,
She swallowed the scream and it settled within her peacefully.

The people came out to see what had happened. They saw the mad-woman who had been possessed by the legion of alien spirits, sitting there clothed in her right mind; and they were afraid. The spectators told them how the mad-woman had been cured.

As the Healer was leaving, the woman who had been possessed of alien spirits begged to go with her. The Healer would not allow it, but said to her, "Go home to your own folk and tell them that once your were divided against yourself and now you are whole." The woman went off and spread the good news: "It is right and good that I am Woman." And they were all amazed.

WOMEN'S STORIES
A WALK THROUGH THEIR RELIGIOUS PAST

SHAKING THE TREE
Sophia Serrena

I was raised in a patriarchal, atheist family. My father taught me that God was for the weak, for those who "need a crutch." Having survived many traumas of W.W.II and the Korean War as a young man, he had not only proved the inherent evilness of man, but of God and the church also, both of which allowed such horrors to exist. He shunned his Christian upbringing and encouraged his then young bride, my mother, to question her own deep devotion to the religion of her childhood, Catholicism. As a result of her research and soul-searching, she left the church.

In spite of my atheistic upbringing, the vapor of patriarchal, Christian religious culture permeates and pervades all aspects of living, for although I escaped much of its traumas, it still touched my life. I can't pinpoint exactly how this happened, perhaps it was a teacher's attitude, or a little girlfriend's story about sins being "black marks on the soles of her feet" (a child-like misunderstanding of "black marks on the soul?"); or a second-hand account of Eve. I felt smug that I didn't have to sit through church every Sunday, yet I secretly envied people who had a relationship with God, and I didn't. This was the cost of being raised anti-spiritually.

Another cost to me was sisterhood and feminine support. My father taught me to question everything, and for that I'm grateful. In my eagerness to please him, to be strong and in control, I neglected my relationship with my mother whom I considered weak and wishy washy. My dad felt threatened by strong women and passed his suspicion of them on to me. When I was about 13, I wanted to participate in the development of a woman's center, called "A Woman's Place," in our home town. When I expressed my interest, dad had a fit and forbade me to go, deeming it a center for a "bunch of lesbians." Choosing not to defy him, I didn't go to the center. To this day, I'm sorry I didn't participate. I left my quest for sisterhood behind then.

I wasn't able to develop deep, lasting, and trusting relationships with women until I married and sought the companionship of other new mothers. I neglected my feminine side and had no space for religion or spirituality at all, a condition which I find as unhealthy as rigid fundamentalism. I was concerned about having a girl child of my own. I felt that my limited woman-education would affect my parenting of a daughter.

My husband was raised Catholic, and when we married I promised him we would raise the children Catholic. I even tried the Catholic convert program to make the parenting decision more comfortable. It didn't work.

I could not reconcile all of the male stuff with my inner voice calling for a feminine, woman-affirming spirituality. At the same time, I didn't have an effective method for expressing what I felt about spirituality. I thought I had nothing to contribute to our kids' spiritual training. I was bound and determined, however, that my daughter would not be raised with all the woman-shame that I had come to despise about the church.

A God Who Looks Like Me introduced me to the feminine face of the divine. I found many woman-affirming passages that I use with my daughter to reinforce positive attitudes about herself and womankind. The book gave me a voice to address the conflicts I encounter as I keep my promise to "raise" the children Catholic. Encountering the divine feminine also unlocked my relationship with women in general, and my mother in particular. I was able to have an honest conversation with my mother and ask her forgiveness for demeaning and condemning her woman-like characteristics. Finally, I can let my own femininity shine through, and relish my mother's femininity. I feel closer to my mother now than ever before.

Like most parents, I want my children to find self-fulfillment and happiness, and beautiful spiritual truth that supports them in their lives. In the meantime, I am doing all I can to teach them that God resides within them, in their highest Consciousness, and that they are loved unconditionally for their inherent worthiness. I still have to psych myself up for when we attend Mass or share holidays with my husband's deeply religious family. Yet I've found a way to bring my own spiritual understandings with me by viewing Mary as the Goddess she is and by acknowledging silently the pagan roots of each so-called Christian holiday.

MARY AND EVE   *Cristina Goulart*

Mary and Eve were the women acknowledged in my religious background. There were images of Mary in almost every room of our home. She was calm and loving, and her hands were folded in prayer. In the church, a life-sized Mary wept over her dead son as he lay limp in her lap. Mary was the perfect one. She was a virgin even in motherhood. I prayed to her; she was my comfort.

The image of Eve was not in our home or church, but she was spoken of regularly. I often heard the story of how she had been tempted by the serpent who was the devil in disguise, and how she had disobeyed God's commandment not to eat of the tree of knowledge. We were told that Eve's disobedience caused the suffering that women and men continue to experience today.

Our religion was one of fear and shame. I was terrified of the devil who tempted people to commit evil acts or to have evil thoughts. I was terrified of hell where I would be sent for all eternity if I wasn't pious enough. Even my thoughts could be considered sinful as God knew each and every one of them. Mary was my only comfort in this world of fear. She was Divine, yet she did not punish. I prayed my rosary to her.

As I got older I was taught a new fear—the fear of being called a "whore." Although to commit sex outside of marriage was a sin for everyone, I was taught that it was a worse sin for women. A man was almost expected to "fall from grace" and have premarital sex, but if a woman did the same, she became a whore. Once a girl was branded a whore, she was marked for life and that title would always come back to haunt her even if she were "lucky enough" to find a man who would marry her in spite of her reputation.

As a teenager, I became enraged as I reread the story of Adam and Eve. Why was Eve's act of bringing knowledge into this world considered sin? Why were Eve and all of her daughters for the rest of time held responsible for that act when Adam had eaten the fruit too? I knew the story must be some kind of lie—I knew a true God wouldn't do that to his children. I asked the adults in my life about it. They all seemed to agree that Eve's treatment was unfair and that men get away with more than women do. I was told, "It's not fair, but that's just how it is. Play along so you won't be called a whore, so you can get a good husband."

I became furious and resented all the adults who went along with this injustice. I vowed to denounce my Catholic faith and refused to go to church. My mother let me stay home, but my grandmother constantly reminded us that my refusal to go to mass was a sin and that I would surely burn in hell for it.

GETTING SAVED   *Elena Louise Richmond*

My mother always claimed that when I was four years old, I Accepted Jesus Into My Heart. I have no re-collection of this conversion. I have a feeling it was a confession wrenched from me in a maternal interrogation. My mother desperately needed me to exist in that peculiar Christian state of Having Jesus in Your Heart, i.e., Salvation. I on the other hand, needed a mother.

In my quest to find my mother's heart I became as obsessed with Being Saved as she was. I remember sitting at age seven, in Sunday School at Highland Covenant Church and having an experience of paralyzing terror that I had not accepted Jesus and that I would go to hell if I were to die because I had passed the age of six. Age six was the cut-off point for automatic pardon of sin. My brother called it the Age of Consent. Before age six, sin was not actually Sin because you weren't suppose to understand what you were doing. God, being reasonable, wouldn't hold you accountable.

So, at age seven, it suddenly hit me that I might not be saved from eternal damnation since I had no memory, only my mother's assertion that I had Accepted Jesus at age four. I could no longer plead innocent because I had passed the Age of Consent. I did a quick one, saying to the spirit world at large, "Jesus, if you haven't already come into my heart, do it now." It had been a close call, but I was now saved.

Of course, I was Saved many other times in my life. For example, guilt and uncertainty welled up inside of me at a Billy Graham Crusade when I was ten. Maybe I hadn't done it right that other time. The Crusaders were well into "Just As I Am," and sinners were streaming to the front of the arena. I was doing a ten year old version of wringing my hands; feeling hot, uncomfortable, and Convicted.

"Do you have to go to the bathroom?" my mother whispered to me.

"No, I think I need to go down there."

"You were saved when you were four."

"I'm not sure."

She looked at me as though to say, "You should have taken care of this before we came. We'll never get out of this crowd." Billy Graham always said that "if you're with friends, they'll wait," so my mother was in a dilemma. I was in a dilemma too.

In the end, solving the immediate dilemma took precedence over the larger issue of my soul. I didn't want to be prayed over by some smarmy pastor's wife with big teeth. I said to my mother, "I'm all right." "Good," she seemed relieved. "Let's leave now before everyone else does. I hate to get caught in traffic." As we filed out of the arena, I tried to reassure myself that I had most likely done it right when I was seven and that it would probably stick. If not, I was certainly in the right religion for booster shots of salvation.

The churches my family attended—and there were several because my mother would move us every time she thought a pastor had backslidden—were fundamentalist, Bible-breathing organizations. The raison d'être of these fundamentalist churches were altar calls. There were altar calls at all the services, but also at swimming parties and when the maintenance board met to discuss flooding in the basement. In Fundamentalist churches, you have the opportunity to get saved pretty much whenever you feel a need to. As a child, my need for reassurance was so great that I tended to take advantage of those opportunities. But genuine salvation as well as my mother's love continued to elude me throughout my childhood and early adult years. God was Lord of her universe, but he wasn't clever enough to succeed as middle-man between my mother and me. I never managed to get the assurance I needed. In the end, I have had to find my salvation elsewhere.

A WALK THROUGH YOUR PAST
Exorcising Alien Energies

There is no room for goodness to express itself,
no energy to act in positive ways, and no hope of health
with this self-critical tirade going on in my head.
I need an exorcism.

—RETREAT PARTICIPANT

Each critical religious word, image, experience, and expectation lodges within us as an alien energy, cluttering our inner landscape. They become our inner accusers and must be exorcised on our way back to self-possession. Gather the religious words, images, experiences, and expectations that you remembered as you walked through your religious past or go back through the chapter now to acknowledge and record your accumulation of "alien energies." Read through the following ritual to review its content, highlighting the words and phrases that speak to your experience, and adding your own to the list.

When ready, invite a friend to be your healing partner as you enter into the imaginative exorcism. Imagine the Healer—represented by your friend—approaching you among the tombs, approaching your hiding places. She turns toward you with her strong and loving gaze and invites you to name the alien energies that clutter your inner landscape. Name them aloud in the presence of your healing partner.

The Healer asks you, "What is your name?"
"My name is Legion," you answer, "there are so many of us."

"Speak their names-one by one-and be healed."
Original sin. Universal sin. Hereditary sin. Actual sin. Venial sin. Mortal sin. Unpardonable sin. Unforgivable sin. Ultimate sin. Blasphemy against the holy spirit. Four sins crying to heaven for vengeance. Six sins against the Holy Spirit. Seven Capital or Deadly sins. Nine ways of being accessory to another's sin. Eve, responsible for humankind's fall into sin. Eve, scapegoat for all of humanity. Eve, instigator of evil. It was Eve's fault. All because of Eve. It all goes back to Eve. Born evil. Born sinful. Born wayward.

Pollution of parental intercourse. Pollution of passing through the female body. Pollution of inheriting original sin. Completely, irrevocably flawed. Sinful without having taken any willful or conscious action. Sinful merely by reason of being born. Bad in the womb. Children are naturally wicked, willful, and sinful. Parents, like God, must punish and reward. God holds parents responsible for discipline of children. Whipping children keeps them out of hell. Spare the rod and spoil the child. God is always watching. Judgment of God. One can never escape the wrath of God. Life-threatening calamity. Go to hell. Sin. Sinner. Sinful. Unworthy person. A wretch like me. Stepped off the track. Missed the mark. Unclean heart. Dark mark on the soul. Atone for Eve's sin.

Bless me, Father for I have sinned. Examine your Conscience. Monitor your speech and action. Imperfections. Inadequacies. Shortcomings. Impure thoughts. Public confession. Ineligible to partake. Be pure and chaste. Sex is sinful and dirty. Don't play with the naughty parts of your body. Good people control such behavior. Pray to God for the strength to give it up. Masturbation is a sinful and selfish pleasure. Terrible things may happen to you if you touch yourself. Imperfect. Inadequate. Not good enough as is. Never quite good enough no matter what you do. Rise above all that it is human.

A bearded God with his arms outstretched, ordering the world into being. The woman Eve emerging from the sleeping Adam's side. Abraham holding a knife above his son's body poised to kill him. Jesus carrying the cross to Calvary. Jesus on the cross with his head lowered, his body uncovered except for the cloth around his waist. Jesus on the cross wearing the crown of thorns on his head, blood dripping from his brow. Jesus dead on the cross. Mary wearing long robes, covering her entire body including her head. The flames of hell burning people who are crying and pleading. Nuns in long black robes and black shoes.

God, the unseen power behind the scenes. God, at the top, in the highest heavens. God, everywhere, in my mind and heart and body. God, seeing every thought and feeling, wish and dream. God, watching every move. God, searching the depth of my being to find sin; God, the judge. God, looking upon my actions and counting my steps. God, from whom no thought is hidden. Father God, sentencing his only begotten son to die on the cross. God's repulsion for sin pouring out on Jesus at the cross. An angry God. A furious God. Mountains tumbling down before God's anger. God in anger turning his back on Jesus.

The Healer addresses Legion, "Out, alien spirits, come out of this woman!" The alien spirits come out—one by one.

"What is your name?" the healer asks again.
"My name is Woman," you answer.

"Go and spread the good news:
"It is right and good that you are woman."

Afterward:
Place the papers on which you recorded the critical religious words, images, experiences, and expectations in a wok. Burn them in silence and then bury the ashes in the earth or in your garden. The burial is your final good-bye to them. Play Brahm's "Requiem."

After the burial, play "Since I Laid My Burdens Down" from the audio cassette by Sweet Honey and The Rock. Dance with your healing partner as you celebrate the reclamation of your inner spaces. As a final benediction, say to each other, "Go and spread the good news: It is right and good that you are woman."

4

FORBIDDEN ACTS: ASSUMING THEOLOGICAL EQUALITY

*Take the snake, the fruit-tree and the woman from
the tableau and we have no fall, nor frowning Judge, no inferno,
no everlasting punishment, hence no need of a Savior.
The bottom falls out of the whole Christian theology.*

—ELIZABETH CADY STANTON,
The Woman's Bible

Imagine for a moment that it didn't happen the way they told you in Sunday School, Catechism Class, or Hebrew School. Imagine Eve walking among us outside the symposium. In the depths of your imagination, listen as she commits the forbidden acts of breaking out of traditional religious interpretation, telling her own story, and reclaiming her former glory as the Mother of All Living. Imagine the bottom falling out of Christian theology!

I am Eve, the Mother of All Living, culmination of creation.
I hold and nurture life within me.
In the fullness of time, I thrust and push life from me.
And all that I have given birth to is good, it is very good.
  Honor all that has been demeaned.
  Receive all that has been cast aside.

85

I was once known throughout the world as the Mother of All Living. The wisest among you have always honored Me in your myths of beginnings. I have been called by many names, Fertile One Who Births All Things, The Great Mother, Law-Giving Mother, The Bearing One, She Who Gives Birth to the Gods, Queen of Heaven, True Sovereign, Mother of the World, Queen of the Stars. I was called Inanna in Ur; Ishtar in Babylon; Astarte in Phoenicia; Isis in Egypt; Womb Mother in Assyria, and Cerridwen among the Celts.

I was worshipped for many centuries before the God of the Hebrews was imagined into being. As men became threatened by My power and by My intimate involvement in the origins of all life, they swallowed My stories into their unfolding mythologies and twisted My truth. My original power and glory are hardly recognizable in the stories you heard about Me in the churches, synagogues, and homes of your childhood. The image of a Father God ordering the world into being was firmly imprinted on your imaginations. Did you even notice the absence of the Mother?

According to the Genesis myth, I was born of the man, from his rib they say. I am outraged at this twisting of the truth. Who among you was not nurtured in My womb? Who among you has forgotten the source of your life? Jehovah was ignorant of his mother. In his foolishness he said, "I am God. There is none beside me." His arrogance has always troubled Me.

As the Mother of All Living. I exist before all things. From My body, all that is proceeds. Every mother who bears a child is the embodiment of Me. In her pregnancy, she holds and nurtures life within her. In her labor, she thrusts life from her. She is woman, strong and powerful. She is the Mother of all Living. I am outraged that woman's good strong body, containing all things necessary for life, and the body of Mother Earth, which receives back all good things to Herself, are objects of disgust and fear to be controlled and dominated in the Genesis story.

Honor all that has been demeaned.
Receive all that has been cast aside.
The Mother is good. She is very good.

I was given a pivotal role in men's developing mythology. They say that out of feminine weakness I ate the fruit and then seduced Adam. That I set in motion a series of events that resulted in our expulsion from the garden and the release of misery and death into the world. They say I am guilty, and that evil is grounded in my very existence and nature. Of me was written, "From a woman was the beginning of sin and because of her we all die." For thirty centuries of Jewish and Christian history, I have carried the burden of humankind's guilt and shame. No More!

The snake is my wise advisor, counselor, and the interpreter of dreams. Symbol of Sophia, of wisdom, the snake is the bearer of immortality. Life is renewed in the shedding of its skin. Worn on my forehead, held in my hands, and coiled around my body, the serpent has always been my special companion and the symbol of my life-renewing powers.

The myth-makers recognized the importance of the serpent to me. My trusted advisor was no longer to be trusted. Our special connection was demeaned. Instead of trust, they placed enmity between the snake and the woman. And the interpreters of Scripture renamed the snake, "devil," to be feared and eventually crushed.

Honor all that has been demeaned.
Receive all that has been cast aside.
The snake is good. It is very good.

In the very beginning, the sacred grove was the birthplace of all things. Its trees of knowledge and life were intimately connected to my worship. They were not my private property, nor did I wish to control humankind's access to their wisdom. We honored the trees of the grove. We cared for them and caressed them. They held within them the secrets of life, the wisdom of the Earth and her seasons, and the awareness of sexuality.

Many Hebrews worshipped in my sacred groves. Hebrew women followed me. Some, in the secret of their hearts. Others boldly rejected Jehovah and convinced their husbands to follow me. When King Solomon grew old, his wives turned his heart toward the Goddess. He did not remain loyal to Jehovah as his father David had done. He built hill-shrines in my honor. The myth-makers twisted the truth to serve as a warning to the Hebrew people not to visit my sacred groves nor to eat of the fruit of its trees. And the most zealous of Jehovah's prophets cut down my groves and burned the bones of my priestesses.

To eat of the fruit of the tree was to eat of my flesh and drink of the life-giving fluid that flows through me. In the woman Eve you catch glimpses of my former glory. She was intelligent, curious, eager, and strong. She ate of the fruit and received the wise secrets of life and the awareness of sexuality. For some this may be the forbidden fruit. For those of us who are Wisdom's daughters, it is a fruit of rare beauty and goodness.

Honor that which has been demeaned.
Receive all that has been cast aside.
The tree and its fruit are good. They are very good.

As the Mother of all Living, I pick the fruit of life. It is good and satisfies hunger. It is pleasant to the eye and offers pleasure. It is wise and opens the way to self-discovery and understanding. Those among you who are curious, who lust for life in all its fluidity. Dare with me. Bite into life. Eat of the fullness of its possibility. Open to the depths of goodness within you. Believe in your goodness. Celebrate your goodness. Live out of the abundance of who you are as a Child of Life. Affirm the original goodness of your children and your children's children until the stories of old hold no power in their hearts.

I am Eve the Mother of All Living, culmination of creation.
I hold and nurture life within me.
In the fullness of time, I thrust and push life from me.
And all that I have given birth to is good. It is very good. [57]

FORBIDDEN ACTS

For over a thousand years, women have been biting into the Genesis texts and reinterpreting them from a woman's perspective. Beginning with the unnamed women of the heretical Montanist sect who claimed Eve as their champion, women have recognized that their destinies were inextricably bound to Eve's story, and that to reclaim themselves, they must reclaim her. These women laid the groundwork for us. Their rebellious spirits inspire our forbidden acts.

Some women courageously challenged the prevailing views of women from within the religious community in their writings and in their assumption of equality with the male translators, interpreters, and commentators of the Bible. Others stepped outside of the patriarchal world-view of the Judeo-Christian tradition. Matilda Joslyn Gage and Elizabeth Cady Stanton published the *Woman's Bible* in 1898. They were outraged at the interpretations of the Bible used to support women's inferior position in home, church, and society. *The Woman's Bible* is composed of a series of commentaries and essays dealing with portions of the Bible that had the most impact on the lives of women, either in its degraded portrayal of them or in the glaring absence of their stories and concerns.

As a result of her forbidden act of challenging the infallibility of the Bible, Elizabeth Cady Stanton became alienated from the Women's Rights movement to which she had committed her astounding gifts and tenacious activism. She could no longer tolerate the reluctance of the religiously conservative suffrage movement to "take an advanced step" of challenging religion's entrenched misogyny.[58] Exhilarated by her soon to be realized freedom, she wrote, "Once out of my present post in the suffrage movement I am a free lance to do and say what I choose and shock people as much as I please."[59] She joined the Women's National Liberal Union. Its positions were more in line with her growing skepticism toward all religions. Assuming equality, one of its resolutions read: "That the Christian Church of whatever name, is based on the theory that woman was secondary and inferior to man and brought sin into the world, thus necessitating the sacrifice of the Savior. That Christianity is false and its foundation a myth which every discovery in science shows to be as baseless as its former belief that the earth was flat."[60]

Inspired by Eve and the courageous community of women who have gone before us, we take our next step on the journey from self-criticism to self-celebration by assuming theological equality with the traditions that have shaped our self-critical attitudes. We take our place in the noble line of self-possessed and free-thinking women by committing the forbidden act of designing a personal and communal spirituality based on our experience, wisdom, and authority as women.

Some women remain within the Judeo-Christian framework to do this essential work. They confront the "powers that be" in theological and liturgical terms, challenging the idolatry of God the father and calling for the use of inclusive language in the church's liturgy. Others step outside of the lines as Gage and Stanton did before them. These women hunger for a personal connection with "spirit." Refusing to surrender to a god or higher power removed from their lives, they have turned inward to discover untapped spiritual resources.

Imagine a woman who assumes theological equality with the traditions that at one time marginalized her. A woman who uses her newly recovered time, energy, and resources to challenge traditional religion's imbalances and to design a personal spirituality that works for her. Who commits the once forbidden acts of re-imagining her beginnings, re-claiming the divine feminine, re-defining sin, and re-writing the scripture.

Imagine a woman who bites into life and the fullness of its possibility for her daughters, granddaughters, and nieces. A woman who surrounds the girl-children in her life with woman-affirming images, and words, and challenges. Who seeks out spiritual communities that welcome the girl-child's birth, encourage her participation in religious rituals, and celebrate images of a god who looks like her.

Imagine yourself as this woman as we consider four essential forbidden acts:

Re-imagine Your Beginnings
Re-claim the Divine Feminine
Re-define Sin
Re-write the Scripture

RE-IMAGINE YOUR BEGINNINGS

In the very beginning was the Mother.
On the first day, she gave birth to light and darkness.
*   They danced together.*
On the second day, she gave birth to land and water.
*   They touched.*
On the third day, she gave birth to green growing things.

They rooted and took a deep breath.
On the fourth day, she gave birth to land, sea, and air creatures.
They walked, swam, and flew.
On the fifth day, her creation learned balance and cooperation.
She thanked her partner for coaching her labor.
On the sixth day, she celebrated the creativity of all living things.
On the seventh day, she left space for the unknown.[61]

These simple words hang in poster form outside my friend's hair salon. She enjoys watching the faces of passersby who stop to read the poster and then move on. Looks of delight, confusion, anger, the whole gamut of feeling and response are touched by these simple words. The other day she happened to be outside the salon when a man stopped to read the poster. She asked for his opinion of the poem. "The writer has quite an imagination," was his response in a dismissive tone.

Together we imagined this man reading the Genesis creation account from the pulpit one Sunday morning. "Hear the word of God," he begins: "And the Lord God caused a deep sleep to fall upon Adam, and he slept; and he took one of his ribs, and closed up the flesh thereof. And the rib which the Lord God had taken from man, made he a woman, and brought her unto the man. And Adam said, This is bone of my bone, flesh of my flesh: she shall be called woman because she was taken out of man." We wondered if after reading the story, he had ever exclaimed, "The writer of Genesis had quite an imagination!"

Probably not, we concluded. A creation story constructed from men's limited experience and imagination, excluding the mother and reversing biological process was elevated to the level of divine inspiration by Christianity. And yet, the creation stories of women, who are re-imagining their beginnings, continue to be relegated to the "lesser" categories of invention, imagination, and poetry; or to the morally questionable categories of fabrication, false teaching, and vain imagining; or to dangerous categories of heresy, blasphemy, paganism, and male bashing.

A young woman was visibly uncomfortable as I read "In the Beginning Was The Mother" in a Princeton bookstore. I invited her to recount her experience. She shared the intense discomfort she felt just listening to the story. The act of listening as well as the story itself felt dangerous to her. Puzzled by the intensity of her emotion, she stayed with the process rather than leave the bookstore. She remembered childhood warnings about heresy and blasphemy. Words paraded through her mind: "Thou shalt have no other Gods before me" and "As it was in the beginning, it is now and ever shall be, world without end amen." After a while the feelings of discomfort and fear dissipated. She reread the story to herself from the handout while I moved on with the performance piece. For a few moments, she was able to distance herself from those childhood warnings and acknowledge that the simple story made intuitive sense to her, that it required less of a leap of faith to imagine the mother giving birth to the world than it did to imagine the father ordering the world into being by a series of verbal commands.

While at Princeton Seminary, I distanced myself from those very same childhood warnings. I was not been told the whole truth in the churches of my childhood; whole areas of history, archaeology, and mythology had been off-limits to me. In my study of the Old Testament at Princeton, I was introduced to the creation mythologies of our earliest ancestors. They imagined the Great Mother as the source of life. She held and nurtured all of life within her, and in the fullness of time, she thrust life from her cosmic womb. Evidence of our ancestor's reverence for the Great Mother reaches back 30,000 years, beginning in the Ice Age and flourishing throughout the Neolithic Age. This story reaches back before the Hebrew and Christian Scriptures were written. Long before Jehovah ordered the world into being by a series of verbal commands, there was the Mother.

Inspired by a view of history that reaches beyond the beginning defined by men, women are assuming theological equality with religious traditions and reclaiming the richness of their own imaginations. We have come to believe that the theological tasks performed by men throughout the ages were not inspired by a god out there somewhere. Rather they were prompted by a very human and natural inclination to answer existential questions and to order disparate experiences into a coherent whole through religious imagination. Humankind's religious imagination has always given birth to goddesses and gods and to stories making sense of our beginnings and endings. No longer held hostage by a truncated view of history or by the dominance of the Genesis account of creation, our imaginations are once again free.

RE-CLAIM THE DIVINE FEMININE

Imagine walking into church each Sabbath and being greeted by an image of the divine feminine above the altar and pulpit, in the stain glass windows, and in the storybooks read to you in Sunday school. Imagine learning about her in sermons and church school lessons as the embodiment of three aspects of a woman's life: Maiden, Mother, and Crone. Imagine encountering her in the depth of your being, knowing she is intimately acquainted with your woman-tears and laughter, your woman-dreams and desires, your woman-challenges and transitions. Imagine learning a series of movements in acknowledgment of the three aspects of the divine, to be offered each time you stood before her image in the church, synagogue, or home of your childhood:

In the name of the Mother of All Living,
Touch your womb center in honor of the mother's intimate
involvement in the origins of life.

and of the Divine Daughter,
Touch your breasts in honor of the daughter's developing body.

and of the Wise Old Woman,
Touch your eyes in honor of old woman's wise inner vision
acquired through the accumulation of years.

As it was in the very beginning, may it be now.
Open your arms to honor All That Is.

A God Who Looks Like Me

As Christianity spread through Europe, it had to reckon with the Mother Goddess. She was so deeply rooted in the people's consciousness that the Church fathers eventually realized they were powerless to exorcise her. Their "masculine" religion was unappealing because it did not offer any feminine images comparable to the Goddess, except Mary. Although the architects of Christianity paid little attention to Mary after her participation in the birth of Jesus, she was not forgotten by women. Stories about her mingled with stories of the Goddess. To women, Mary became the manifestation of the Goddess. She was the accessible God who looked like them, who understood them because she was a woman.

In order to "market" their relatively new religion, the Church fathers blended together two powerful feminine images: the image of Mary, the mother of Jesus, and the image of the Goddess. Layered atop the meager details of Mary's life are centuries of imaginative renderings in which she has been reconstructed as the Queen of Heaven. To appease followers of the Goddess, the Church fathers wove into Mary's image some of the Goddess' qualities while eliminating others disturbing to their world-view—namely, her sexual autonomy and her willfulness!

The Queen of Heaven developed a life of her own among the people. She was the Goddess reborn. She refused to stay in her place as defined by the Church fathers. She refused to allow them to dictate the terms of her existence. The people worshipped her as God. Upset, the Church fathers attempted to contain her. Eventually though they recognized that the worship of the Goddess, reincarnated as the Queen of Heaven, could not be stopped. So they incorporated the festivals, beliefs, and images of the Goddess into their developing theologies. And they transformed her ancient shrines into the chapels of the Queen of Heaven.

Women are reclaiming the divine feminine today. Surrounded by women from every age and inspired by their courage, we are committing the forbidden acts of naming and imagining the god of our understanding as Goddess, Woman God, and God the Mother. Although we are not all devotees of the Goddess, it has been essential for us to extend our historical and theological vision to include the divine feminine. Some find her within traditional religion in the images and stories of Eve and Mary, Sophia and Shekhinah, Miriam and Esther, Naomi and Ruth, Tamar and Susanna, and of countless unnamed women. They are incorporating these women's stories into their liturgies and prayers. Others find her on the margins of patriarchal history in the images and stories of the Goddess. They are incorporating her images into their paintings and songs, their altars and prayers, and they are weaving her ancient festivals and beliefs into their unfolding spirituality.

In Search Of The Mother

I heard rumors of the Mother throughout my stay in Salt Lake City. A country western DJ introduced her to me on his show by reading a Mormon Sunday School hymn, acknowledging the mother in heaven. "We don't have to work as hard as the rest of you to conjure up feminine images of the divine," he told me. "We have always acknowledged the Mother."

I asked the waiter at my hotel restaurant about the Mother. He acknowledged that if there was a father-god there must be a mother-god. "But she stays at home and lives a quiet life," he explained.

"Why is that?" I asked.

"God the father is exposed to all manner of blasphemy and evil speaking. We don't want the precious mother to be exposed to such things."

I shuddered, remembering that similar arguments were used to oppose a woman's rights to be educated, to vote, and to work, and knowing that pedestals are a precarious invention designed to keep us quiet and in our place.

I learned that Mormon women were challenging the patriarchs of their faith to allow Mother God out of hiding, to allow her a public presence within the Mormon community. At my last engagement in Salt Lake City, I asked about these courageous women. I wanted to speak to them, to let them know that they were not alone, that they were supported in their forbidden act of re-claiming the divine feminine from within their tradition. A woman approached me after the event and revealed that the "ringleaders" of the group were in the process of being excommunicated from Mormonism.

Men are not the only ones threatened by our reclamation of the divine feminine and our dismantling of the idolatry of God the father. Invited to Canada to offer a critique of religion's exclusively male god-language and imagery and it effects on women's psyches, bodies, and lives, I stood before an audience of therapists, ministers, lay women and men, and Salvation Army officers. My opening words were:

> "Our imaginations have been held hostage by God the father. 'He' has been an undisturbed idol for too long. His image has been used to convince women that they are excluded from the divine, that they are inferior to men, that they are in need of a male savior, and that to name and imagine God in any other way than he has always been known is blasphemy. A woman's inability to imagine a Woman God who looks, bleeds, feels, thinks, and experiences life as she does is an indication of how deeply she has been injured by her religious past."

As I finished these words, two women walked out. I found out later that they were offended by the words "Woman God."

We tread on dangerous ground when we call into question the exclusively male language and imagery for the divine that permeates our religious and cultural life. For many, the male God of traditional religion has been a rich and meaningful concept. And the roots of these god-words reach deep into the Hebrew and Christian traditions. The ground becomes even shakier when theologically arrogant women name their own gods, claiming "the supreme hubris which asserts to itself the right to reorder the world. The hubris of the godmakers . . ."[62]

Moving Beyond Gender

I offered a workshop in New York City, surrounding women with images of the divine feminine and reflecting on the influence of these images on their bodies, relationships, and self-understanding. Using storytelling, sacred drama, image-making, movement meditation, healing ritual, and creative group interaction, we encountered Eve, the Mother of All Living; Lilith, the Rebellious First Woman; Mary, She Who is Complete in Herself; The Divine Girl-Child; The One Who Shed Her Blood; The Wounded Healers; and The Wise Old Woman.[63]

Afterward a woman shared her discomfort. "I believe it is important to move *beyond* gender in our understanding of God in order to bring us all together as men and women rather than to divide us." Her colleague was listening to our conversation and responded, "You sound like the critics of affirmative action we have to deal with everyday in our diversity work. They say, 'Let's move beyond all this color stuff. We live in a color blind society.' And you and I know that color blind means the same old white dominance and privilege because there isn't a level playing field yet." "That's right," I continued, "and there isn't a level playing field in the heavens yet either." She got it and smiled a knowing smile.

We avoid two essential and potentially uncomfortable steps when we move prematurely to a genderless sense of the divine. First of all, we must dismantle the idolatry of God the father in the society, church, and family, and within us. And secondly, we must encounter the divine feminine to restore our personal and collective balance. Yes, just as it is necessary to dismantle racism and its personal and systemic consequences before affirmative action programs are set aside, so it is necessary to dethrone the male God of traditional religion and invite the exiled feminine to take her rightful place beside him before we consider moving on to a genderless sense of the divine.

And even then it may not be possible or even desirable to eradicate all images of the divine. As a human community we have always employed our imaginations to give shape, form, and meaning to our noblest visions. This is a tenacious human impulse. Rather than eliminating all names in an artificial attempt to be "spiritually correct," we have developed a ritual that welcomes many names of the divine. Each of us is free to share the God of our understanding in our own language and imagery. In our circles it isn't unusual for a feminist to refer to the divine as Goddess, a fundamentalist to acknowledge God the father, a Buddhist to share her sense of connectedness to all beings, and an atheist to ask for silence in acknowledgment of all that cannot be named. Join us.

Let us "bring many names" always mindful that the ultimate truth, wisdom, and mystery of the Universe is far deeper, higher, wider, and richer than any name or image we use to refer to it. Mystery cannot be confined within a language.

Bring many names . . . moving us beyond the limitations of gender: Deeper Wisdom, Higher Power, Wise Energy, Source of Life, Community of Support, Sacred Breath.

Bring many names . . . retaining the relational quality of the divine: Loving Wise One, Welcoming Friend, Compassionate One, Nurturing One, Counselor, Seeker of the Lost.

Bring many names . . . weaving traditional names into an unfolding spirituality: Loving Father; Abba; Jesus; Holy Spirit; Mother-Father God; Creator, Redeemer, and Sustainer.

Bring many names . . . challenging the idolatry of traditional religion: Goddess, Woman God, Sister God, Sophia, A God With Breasts Like Mine, Mother of All Living.

Bring many names and no names at all . . . In the silence let us leave space for the unknown.

Re-Define Sin

Imagine hearing Eve's words introduce the communion service one Sabbath morning: *"As the Mother of all Living, I pick the fruit of life. It is good and satisfies hunger. It is pleasant to the eye and offers pleasure. It is wise and opens the way to self-discovery and understanding. Those among you who are curious, who lust for life in all its fluidity, dare with me. Bite into life. Eat of the fullness of its possibility."*

After Eve's words are read, the elder women of the congregation give an apple to the first person in each pew. As the crone hands you an apple, she looks into your eyes and says, *"Take and eat of the good fruit of life. You are good. You are very good."* You bite into the apple, savor its sweet juiciness, and pass it on to the person next to you with the same words.

After all have partaken of the good fruit of life, the benediction is spoken, *"Open to the depths of goodness within you. Believe in your goodness. Celebrate your goodness. Live out of the abundance of who you are as a child of life. Affirm the original goodness of your children and your children's children until the stories of old hold no power in their hearts. Bite into life and the fullness of its possibility."*

Sin, Salvation, and Surrender

As we dismantle the throne of God, traditional religion's hierarchically-based answers to the fundamental questions of human existence must be reformulated from our own experience. As the image of the big guy in the heavens, scrutinizing our every thought and action dissolves, and as his system of rewards and punishments, keeping us in line is disbanded, women are reframing traditional religion's definitions of sin, salvation, and surrender.

Ascent has been the journey of men. They erect ladders and monuments, reaching toward the heavens. They name their gods "Higher Power" and "God of the High Places." They have accurately defined their sin as pride, the willful pursuit of power, and the desire to be like God. In a society that worships a male God, these have not been our sins. God-likeness has never been an option for us. Our place has been clearly secondary and supportive. The root of our sin has been an alienation from ourselves and an accompanying self-critical spirit. We have internalized the carefully designed systems of thought and belief that take for granted our defectiveness and inferiority. We sin by our own participation in a hierarchical paradigm that at its foundation is not woman or life-affirming and by our cooperation in the maintenance of this paradigm in the training of our daughters and granddaughters.

We sin each time we ask "what's wrong with me;" each time we waste a precious resource of time, money, or energy in our frantic search for remedies; each time we twist ourselves out of shape in response to an "expert" opinion. We sin as we hide our bodies beneath layers of clothing, our natural processes beneath layers of secrecy, our sexuality beneath layers of passivity, our opinions and thoughts beneath layers of conformity, and our feelings beneath layers of restraint. We sin as we hide the reality of our lives beneath layers of seething resentment in response to and in avoidance of the persistent scrutiny of the culture, of God, and eventually, of ourselves.

As women redefine sin, they rethink the remedies put forward to alleviate our sinful condition as well. Men's sins have been pride and grandiosity so it makes sense that ego-deflation, denial of self, and "surrender to God's will" have been considered appropriate remedies. Our two-fold sin of alienation from self and of an all-consuming self-critical attitude require a conversion of sorts. Women are turning inward—instead of looking to a god or higher power outside of our lives for salvation, we journey "home" to ourselves. Instead of ascending to enlightened states of being that involve the denial of the self, we have discovered that ours is a journey of descent—we look deep within to reclaim forgotten aspects of ourselves. We reach beneath our obsession with flaws, beneath the accomplishments that mask our sense of unworthiness, beneath years of alienation from ourselves, toward the goodness at our center. We discover that the good is deeply embedded within us. As we embrace our original goodness, our inner spaces are cleared out and reclaimed as our own. We find rest within our own lives and accept all of ourselves as worthy.

In our descent, we rediscover Wisdom or Sophia, which is the Greek word for wisdom. She is a feminine aspect of the divine presented in the Hebrew Scriptures. Her presence in the male pantheon of gods has been obscured but not completely eradicated. In the Gnostic writings, considered heretical by the "orthodox" church, Sophia was present at creation, all things were conceived in feminine power and wisdom. After creation, she escorted Adam and Eve toward self-awareness. Women are reclaiming Sophia as a representation of their own inner wisdom. No longer is "God's will" imposed from outside of their lives—wisdom unfolds from within them and is in sync with their own natural gifts and capacities. No longer available to turn their lives and wills over to gods, gurus, and experts, they are refusing to surrender except to Wisdom's urgings. No longer abdicating responsibility for their lives, they are employing their own willfulness in harmony with Wisdom's ways. No longer scrutinizing every facet of their beings to figure out what is wrong, they are celebrating themselves as powerful and gifted children of life.

Re-Write the Scripture

Imagine if you had heard this passage read from the "Book of Woman" one Sabbath morning:

In this hour everything is stillness.
There is total silence and awe.
We are overwhelmed with a great wonder. We keep vigil.
We are expecting the coming of the Divine Girl-Child.

In the fullness of time, she is born.
She shines like the sun, bright and beautiful.
She is laughing a most joyful laugh.
She is a delight, soothing the world with peace.

Become bold. Lean over and look at her.
Touch her face. Lift her in your hands with great awe.
Look at her more closely. There is no blemish on her.
She is splendid to see.

She opens her eyes and looks intently at you. A powerful light comes forth from her eyes, like a flash of lightning. The light of her gaze invites the hidden one to come into the light. The sleeping one to awaken. The frozen one to thaw. The buried one to emerge. The hard and protected one to soften. Receive her healing gaze deep within your being.

Suddenly there appears a multitude of heavenly beings singing:
Glory to the Mother of All Living and to her Daughter.
She has arrived. The Divine Child is among us.
She will bring peace and inspire goodwill among all people.

Welcome her joyfully. Shout with a loud voice:
You belong here among us. We're glad you're alive!
Surround her with goodness, safety, and laughter.
She is the Divine Child, come among us this day.

Sacred Words

"Do you believe in Jesus?" is another one of those inevitable questions asked on radio call-in shows. I acknowledge that I am Jesus-friendly *and* that I don't believe he is the son of God. Since the dethronement of God the father, the son has taken on more human proportions in my self-defined spirituality. And so has the book claimed to be the inspired "word of God."

It matters the books we consider sacred. The Bible I read daily as a child, adolescent, and young adult was filled with men's words, stories, and interpretations of the divine. There were two impulses within me during those years. On the one hand, the vulnerability of my status as "orphan" required that I learn the party line and conform to it. Yet a deeper part of my being remained untouched by their teachings. It was accumulating courage for the day when I would leave the suffocating world of fundamentalism and venture into the open spaces of a life-affirming spirituality.

My secret courage was nourished as I gathered an alternative scripture from the works of poets, artists, and writers. Given my early identification with men, it makes great sense that Walt Whitman, Rainier Rilke, Chaim Potok, and Herman Hesse were the first to feed my suspicion of the so-called word of God. I discovered these men on my own as our church did not encourage dialog with non-biblical sources. They became the non-punitive face of the divine in my life. Unlike the rigid teachings of my childhood and adolescence which imprisoned God and prescribed my responses, the life-affirming visions of these men employed open language and unfolding imagery. Their words deepened my longing to venture out beyond "orthodoxy" and their images inspired my imagination.

From Chaim Potok's *Book of Lights*:
The smug superiority of those certain of salvation...teaching the road map of relationship with Higher Power, carefully delineating each turn and bend, a frightened joylessness, everything known, no new lights, no unexpected visions that chill the spine, no bursts of surprise, no escape from the choreographed landscape of texts and commentary.

From Walt Whitman's *Leaves of Grass*:
I celebrate myself and sing myself.
And what I assume you shall assume.
For every atom belonging to me as good, belongs to you.

From Rainier Rilke's *Letters To A Young Poet*:
How should we be able to forget those ancient myths that are at the beginning of all peoples, the myths about dragons that at the last moment turn into princesses; perhaps all the dragons of our lives are princesses who are only waiting to see us once beautiful and brave. Perhaps everything terrible is in its deepest being something helpless that wants help from us.

From Herman Hesse's *Sidhartha*:
The world is not imperfect or slowly evolving along a path to perfection. No it is perfect at every moment, every sin already carries grace within it, all small children are potentially old, all sucklings have death within them, all dying people-eternal life. Therefore it seems that everything exists is good-all death as well as life, sin as well as holiness, wisdom as well as folly. Everything is necessary, everything needs only my agreement, my assent, my loving understanding.

As the face of God changed in my experience and my longing for women's voices deepened, I searched for the stories of women in religion's sacred texts, reclaiming them from the margins of religion and history. I added the stories of Eve, Lilith, and Mary; the Divine Girl-Child and The One Who Shed Her Blood; Tamar, The One Who Was Cut into Pieces, and the Wise Old Woman to my personalized scripture.[64] I sat in circles of women in churches and centers throughout the country and listened to women's untold stories, the truth of their lives found its way into "The Book of Woman" I was developing.

As I imagined what it would have been like to experience religious songs, images, words, stories, prayers, and liturgies that included women and their experience, I rewrote the familiar "canon" from a woman's perspective, moving beyond mere replacement of pronouns to profound paradigmatic alterations. Over the years, I have gathered many of the rewritten bible verses and stories, traditional liturgies and hymns into the "Imagine" performance piece. I will close the chapter with it. Imagine walking into a church, bookstore, or women's center and receiving the following "Order of Service."[65] Participate as the spirit moves you.

IMAGINE

THE MOTHER OF ALL LIVING: IN THE VERY BEGINNING

Reader

Imagine hearing a creation myth in which the Mother is present. Imagine if you had heard these words in the synagogue, church, or home of your childhood.

Dance and Voice Choir

In the beginning was the Mother.
On the first day, She gave birth to light and darkness.
  They danced together.
On the second day, She gave birth to land and water. They touched.
On the third day, She gave birth to green growing things.
  They rooted and took a deep breath.
On the fourth day, She gave birth to land, sea, and air creatures.
  They walked and flew and swam.
On the fifth day, Her creation learned balance and cooperation.
  She thanked her partner for coaching her labor.
On the sixth day, She celebrated the creativity of all living things.
On the seventh day, She left space for the unknown.

Reader

Together let us pray,

All

Our Mother, who art within us, we celebrate your many names.
  Your wisdom come.
Your will be done, unfolding from the depths within us.
Each day You give us all that we need.
  You remind us of our limits, that we might let go.
  You support us in our power, that we might act with courage.
For thou art the dwelling place within us,
  the empowerment around us, and the celebration among us.
As it was in the very beginning, may it be now.

THE DIVINE GIRL-CHILD: A NEW BIRTH

Reader

Imagine hearing stories of the Divine Girl-Child whose birth was announced and celebrated by angels, whose coming merited visitors and precious gifts, and in whose honor the peoples of the world gather for a yearly retelling of the story of her birth. Imagine if you had heard these words in the synagogue, church, or home of your childhood.

Dance and Voice Choir

In this hour everything is stillness. There is total silence and awe.
We are overwhelmed with a great wonder. We keep vigil.
We are expecting the coming of the Divine Girl-Child.

In the fullness of time, she is born.
She shines like the sun, bright and beautiful.
She is laughing a most joyful laugh.
She is a delight, soothing the world with peace.

Become bold. Lean over and look at her.
Touch her face. Lift her in your hands with great awe.
Look at her more closely. There is no blemish on her.
She is splendid to see.

She opens her eyes and looks intently at you. A powerful light comes forth from her eyes, like a flash of lightning. The light of her gaze invites the hidden one to come into the light. The sleeping one to awaken. The frozen one to thaw. The buried one to emerge. The hard and protected one to soften. Receive her healing gaze deep within your being.

Suddenly there appears a multitude of heavenly beings singing:
"Glory to the Mother of All Living and to her Daughter.
She has arrived. The Divine Child is among us.
She will bring peace and inspire goodwill among all people.

Welcome her joyfully. Shout with a loud voice:
You belong here among us. We're glad you're alive!
Surround her with goodness, safety, and laughter.
She is the Divine Child, come among us this day." [66]

All

For Mother God so loved the world that she sent into its midst the Divine Girl-Child. Whosoever believes in Her goodness, listens to Her wisdom, and celebrates Her power will be awakened to the abundance of gifts within them. (John 3:16, adapted)

THE ONE WHO SHEDS HER BLOOD: THERE'S POWER IN THE BLOOD

Reader

Imagine the sacraments and rituals of childhood commemorating the monthly shedding of a woman's blood, her sacred blood that holds within it both life and death. Imagine singing songs and spirituals that celebrate the beautiful, powerful blood of woman. Imagine if you had sung these words in the synagogue, church, or home of your childhood.

Voice Choir

Would you be free from the burden of lies?
   There's power in the blood, power in the blood.
Would you receive deep healing within?
   There's wonderful power in the blood.

Chorus
There is power, power, wonder-working power
   in the blood of the woman.
There is power, power, wonder-working power
   in the precious blood of the woman.

Would you be wiser much wiser than now?
   There's power in the blood, power in the blood.
Shame's stains are lost in her life-giving flow.
   There's wonderful power in the blood.

Chorus
There is power, power, wonder-working power
   in the blood of the woman.
There is power, power, wonder-working power
   in the precious blood of the woman.[67]

THE WISE OLD WOMAN: GATHERING THE YEARS

Reader

Imagine the rituals and sacraments of the churches and synagogues of our childhoods presided over by wise old post-menopausal women. Women who, as in ancient times, were considered the wisest of the wise because they permanently held within them their life-creating wise blood. Imagine if you had heard these words from the wise old woman every Sabbath.

A Circle of Crone Guides

Let us gather our years. Move forward through the years of your life, beginning with your birth. Pay special attention to the years that hurt as you pass through them. Bless the bruised and wounded years. Call out those years. (*Pause for group to call out the years.*)

Now travel again through the years, beginning with your birth. Pay special attention to the years that delight you as you pass through them. Celebrate the bright and comfortable years. Call them out. (*Pause for group to call out the years.*)

Gather all the years of your life in a bundle, the bright and the bruised. Bring that bundle of years into this room. Call out the years you have lived. Fill this sacred space with the accumulation of your years. (*Pause for group to call out the years.*)

Reader

Together let us remember,

All

In the name of the Mother of All Living,
(Touch your womb center in honor of the mother's intimate connection to the origins of life.)

and of the Divine Daughter,
(Touch your breasts in honor of the daughter's developing body.)

and of the Wise Old Woman,
(Touch your eyes in honor of the wise inner vision acquired through the accumulation of years.)

As it was in the very beginning, may it be now.
(Open your arms to receive All That Is.)

WOMEN'S STORIES
ASSUMING THEOLOGICAL EQUALITY

TAKING OF THE TREE   *Cristina Goulart*

Since my rejection of Catholicism, I have ached for a spiritual path that would satisfy me. I longed to feel closer to God, but needed a religion that was fair and that supported my equality to men. I discovered Buddhism and Hinduism. I practiced yoga and meditation. These spiritual paths felt better to me than my childhood religion, but they still didn't fit. I searched some more and explored Native American religions. While I burned sage and smoked tobacco, I felt as though I were stealing a tradition from a people who had everything else stolen from them.

I then stumbled onto the Goddess, she who was worshipped in the land of milk and honey before the Hebrew tribes killed her worshipers and confiscated their land. I discovered images of Cretan women, praying to the Goddess with their arms outstretched and snakes in their hands. I read that the Goddess gave sexuality to her children as a gift. I met women who were worshipping the Goddess today, treating the earth as sacred and feeling joyful in their bodies. I fianlly found my way to a spirituality that fit. I now pray to the Goddess. She creates in love, and wishes us to live in love. I make offerings, but do not bow my head in shame. I pray with my head upturned and my feet planted on the ground.

Recently I participated in a ritual with some dear friends who are companions on the path to the Goddess and to wholeness. We committed the forbidden act of honoring ourselves, the Goddess, and Eve. We sat in a circle with candles burning. We each took an apple or a fig into our hands. I portrayed Eve as I read from the "Encounter With Eve:" Take, eat of the good fruit of life . . . Believe in your goodness. Celebrate your goodness. Live out of the abundance of who you are as a child of life . . ." For a moment I felt panic—just having read those words made me fearful of being called a whore or of being condemned as a witch to be burned at the stake. I looked across the table at my friend Mimi who was also hesitating. The same look of fear and uncertainty was on her face. Then I heard one of the women bite into a crisp apple. I followed suit, and bit into my fig. My beautiful friend across the table bit into hers.

I could not have bitten into the fruit without the support of my friends. Together we did it. And as I ate the luscious flesh of the fig, I felt myself reclaiming my truth and becoming whole again. I have willingly eaten of the fruit of knowledge, the fruit of life, and I will again.

APPLES AND FIGS   *Mimi Carlson*

After discussing the Adam and Eve story from Genesis, our women's group passed a basket of apples and figs around the circle. As we each took a piece of fruit, I suddenly realized we were going to take a bite, just like Eve. I hesitated . . . original sin was a long time ago, it was not my fault, if I enact the whole thing again does that make me really BAD? Now I understood what another woman said earlier, "This could be scary." Then I thought about how the legend had been distorted, how serpents and goddesses used to be considered "good," and how self-serving the patriarchal story really was. I took a bite and it felt empowering. The fig was delicious, and I was surrounded with support.

BECOMING MY OWN AUTHORITY   *Debby Ostlund*

I have read many books about the Goddess and women's spirituality. They spoke to my intellect and opened my eyes to new possibilities and realities. But none of these books helped heal the incredible wounding perpetrated by patriarchal religion. Although I discarded my religious heritage years ago, its influence remained. What I longed for and needed were words that spoke not only to my head but to my body, experience, and self-image, the places where the scars ran the deepest. What I longed for and needed were words and images to heal the split between myself and the divine. What I longed for and needed were *inspired* woman-affirming words of healing, wisdom, comfort, AND authority. What I longed for, I finally found in the book *A God Who Looks Like Me*. Its words were both a source of wisdom on my journey toward a woman-affirming spirituality and a source of practical support to help me truly embody the transformation I experienced in imagining the divine as woman, as ME.

The most profound healing began for me as I read the reworking of traditional scriptures into woman-affirming passages, especially the retelling of the story of Eve. I had long been aware of the injustice and manipulation of blaming Eve for the sin of all humankind. Time after time, as I read Eve's *new* story aloud to myself in which she assumes equality and sets the record straight. I felt her outrage and her courage and they became my own. It was necessary to speak these words aloud to counter all the times I had heard the evil and blaming words. I sobbed as I became Eve and she became me. Together we began the *real* journey toward healing the shame of being born in a woman's body.

In its pages I continue to find the words of wisdom, inspiration, and authority I need to stay on my spiritual path. When I am challenged and I begin to feel unsure about my "right" to live and to speak as my own truth dictates, I do not turn to the scriptures of old but to my new scriptures. I find there beautiful words of inspiration, wisdom, healing, and courage to assume equality and to become the authority in naming my own experience.

I support my daughters to name their own experience and to retain the freedom of their imaginations. As you read the creation myth my daughter Andrea and I wrote, imagine your family gathered around a fire or dinner table, in a sacred grove or open meadow, to spin stories of your beginnings, stories that include the mother:

"The Very Essence of All"

In the very beginning, in the time before time, was the Mother. The Mother was all things. She was time itself. She was the Sun and the Moon. She was the darkness and the light. She was the Earth, and all seasons, winter, spring, summer, and fall. She was the highest mountain and the fertile valley. She was the river and the ocean into which it flowed. She was the trees and the flowers, the vegetables and herbs. She was all because she created all and was the essence of all. She was the very breath of life itself.

The Mother was also all manner of being. She was the fierce and the gentle. She was laughter and she was tears. She was innocence and she was wisdom. She was life and she was death. Above all, she was love. She was truly the light of love. She had so much love to give that even though she cherished all she had created so far, she longed for something more. She longed for a special kind of being to love and to be loved by in return.

One night as she slept, wisdom showed her beautiful creatures of all kinds in a dream, creatures of land, air, and sea. When she awoke, she was moved to create all that she had seen in her dream and being the Mother, she knew instinctively how to do so.

She knelt, touching the earth, and gave birth to the Earth creatures. She swam in the waters and gave birth to all water creatures. She danced through the air and gave birth to all air creatures. She lay gently on the earth and in the fullness of time gave birth to all humankind.

She saw all that she created was beautiful and good and she was overwhelmed with feelings of great joy. She nourished and loved all of her creation and they grew and lived together in peace, harmony, and love.

MOVING INWARD   *Jane Sterrett*

I stand in the shower, and suddenly I'm singing a hymn I haven't thought of for years. What power the old words have, what metaphors and imagery. How can I deny their place in my unconscious? I must know all the words, every line and comma. I drag out the old hymnbook with my first husband's name in gold on the soft leather cover, and I sing all the verses. The words come back as if it were 1942 and I were still ten years old. "Watch with Him one bitter hour." We are to feel guilty for our sin of abandonment.

The towel around my hair is soaking through, and I'm shivering in the cool house. I'm shivering with the knowledge that this hymn and many others are deeply embedded in my mind, troubling my days with their messages of guilt and shame. I dry my hair, pull on a sweatshirt, sit down at the computer and begin typing a new version. No, I won't have a male as the ideal image. I will change the words, and it will be an exercise and an exorcism. I put the new words away, angry and only a little satisfied. The bloody image of the cross remains. Sin and guilt remain.

Months pass. I join a Goddess group, where I find new imagery, and another stifling institution that I must leave. Then I attend a reading by Patricia Lynn Reilly, a performance-reading. She has read my heart. She has struggled as I have. I drive home late, pull up the hymn on my computer and try again. This time there will be birthing instead of dying, and I will affirm my life.

The Original Hymn
Go to Dark Gethsemane

Go to dark Gethsemane
Ye that feel the tempter's power;
Your Redeemer's conflict see,
Watch with Him one bitter hour;
Turn not from His griefs away,
Learn of Jesus Christ to pray.

Follow to the judgment hall,
View the Lord of life arraigned;
O the wormwood and the gall!
O the pangs his soul sustained!
Shun not suffering, shame or loss,
Learn of Him to bear the cross.

Calvary's mournful mountain climb,
There, adoring at His feet,
Mark that miracle of time,
God's own sacrifice complete;
"It is finished," hear the cry.
Learn of Jesus Christ to die.

Early hasten to the tomb
Where they laid his breathless clay;
All is solitude and gloom,
Who has taken Him away?
Christ is risen! He meets our eyes.
Savior, teach us so to rise.

My First Try
Go to Dark Gethsemane

Go to dark Gethsemane
You that fear the darker power;
your true nature's conflict see,
watch with her one bitter hour;
Turn not from her grief away,
Learn of your true self to pray.

Follow to the judgment hall,
View the Goddess there arraigned;
O the wormwood and the gall!
O the pangs her soul sustained!
Shun not suffering, shame or loss,
Learn of her to bear the cross.

Calvary's mournful mountain climb,
There, adoring at her feet,
Mark that miracle of time,
Your own sacrifice complete;
"It is finished," hear the cry.
Learn of your true self to die.

Early hasten to the tomb
Where they laid her breathless clay;
All is solitude and gloom,
Who has taken her away?
You are risen! You meet our eyes.
Goddess, teach us so to rise.

My Total Rewrite
Go to Your Deep Memories

Go to your deep memories
you who fear the darker powers.
Your true nature's conflict see,
stay with her through bitter hours.
Turn not from her grief away,
Learn of your true self to pray.

Follow to the birthing place.
See the Goddess there restrained.
O the pilferers of grace!
O the anesthetic chains!
Hold her close through loss and blame.
Take away all guilt and shame.

Mountains challenge. Dare to climb
toward your woman strength and pride.
Trust the miracle of time.
Healing comes. No longer hide
your beauty from us! You can give
your true nature ways to live.

And when age and wisdom fill
memory with power and glories,
paint the sky with your strong will,
write your songs, tell your stories!
Blessed be, self, Goddess wise.
Teach your daughters so to rise.

REWRITING THE SCRIPTURE   *Freda Rhodes*

For as long as I can remember, I have received comfort and healing from writing. And it was through the writings in my personal journal, including the writing of "The Book of Mary" that I was able to heal a major wound in my life.

After nearly five years of working to heal from childhood sexual abuse, I had slowly begun to regain courage, commitment, and self-acceptance. But it wasn't until after I read the chapter on Mary in *A God Who Looks Like Me* that I realized that a lack of self-will was the "missing link" I needed to reclaim my power, and reconnect to a healing spiritual presence.

When I first wrote "The Book of Mary" in my journal, it was filled with raw, violent sexual imagery, showing Mary as helpless victim. Over the next few months, however, it began to slowly change from a mere retelling of the horror of abuse to a story of healing and empowerment. My purpose in writing this story is to reclaim power and healing for myself and all wounded women in a way that honors our capacity to love and to create ON OUR OWN TERMS.

Since I completed the final version of this piece, I have taken many bold steps to make my dream of becoming a full-time writer a reality. In early 1996, I completed a book of poetry. I am currently working on a second book that will "get to the bone" of my relationship with my mother and the rest of my spiritual motherline. I am currently working as a word processing specialist by day and a "wild poet" by night. I live with my husband in suburban Detroit.

The Book of Mary

God's Will

Father God crept into the room where Mary slept. He took off his robe and stood tall over her. When she awoke, her eyes grew large with terror as she looked at him in all is stark and massive nakedness. And with hardly a word, Father God climbs on top of Mary. When she opens her mouth to scream, the Father God presses his fingers to her lips. "Now hush sweet Mary. This is the Lord's will."

And Mary, with tears in her eyes proclaims, "But Father, I am yet a virgin. If you do this to me, you will surely destroy me. I beg you, let me remain a virgin." But it was as if the Lord did not hear her plea. He simply smiled and said, "Don't worry. I'll be sure that even after I am done with you, you will still be a virgin. Why, I'll even make you Queen of Heaven!"

And with those words, Father God spread apart Mary's trembling legs. The silent night filled with his moans of delight. Yes indeed, this was a most tender virgin. And Father God was well pleased. And underneath Father God in all of his massive nakedness, Mary wept, and prayed for daylight.

And it came to pass that right before dawn, the Lord loosed his fire within Mary. So abundant was his seed in Mary, there was no room left for her tears.

And within the wink of an eye, the Father Lord vanished.

Under the bright sun's warming rays, Mary feels dark and cold. And when her mother asks, "What's wrong?" Mary cast her eyes downward. "Nothing is the matter Mother. Everything is fine." And when her betrothed Joseph asked, "Why are you so sad, Mary?" her face flushes with the scarlet red of shame. "Nothing is the matter, my love. Everything is fine."

In the middle of a moonlit night, Mary stood by the river. Her reflection bore her swollen belly, growing with the baby Jesus. Suddenly the Lord appeared. "Father what shall I do? Soon Joseph and everyone else will know and I will be destroyed." And Father God said, "There, there my child. Do not worry. I'll take care of everything. Why, everyone will still believe you're a virgin. Relax, everything will be just fine."

True to his word, Father God did make everything OK. No one spoke of Mary's swollen belly. Each smiled when they passed her in the village, greeted her, then continued silently on their way. Why, even Joseph seemed to be accepting.

Then came that night, inside a stable, baby Jesus was born of Mary. Mary is filled with pain and terror. They say on that night in the manger she lost much blood—and part of her soul.

And on that cold and lonely night, Mary wept.

Soon after, Father God came to visit Mary and the baby Jesus. "Well done," he said, holding baby Jesus up towards the Heavens. And although she was hurting, Mary was eager to accept her role as queen. She spoke humbly unto the Lord, "OK, father, I am ready to accept my role as queen. Please show me to my throne."

And Father God looked at Mary and said, "No, no, dear Mary. You misunderstood. I said you would be a queen someday—when you are DEAD. But first you must raise the baby Jesus so he can do his work in the world."

Mary panicked. "But Father, Joseph and I are poor! Who will pay for the things your child needs—the things fit for a royal child?" And Father God bellowed, "Well, he'll just have to make do. Now do as I command because I am the Lord. It is MY WILL."

Upon hearing of her talk with the Lord, Joseph sits silent and stunned. He had been duped. And on that cool autumn night, he consumed a bowl of bitterness. And Mary swallowed spoonfuls of sorrow.

And in this house of bitterness and sorrow, Jesus grew to manhood. He preached the word, healed the sick, and raised the dead. "Who is my REAL father?" he once asked Mary. For surely, a mere carpenter could not be responsible for creating a child who could perform such miracles in the world. But Mary's lips, just like her soul, were sealed, and she never told Jesus who his real father was. And Father God never once stepped forward to claim him, or bestow on him the earthly riches or recognition befitting a king's child.

Then it came to pass that Jesus stood accused. And when the Ruler of the Land asked if he was indeed the son of Father God, Jesus feebly said, "I Am, I am . . ." but could not finish the sentence, for he didn't know who he was at all.

And he was hung from a cross, made to suffer because his father would not claim him. "Father, why have thou forsaken me," he cried in anguish. And being forsaken, on that day he died.

And on that day Mary went out into her garden. And there among the lilies she vowed, "From this day forward I will never again speak to Father God in heaven. I well return to the one who loves me—the Goddess of my home, the earth." Mary fell upon the ground weeping and begged her long forsaken Mother for comfort and guidance.

And on a quiet moonlit night, Mary wept. And Mother God wiped away her tears.

Mary's Will

Mary called together the 12 disciples: Sarah, Ruth, Naomi, Eve, Lilith, Rachel, Miriam, Kali, Demeter, Helen, Pandora Mary Magdelene. The room was fragrant with the smell of healing herbs. And looking around the room of these humble, yet powerful women, Mary arose and spoke: *"You are all wise women. I have called you together to carry forth into the world an important message."*

Mary lovingly poured a bowl of soup for each disciple. Then she opened up a red embroidered cloth that lay before her. The women looked in awe. Inside was the umbilical cord from the body of the baby Jesus. Mary had saved it on that cold night in the stable so long ago, though until this very moment, she knew not why. As they looked upon the cloth, she spoke to them again, proclaiming: *"I now ask that you cut off a piece of this cord, then place it in your soup. Then slowly, quietly, sip it." And so each disciple, one by one, did this. And in eating the soup, each was consumed with a feeling of power and courage beyond any they had ever known.*

And Mary spoke one last time: "You have drunk from the nectar of spirit's divine child. Now I ask you to go out into the world and teach every women, every healer, every midwife, that the cord of each newborn child is to be saved. For you see, every child is a divine child. I charge you with carrying forth this message. "It is Mother God's will."

And each disciple bowed and prayed, "Mother God, thy will be done."

Afterward

Mindy closed her Bible and her heart was happy. Just as it always was when she read the Bible. It was now well past midnight. As Mindy walked through the village, she smiled at the women gathered in small groups in front of their homes, making offerings to the moon on this star-filled night. As she approached the center of the village, Mindy knelt in front of the statue. She traced a circle around her heart and belly and looked up at Mary holding the baby Jesus in her arms. He hung onto her breast, looking content and loved. And between them was the divine cord that ran from the Divine Mother Mary to the Baby Jesus. Mindy was glad to be alive. Glad because she knew she had been born with a divine cord. Just like the baby Jesus. She knew she would be blessed forever.

As Mindy walked from the square, she caught a glimpse of the statue out of the corner of her eye. And in that brief and magic moment, Jesus laughed.

And Mary winked.

HEALING INTO THE PRESENT
A RITUAL IN CELEBRATION OF EVE'S FORBIDDEN ACT

Eve's Forbidden Act: As the Mother of all Living, Eve picked the good fruit of life. It was good and satisfied hunger. It was pleasant to the eye and offered pleasure. It was wise and opened the way to self-discovery and understanding. She invites those among us who are curious, who lust for life in all its fluidity, to dare with her by biting into life and the fullness of its possibility. She speaks from the depths of us, "Bite into your life and the fullness of its possibility."

Our Forbidden Acts: With Eve, we reject the dominance of a creation myth, portraying women as the instigators of evil and excluding the Mother from the creation of the world. We reject the sin-based messages of family, religion, and society, stressing our wrongs, our defects, and our insufficiencies. We embrace a woman-affirming spirituality, celebrating the Mother's intimate involvement in the origins of life and reminding us of our original goodness.

Recall a time when your mother reached for the apple, a moment when she bit into her life and the fullness of its possibility.

Individual Response: My mother bit into the apple when she _____.
   Examples: My mother bit into the apple and went to law school at 58.
         My mother bit into the apple by going away alone one
         weekend a month for personal retreat.

Communal Response: Mother, we celebrate your act of courage.

Recall a time when you reached for the apple, a moment when you bit into your life and the fullness of its possibility.

Individual Response: I bit into the apple of my life when I _____.
   Examples: I bit into the apple and acknowledged my love for a woman.
         I bit into the apple by working only three days a week
         and painting the other four.

Communal Response: Sister, we celebrate your act of courage.

Receive Eve's Support: Pass Eve's apple around the circle. Commit the forbidden act of biting into your life.

Individual Response: I will bite into the apple of my _____.
   Examples: I will bite into the apple of my creativity and write a book.
         I will bite into the apple of my sexuality and celebrate
         my body's responses.

Communal Response: Sister, we support you to act with courage.

HEALING INTO THE PRESENT
A Litany of Remembrance

Courageous women have challenged the prevailing views of women from within the Christian community for over a thousand years by assuming equality with the male translators, interpreters, and commentators of the Bible. Read through the following "Litany of Remembrance," acknowledging these women. Instead of reading another self-improvement book, go to the library and pursue their writings and stories. The litany was inspired by Chapter 7 in Gerda Lerner's *Creation of Feminist Consciousness*. Begin your exploration there.

At your next women's gathering or church forum, acknowledge the courage of these women by naming them aloud in your circle. After the entire "Litany of Remembrance" has been read, conclude by saying, "*Sisters, we remember you. We celebrate your forbidden acts.*"

Unnamed Montanist women (2nd Century)—Assumed prophetic roles in the church, claiming Eve as their champion.

Hildegard of Bingen (1098-1179)—Brilliant mystic, abbess, preacher, teacher, counselor, and prolific writer.

Christine de Pizan (1365-c.1430)—Single mother, biographer, illustrator, biblical commentator; Defender of women.

Isotta Nogarola (1418-66)—Learned Renaissance women and biblical commentator; Defender of Eve.

Laura Cereta (1469-99)—Woman Humanist and mathematician; Defender of Eve.

Marguerite d' Angouleme (1492-1549)—Queen of Navarre and humanist author, feminist theologian.

Anne Askew (16th century)—Defender of a woman's right to interpret scripture; Burned as a heretic in 1546.

Jane Anger (16th century)—Biblical commentator and pamphleteer; Defender of Eve's superiority.

Rachel Speght (17th century)—Brilliant deconstructionist of misogynistic views; Defender of Eve's equality.

Ester Sowernam (17th century)—Aggressive deconstructionist; Defender of Eve as "the mother of all living."

Sarah Fyge (1669-1722)—Banished from her father's house for writing a poem that celebrated Eve's goodness.

Antoinette Bourignon (1606-80)—Pietist preacher and religious writer; Defended of the androgynous image of god.

Margaret Fell (1614-1702)—Quaker teacher, preacher, writer; Defended women's active role in ministry; imprisoned for her beliefs.

Mary Astell (1666-1731)—Biblical commentator; Challenged the authority of patriarchal interpreters of scripture.

Ann Lee (1736-84)—Shaker preacher and teacher; Defender of Sophia, the female aspect of the androgynous divine.

Joanna Southcott (1750-1814)—Prophet; Defender of women who are called to bring the knowledge of the good fruit to humankind.

Julia Smith (1792-1878)—Feminist and abolitionist; Translator of the Bible from its original languages: Greek, Hebrew, and Latin.

Sarah Moore Grimke (1792-1873)—Feminist and abolitionist, Biblical commentator; Defender of Eve's equality, freedom, and intellect.

Sisters, we remember you. We celebrate your forbidden acts.

PART THREE

REVERSING THE QUESTION

5

THE PERSONAL ORIGINS OF THE QUESTION

At the buried core of women's identity is a distinct and vital self first articulated in childhood, a root identity that gets cut off in the process of growing up female.

—EMILY HANCOCK, *The Girl Within*

Our daughters, granddaughters, and nieces remind us that in the very beginning the girl-child is shameless. She comes into the world with feelings of omnipotence, not inferiority. She loves her body, expresses its needs, and follows its impulses. She recognizes and expresses her feelings. She tells the truth. She is interested in herself and enjoys private time. She is involved with herself and her own pursuits. She celebrates herself and expects acknowledgment for her creativity and accomplishments.

The question "what's wrong with me" trickled down through the centuries into the sermons and lectures our parents heard, the bibles and "how to" books they read, and the personal experiences that shaped their parenting styles. The question was then absorbed by us. Their critical words and expectations—like the steady drip of an IV inserted at birth—exposed, scrutinized, and judged our natural needs, desires, and capacities as inferior, inadequate, and never quite good enough. It is from our parents that we learned the language of self-criticism.

While in Seminary, I read a parable, reminding me of the sad reversals of childhood. In an adapted form, it has followed me through the years, finding its way from one journal to the next:

> In the dark of the night thieves entered a store and did their work without detection. In the morning the store opened at the appointed time. It was obvious to the clerk that the store had been entered and yet nothing seemed to have been taken. As the day progressed and customers brought merchandise to the counter, the storekeepers began to notice a curious phenomenon. The merchandise of least value wore the tags of greatest value. And the items of greatest value carried the tags of least value. By the end of the day the puzzle had been solved. The thieves had reversed the price tags.

Sadly, a conformity-based childhood reverses the price tags. The natural and essential self, a priceless treasure, is demeaned and set aside, and the artificial and constructed self grows in value. Image is more valuable than essence; conformity more priceless than originality; and lies are celebrated as truth. Mary Ellen was accused of stealing the music teacher's check. She had been chosen to deliver the check and for some reason the music teacher could not find it. Everyone assumed Mary Ellen had stolen it. She was interrogated by the principal and proclaimed her innocence. She was sent home and her mother continued the interrogation for two days. Exhausted, Mary Ellen made up a story, taking responsibility for the missing check. "Finally the truth," her mother said. She was required to apologize. Her lie was celebrated as the truth. Throughout childhood we were offered a monumental choice: to tell the truth and be who we were, risking abandonment and rejection, or to conform by developing an artificial self in order to win the approval of important adults and to survive childhood.

Both boys and girls experience the sad reversals of childhood. Yet due to the trickle down effects of Western civilization's tenacious belief in the inferiority of women and our "B" status in the hierarchic scheme of things, the girl-child's experience is particularly disturbing. Throughout the communal and religious history we have reviewed, women's natural needs, desires, and capacities were dissected, defined, and then judged as inferior and defective based on the definitions of men. Consider again Freud's requirement that the girl-child repress and eventually discard her autonomous "masculine sexuality" in order for her passive and receptive feminine sexuality to emerge. Those who "obstinately" clung to the excitability of the clitoris were considered sexually crippled and "unfeminine." Those who were unable to experience a vaginal orgasm were diagnosed as "frigid."

In this way, a woman's natural impulses to retain a relationship with her own body and to enjoy her sexual autonomy were judged as unfeminine and aberrational. The function of the clitoris in female sexuality was dissected and defined by men "regardless of the subjective statements of the women."[68] Our mothers and grandmothers were immersed in these distorted understandings of female sexuality. By adolescence many of us became convinced something was wrong with our sexuality—prompting us to hide our "unfeminine" knowledge of our bodies and our ability to meet our needs for sexual satisfaction.

Lest we think these "reversals of value" are relics of our own pre-women's movement socialization, consider the sobering words of Mary Pipher:

> "America today is a girl-destroying place. Everywhere girls are encouraged to sacrifice their true selves. Their parents may fight to protect them, but their parents have limited power. Many girls lose contact with their true selves, and when they do, they become extraordinarily vulnerable to a culture that is all too happy to use them for its purposes."[69]

EIGHT NATURAL CAPACITIES

From my own experience as teacher and friend of children, as workshop facilitator and spirituality counselor, and from the experience of the women whose stories I have read and listened to in countless circles, I have pinpointed eight natural capacities that constitute our potential for health and fullness. In some of our homes, these capacities were supported to develop and to flourish. In conformity-based homes, the price tags were reversed: the natural and essential-self was criticized and expected to be discarded on our way to becoming an acceptable female. Each natural capacity will be introduced in this chapter as we explore the third path on our transformative journey from self-criticism to self-celebration. We continue to acknowledge the past's influence on the present by walking through our personal past, actively engaging the "reversals of value" embedded within our family experience, reversals that shaped the question "what's wrong with me."

A LIST OF CAPACITIES

1. The Girl-Child is Body-Centered.
A Reversal of Value: The restraint of the girl-child's natural body centeredness. The development of the restrained-self.

2. The Girl-Child Expresses Her Needs.
A Reversal of Value: The dismissal of the girl-child's organic needs. The development of the disembodied-self.

3. The Girl-Child is Sexually Autonomous.
A Reversal of Value: The repression of the girl-child's erotic potential. The development of the passive-self.

4. The Girl-Child Expresses Her Feelings.
A Reversal of Value: Recognition of the inferiority of the girl-child's emotions.The development of the acceptable-self.

5. The Girl-Child Tells the Truth.
A Reversal of Value: Recognition of the inferiority of the girl-child's perceptions and thoughts. The development of the dishonest-self.

6. The Girl-Child is Creative.
A Reversal of Value: The relinquishment of the girl-child's creative and original-self. The development of the self-just-like-everyone-else.

7. The Girl-Child is Interested In and Involved With Herself.
A Reversal of Value: The relinquishment of the girl-child's separate-self. The development of the helpful-self.

8. The Girl-Child is Full of Herself.
A Reversal of Value: The relinquishment of the girl-child's celebratory-self. The development of the humble-self.

Along with the eight natural capacities, this chapter will explore the generic "reversals of value" woven into the family experiences of the women with whom I have worked. Their childhoods span five decades—the 1930s through the 1970s. The specific family dysfunctions, aggravating these generic reversals, such as alcoholism and sexual abuse, were explored in *A God Who Looks Like Me* and will not be addressed here except in the personal stories at the end of the chapter. Many women did not experience overt abuse or dysfunction in their childhoods. They wrestle alone with an insidious and unnamed impairment for which no self-help groups exist. To walk the personal path in the company of all women validates their intuition, names their impairment, relieves their loneliness, and supports their decision to heal into the present.

Some women must be convinced of the importance of this "personal" path. According to them, the only effective path to women's liberation is the intellectual-political journey outlined in Chapters 1 and 2. They are comfortable dealing with global issues yet uneasy when invited to bring the global down to the specifics of their family history. They have attempted to ignore the past, considering childhood irrelevant to their adult pursuits. They regard a woman's inability to let go of the past to deal with the "more pressing political issues at hand" as an indication of "feminine weakness." Others are afraid of feeling too deeply, of being overwhelmed with the unexpressed feelings of a lifetime. For them, any display of deep emotion is another evidence of our inferiority. They immerse themselves in political action and achievement to avoid the intimacy of confronting their own personal histories.

We hold every memory, impression, image, word, event, and formative belief of childhood within us. Nothing has been lost or forgotten. It is impossible to ignore the past. It will always make itself known in troubling physical symptoms and persistent ineffective behaviors, as well as in the "splattering" of our unexamined memories and unreleased feelings on both our colleagues and political opponents. In order to be an effective and responsible agent of transformation in the culture, we must walk through our personal past.

The material of Chapter 5 is presented in collage form, in the non-technical language of verbal snapshots and word fragments gathered from the memories, experiences, and writings of women. Many sociological and psychological textbooks examine the harmful socialization of women. They engage only a limited portion of our intelligence. Cognitive understanding alone does not reach to the depths of our self-critical attitudes. We do not remember our childhoods in nice neat developmental categories. We hold the memories and impressions of childhood in our bodies and their sensations; in our tears, trembling, and joy; in the depth and pace of our breath; and in the repetitive and critical self-talk that accompanies our days. Reaching to these levels of remembrance prepares us for a profound transformation of our inner worlds, a complete reversal of everything we have been taught to believe about ourselves.

As you read through Chapter 5, sorting through the "reversals of value" experienced in your childhood, notice the depth of your breath and the sensations in your body. Take note of the phrases of particular significance to you, the ones that trigger your own experience or the experience of your daughter, granddaughter, or niece. Some women find it helpful to note these phrases with a magic marker or highlighter. Others jot them down in their journals.

I have included the questions participants think about as they move through this material. Consider writing or drawing with your non-dominant hand as you reflect on the questions. This technique is an effective means of accessing childhood memory. It bypasses the judgment, criticism, and resistance of the adult. Experiment with the technique. The child part of you has much to say. Her voice will become familiar to you over time; you will recognize it as the voice of the child you once were—in the very beginning.

If you are parent, use Chapter 5 as an opportunity to review your own attitudes toward your daughters and to evaluate the family environment you have created. Are their natural capacities supported to develop and flourish? What is valued in your home: image or essence, conformity or originality, lies or truth? Celebrate the gifts of your parenting style and receive support to address your parenting challenges as you read through Chapters 5 and 6.

THE GIRL-CHILD IS BODY-CENTERED

In the very beginning, the girl-child's body is full of energy, movement, and sound. She lives a body-centered existence and is naturally exuberant. She releases her big bundle of body-energy through movements and sounds. She runs and jumps, climbs and explores, throws and hits. She cries, moans, and screams. She shouts, sings, and hums. And even her occasional "tantrum" at the end of a long day serves to release her pent-up energy before sleep. Every body-movement and expression teaches her where she ends and others begin. Early on she doesn't know the difference between hitting a chair and hitting her brother, between climbing on the couch and climbing grandma's precious antique chair. Her senses are alive and attune to the world around her. She is naturally curious about the sight, sound, taste, feel, and smell of things. Most of what she will learn in the first five years of life, she will learn through her body and its capacities. It is her teacher, healer, and challenge. No separation exists between her mind and her body. They are one within her. The exuberance of the universe pulsates through her. She is full of herself.

Some women have vivid memories of the very beginning. Take a moment to remember your original exuberance and body-centeredness: the times when you ran free like the wind or jumped high like a horse, when you climbed a tree or fearlessly crossed a creek, when you wrestled a friend to the ground and then tumbled down a hill, or when your voice rose up within you and was heard by the whole wide world.

Others have no memory of the girl-child they once were. They ask, "Where is she? Was she ever me? Was there ever a time when I was full of myself?" If you do not remember your childhood, remember the exuberance and body-centeredness of your pre-adolescent daughter, granddaughter, or niece: a time when she followed her own impulse to dance up the aisles of the supermarket without embarrassment or when she needed no instruction to climb the big oak tree in your backyard and refused to come down for lunch. Allow your daughter, granddaughter, or niece to awaken memories of a time when you were full of yourself.

A Reversal of Value: *The Development of the Restrained-Self*

Eventually our natural exuberance and body-centeredness were criticized as unlady-like (not feminine enough) or tomboyish (too masculine) by our families. We were offered fewer opportunities than our brothers to develop our physical capacities and to stretch our bodies to their physical limits. Our brothers were taught to throw a ball. They were encouraged to play baseball. A girl's place was in the home not on the field, we were told. We were expected to wear shoes and clothes that made it impossible for us to run, jump, and keep up with the boys. We were expected to limit the space we took up with our voices: wimpish and passive sounds were encouraged because they reflected our restraint. We were expected to limit the space we took up with our bodies: "ladies" sat still with their legs together or crossed. We were required to conform to these childhood commandments at the expense of our exuberance and healthy body-centeredness.

Some of us conformed and became quintessential females to win the approval of our parents and to survive childhood. Sufficiently restrained, our natural body-energy was directed away from body-activity toward body-grooming, away from spontaneity toward control. Groomed to be "ornamental," we spent inordinate amounts of time and resources twisting our bodies into the acceptable shapes of the culture. Some of us rebelled and refused to twist our bodies out of shape. We identified with the boys and sought to transcend the "weakness" of being female. We assumed an androgynous demeanor and attitude. Thus we were unacceptable to the "ornamental" girls and we never quite fit in among the boys either. Whatever our choice, we became convinced something was wrong with our bodies and their natural impulses toward activity and exuberance. Those of us who chose ornamentalism denied these impulses as "unfeminine." Those of us who chose a male-defined androgyny, embraced them as "boyish." Either way, the girl-child's original goodness was twisted out of shape and labeled unacceptable by her family, and eventually, by herself.

What specific words, images, experiences, and expectations twisted your natural exuberance and body centeredness out of shape and encouraged restraint? Did you conform and become an ornamental female by denying your natural impulse toward activity and exuberance? Were you unprepared for feminism's challenge to love your body, certain something was fundamentally wrong with you because of your inability to "get with the program" and shed the restraint of a lifetime? Or did you rebel in childhood and refuse to twist your body out of shape by hanging with the boys? What were the gifts and challenges of your choices?

THE GIRL-CHILD EXPRESSES HER NEEDS

In the very beginning, the girl-child is one big bundle of needs and she expresses them very clearly. When she is hungry, she lets everyone know. When a food upsets her system, her body offers immediate feedback in the form of a rash or stomach ache, or in the clear dislike of that food in the future. When she's tired, she falls asleep wherever she may be—in someone's arms or on the department store floor. And when she hasn't gotten enough sleep, her whole being is out of balance until her life energy has been restored. When she is cold, she wraps up. When she is hot, she strips down wherever she may be! When she needs to expel gas, she farts or burps without hesitation. When she is ready to eliminate the day's waste, she finds a bathroom however inconvenient to her caretakers! When she wants to be hugged or held, she crawls onto someone's lap. She loves the feel of her blanket touching her face, the feel of the mud and sand touching her feet, and the feel of the water touching her whole body as she swims or takes a bath. Touch is essential to her healthy development. In her mother's womb, it soothed and comforted her. And on her trip down the birth canal, she was pushed, pulled, and hugged her into life by the laboring action of her mother's body. The organic needs and impulses of the universe pulsate through her. She is full of herself.

Pause to remember your childhood awareness of your own organic needs and impulses: a time when your were aware of your need to sleep, to eat, or to bundle up, and expressed it however inconvenient it was for your caretakers; a time when you were certain a food was not what your body needed; a time when you reveled in the feel of the mud, sand, or water touching your body.

If you do not remember your childhood, recall your pre-adolescent daughter, granddaughter, or niece's awareness and expression of her organic needs: a time when she burped or farted without hesitation; a time when she refused to take another step in the department store and fell asleep outside the fitting room. Allow your daughter, granddaughter, or niece to awaken memories of a time when you were full of yourself.

A Reversal of Value: *The Development of the Disembodied-Self*

Eventually the awareness and expression of our natural needs were judged as fussy, needy, or "too sensitive" by our parents. They determined when we were cold or hot; when we were hungry; what foods were good for us; when, where, and how we were to expel gas; and when they were available to hold us. And they were the ones who determined if an expression of need was genuine or "manipulative." From early on, we received direct or indirect messages from our parents that it was not OK to have needs outside of the regulated and acceptable framework of family life based on their schedules and responsibilities.

Without the support of a "village" to assist them in raising us, our overwhelmed parents seldom consulted us about what we needed or didn't need. Instead, they tightened around any spontaneous expression of need, convincing us that something was wrong with our natural "neediness." In an attempt to fit into home and school environments that did not honor the natural needs and impulses of our developing bodies, we learned to ignore its needs and to develop the essential skill of conquering the body by "waiting" an hour to eat, "holding it" until bathroom time, or by censoring our desire to be touched. Compounding our deepening "disembodied-ness," we were groomed to anticipate and then meet the physical needs of others in our training to become housewives and mothers. Preoccupied with the growing demands to service others, we ignored our own body's signals to stretch, to rest, to eat, or to go to the bathroom. Depleted, we lost touch with our own needs.

What specific words, images, experiences, and expectations twisted your awareness of your natural needs and impulses out of shape and encouraged the disembodied-self? Did you conform by denying your needs in order to service the needs of others? Were you unprepared for the recovery movement's dismantling of codependency, certain something was fundamentally wrong with you because of your inability to shed the caretaking habits of a lifetime? Or did you refuse to twist yourself out of shape by becoming a "fussy," and "much too sensitive" girl? What were the gifts and challenges of your choices?

THE GIRL-CHILD IS SEXUALLY AUTONOMOUS

In the very beginning of her life, the girl-child is acquainted with the erotic energy within her. Childhood is not a time of sexual dormancy for the girl-child. From birth, she is capable of sexual arousal and orgasm. These are her birth-rights as a child of life. She says a big YES to life as it pulsates through her. She feels the YES in her curiosity about her body's sensations and in her exploration of its fascinating nooks and crannies, openings and operations. Her body is her closest friend. She discovers her clitoris and receives pleasure from touching it. She experiences her body's sensuality by feeling its smoothness and curves, by touching its lips, by entering its openings, by tasting its juiciness, and by delighting in its natural fragrances. She also feels the YES in her heart, her joy, and even in her tears. It touches every area of her life. The erotic potential of the universe pulsates through her. She is full of herself.

Pause to remember your original erotic potential: a time when you discovered something new and exciting about your body; a time when you touched your clitoris, delighting in your own body; a time when you were unashamed to look at yourself in the mirror with great joy.

If you do not remember your childhood, recall the times when you observed the erotic potential of your pre-adolescent daughter, granddaughter, or niece: the many times she pranced around the house naked, dancing joyously; a time when she wanted to stay in the bathtub for hours, playing with her body shamelessly. Allow your daughter, granddaughter, or niece to awaken memories of a time when you were full of yourself.

A Reversal of Value: *The Development of the Passive-Self*

Eventually, our original erotic potential was judged as unfeminine, immodest, and impure by our parents' words and actions. For those of us who were touched affectionately by our parents, touch was seldom extended beyond early childhood. As we matured and grew out of the "cute stage," our parents became uncomfortable with our developing bodies and most touching abruptly stopped. We created stories to make sense of this withdrawal of affection. We became convinced something was wrong with our bodies, that our growing breasts and pubic hair, and the genital sensations we were experiencing made us untouchable to our parents. For some of us, the incestuous behavior of a parent or relative compounded this growing discomfort.

Early in our lives we discovered the clitoris as a source of pleasure. In adolescence, the vagina became the focus of sexual pleasure in a family and culture that reduced sexuality to genital intercourse defined by the needs and desires of men. We accepted a form of sexuality that required a partner and that did not offer us satisfaction. And because our early body-knowing and erotic autonomy were not cultivated by our parents, we eventually became ignorant of the mechanics of female sexuality and dependent on others to meet our needs. Groomed by our parents to service men sexually, we forgot about the wonders of our own bodies, their rich erotic potential, and their capacity for sensual delight and satisfaction. Our original love of the body, our curiosity about its sensations, and our exploration of its fascinating nooks and crannies, openings and operations were twisted out of shape and labeled unacceptable by our families, and by ourselves.

What specific words, images, experiences, and expectations twisted your original erotic potential out of shape and cultivated the development of the sexually passive-self? Did you conform by denying your sexual needs to satisfy the needs of others? Were you unprepared for the sexual liberation of the women's movement—certain something was wrong with you because of your inability to shed the sexual passivity of a lifetime? Or did you refuse to twist yourself out of shape in adolescence by retaining a relationship with your own body and sexual autonomy? What were the gifts and challenges of your choices?

THE GIRL-CHILD EXPRESSES HER FEELINGS

In the very beginning, the girl-child has the capacity to feel and to express the whole range of human emotion. The primary emotions create sensations and energy tracks through her body. Through her body, she knows her feelings. Through movement and sound, she releases the energy, accompanying each feeling. No separation exists between her feelings and her body. They are one within her. She feels sadness as an ache in her heart and as the tear flowing from her eyes. She feels anger rise up within her and releases it in loud sounds and strong movements. She feels fear in the shortness of her breath and in the fluttering sensation in her tummy. She feels erotic energy in the tingling warmth of her genitals. She feels joy in the warmth of her face, the smile in her eyes, and in the giggle inside of her. Her feelings ebb and flow as naturally as the breath. When she gets angry, she stomps and yells and before you know it, she's smiling and off with a friend. The expression of a full range of human emotion is essential to her physical and psychological health. Her immune system is strengthened by the circulation of her feelings. The feelings of the universe pulsate through her. She is full of herself.

Remember your original awareness and expression of the whole range of human emotion: a time when you were angry and felt it pass through your body and then be gone; a time when your heart ached and you felt comforted as you cried into your pillow; a time when you were happy, sad, and angry all within one day and that was OK.

If you do not remember your childhood, recall your pre-adolescent daughter, granddaughter, or niece's ability to express her feelings: a time when she let it be known that she was angry at her brother for entering her room without permission; a time when she needed to talk about her absent father with tears in her eyes while pounding her fist into a near-by pillow. Allow your daughter, granddaughter, or niece to awaken memories of a time when you were full of yourself.

A Reversal of Value: *The Development of The Acceptable Self*

Our capacity to feel was judged as fickle, too intense, and inferior by our parents. Although we were allowed more room to feel than our brothers, an inherent judgment surrounded our capacity to feel. Feelings were not as important as thoughts. Boys think. Girls feel. Our feelings were tolerated at best and dismissed at worst as evidence of our inferiority. We heard rumors of women who allowed their feelings to keep them from getting a job done, unlike men who mastered their feelings and completed the task at hand; of women who were too emotional and good for nothing especially at that time of the month, unlike men who could be counted on all the time; of women who were fickle, erratic, and unstable because they let their feelings get the best of them, unlike men who were reliable and controlled.

There were good feelings and bad feelings. Responsible for the reactions of others, we sorted through our feelings. Bad feelings were to be controlled and kept inside because they made others uncomfortable. Good feelings could be expressed as long as they weren't too intense. Intensity made everyone uncomfortable. We became aware of boy-feelings and girl-feelings. Girls got hurt and cried a lot. Boys got angry and yelled a lot. If a boy cried, he was called a sissy. If a girl got angry, she was called unfeminine and ugly. Humble, discreet, and considerate, we learned to cry when we were angry and to smile when we really wanted to yell.

What specific words, images, experiences, and expectations convinced you of the inferiority of your capacity to feel; required you to categorize feelings into good/bad, and girl/boy compartments; and allowed only the expression of "acceptable" emotions? Did you conform by swallowing your uncomfortably intense emotions, including those reserved for boys? Were you unprepared for the emotional openness of the therapeutic age—certain something was wrong with you because of your inability to shed the facade of a lifetime? Or did you refuse to twist yourself out of shape in childhood by maintaining a relationship to all of your feelings and expressing them through writing or painting, or in conversations with your best friend? What were the gifts and challenges of your choices?

THE GIRL-CHILD TELLS THE TRUTH

In the very beginning, the girl-child tells the truth about what she thinks and how she responds to the events of life. She is transparent, forthright, and bold. When she doesn't like her food, she spits it out. When she's exhausted from tagging along on a shopping spree, she refuses to take another step. When she doesn't like someone, she tightens in their presence and makes her discomfort known. She has a mind of her own and responds to the events of life with her own set of opinions. She tells her mother, "I get tired when you stay at those meetings so late. Can't we leave earlier?" She tells her father, "I like it when you read stories with me in the morning." She confronts her parents, " When you fight with each other late at night, I hear your voices and it makes me sad and afraid. I wish you wouldn't fight." She tells the truth when she is asked questions:
"No, I don't like the new baby-sitter. She yells."
"No, I don't want to go to their house. I don't like to sit on uncle's lap."
"Yes, I want a room of my own."
The truth of the universe pulsates through her. She is full of herself.

Pause to remember your childhood capacity to tell the truth and to trust your own perceptions and thoughts: the time when you let your mother know it was NOT OK that your grandfather did not ask permission before he hugged you; the time when you told the grouchy neighbor that it was NOT OK to yell at little children; or the time when you requested that your father keep his promise and spend more time with you on the week-ends.

If you do not remember your childhood, recall your pre-adolescent daughter, granddaughter, or niece's ability to tell the truth and to trust her own perceptions: the time when she let you know that your hurried response to her question was not acceptable to her; or the time when she told you that she didn't like the man you were dating and listed the reasons why. Allow your daughter, granddaughter, or niece to awaken memories of a time when you were full of yourself.

A Reversal of Value: *The Development of The Dishonest Self*

Eventually, our capacity to tell the truth was judged as rude and "not nice," and our capacity to think for ourselves as "troublesome" and "rocking the boat" by our families. We learned to question our own thoughts and perceptions and to lie in a compliance-based environment that valued conformity to outdated gender stereotypes and "politeness" more than it did originality and integrity. We kept our thoughts about the events of life to ourselves so there wouldn't be an argument. We strained to like everyone so we wouldn't hurt anyone's feelings. We pretended that we didn't know what we knew so their egos wouldn't be hurt; that we didn't hear what we heard so their secrets wouldn't be exposed; and that we couldn't do what we could do so the masquerade about who was weak and who was strong would be maintained. We were required to be nice and pleasant at the expense of our own healthy integrity. The constant repetition of these childhood commandments censored our natural tendency to tell the truth and to think for ourselves. Humble, discreet, and considerate, we learned to question our truth and to defer to the thoughts and perceptions of others, assuming something was wrong with us.

What specific words, images, experiences, and expectations convinced you of the inferiority of your perceptions and thoughts; required you to categorize them into acceptable/unacceptable compartments; and allowed the expression of only acceptable ones? Did you conform by swallowing your uncomfortable perceptions, opinions, and ideas? Were you unprepared for the intellectual challenges of the women's movement, certain something was wrong with you because of your inability to shed the "deference" of a lifetime? Or did you refuse to twist yourself out of shape by maintaining a relationship to your inner truth and intellectual independence? What were the gifts and challenges of your choices?

THE GIRL-CHILD IS CREATIVE

In the very beginning, the girl-child trusts her vision of the world and expresses it. With wonder and delight, she paints a picture, creates a dance, and makes up a song. To give expression to her creative impulses is as natural as her breathing. She creates in her own language-imagery-movement. She follows no script. She is not bound by the customary way things have been expressed. Her creative intuition is original. She gathers all of life into her inner crucible and mixes it with her unique vision and experience. She produces an original creation. She loves the sounds, movements, ideas, images, and words that emerge from inside of her. Sometimes the creative impulse leads her to share her dance, her song, her picture. She is full of herself as she performs before audiences large and small. Other times she does not want to share her creative expression with anyone. She reads to herself, creates an art showing in the privacy of her bedroom, or dances with her beloved stuffed bears as her audience. The originality of the universe pulsates through her. She is full of herself.

Pause to remember your childhood creativity and its expression: the time when you organized and directed the whole neighborhood's performance of the play you wrote; the time when you choreographed a "routine" and taught it to your girlfriends at a slumber party; or the time when you painted the sunset with berries while vacationing at the ocean with your grandparents.

If you do not remember your childhood, recall the creative expressions of your pre-adolescent daughter, granddaughter, or niece: the time when she made "sculptures" out of the cookie dough you taught her to prepare; the time when she made a collage out of the photos and memories of her best friend who had moved away; or the time when she requested all of your material scraps to use in the design of her first quilt. Allow your daughter, granddaughter, or niece to awaken memories of a time when you were full of yourself.

A Reversal of Value:
The Development of the Self-Just-Like-Everyone-Else

Our capacity to create was judged as impractical, not good enough, and "outside the lines" by our parents and teachers. Very early on, our creative expressions were exposed to the competition-oriented comments of well-meaning others who judged our work as "better than" or "not as good as." Perfection became the goal and anything less than perfect was thrown away. No longer was the emphasis on spontaneous expression rising from our own inner lives, product and performance took center stage. Creative expression became work assigned by parents and teachers with specific performance goals as its motivation. "Being creative" became a job to be done in its proper time and place. As our lives became cluttered with responsibility for others in the family and with the preoccupation with their needs, creativity became scheduled like everything else. Eventually, we lost touch with the spontaneous expressions of our inner lives. There was a particular way things were to be done and if we dared to use our own colors, shapes, or movements, or to experiment with a brand new way of doing something, we were scolded for venturing outside the lines. Humble, discreet, and considerate, we learned to stifle our creative impulses except in service of the careers and projects of our children and lovers, our friends and colleagues. We learned to color inside someone else's lines.

What specific words, images, experiences, and expectations required the repression of your creative and original-self and the development of the self-just-like-everyone-else? Did you conform by coloring in the lines? Were you unprepared for the creative challenges of the women's movement, certain something was wrong with you because of your inability to shed the conformity of a lifetime? Or did you refuse to twist yourself out of shape in childhood by maintaining a relationship to the spontaneous expressions of your inner life through writing, drawing, sculpting, designing, singing, or dancing? What were the gifts and challenges of your choices?

THE GIRL-CHILD IS INTERESTED IN AND INVOLVED WITH HERSELF

In the very beginning, the girl-child is interested in herself and involved in self-motivated adventures. She is a natural explorer of everything in her world. Her ordinary life is interesting enough. Every experience is filled with wonder and awe. It is enough to gaze at the redness of an apple; to watch the water flow over the rocks in a stream; to listen to the rain dance; to count the peas on her plate. Ordinary life is her teacher, her challenge, and her delight. She is never bored. There is always another adventure and project to turn toward. Only on her terms does she want to share a luscious piece of her grandma's cake or a seashell from her chest of special treasures or the letter her favorite aunt wrote to her from Africa. Much of the time, she wants to savor the pleasures of her own life all by herself. The vitality of the universe pulsates through her. She is full of herself.

In the very beginning, the girl-child enjoys the privacy of quiet times, under the cover times, alone times to digest the events and experiences of her life. She is always available to herself so she is never really alone. She keeps some things to herself, holding them in the privacy of her own heart. She has a new idea that's too fragile to share so she keeps it close to her. If she tells someone about it too soon, the fragile blossom may wilt from premature exposure. She has a new friend who's too new to invite into her very private dreams; theirs is still too fragile a connection to hold the fullness of who she is. She has a new relationship with her body as it changes from day to day. She needs private time to befriend each change before she exposes her body to others. She loves the quiet of the night when everything slows down and she has a chance to think about the day, to feel the sadness in her heart, to let her imagination drift to other worlds, to see the dancing images of her night-dreams—all by herself. The solitude of the universe pulsates through her. She is full of herself.

Pause for a moment to remember your original self-interest and self-involvement: the time you sang songs to yourself for an hour straight without interruption, loving your own company; the time when you sat in the attic for a whole afternoon, looking through old picture albums while conversing with your dead grandmother; or the time when you ventured into the meadow beside your house in the morning and forgot all about lunch as you carried on important conversations with your favorite trees.

If you do not remember your childhood, recall the self-interest and self-involvement of your pre-adolescent daughter, granddaughter, or niece: the time when she put a sign on her door that read, "Do not disturb for the whole day. Please leave meals outside door;" or the time when she refused to share with anyone the cookies she made with her visiting grandmother because she wanted to eat one a day for week to remind her of their time together. Allow your daughter, granddaughter, or niece to awaken memories of a time when you were full of yourself . . . in the very beginning of life.

A Reversal of Value: *Development of Helpful-Self*

Our natural self-interest was judged as selfish and self-centered by our families. Nice girls share their cake and treasures. Nice girls include others in their adventures. Nice girls don't hurt the feelings of others. "If you have a piece of chocolate cake and your friend doesn't, she will feel bad so be sure to share." "If you are working on a project and your little brother wants to help, be sure to include him so he won't feel left out." We were required to share at the expense of our own healthy self-interest and to include others at the expense of our own healthy self-involvement. Our healthy narcissism and self-centeredness became crushed under the weight of these conformity-based expectations.

Our natural need for privacy was judged as selfish and unhelpful. We watched our mothers closely and learned that she had no private, under the covers, all by herself time except maybe in the bathroom but even there someone was always barging in with a question or an emergency. Someone was always barging into our lives too. Barging in on our thoughts: "What are you thinking, young lady?" Barging in on our feelings: "Why so sad today?" Barging in on our rooms: "The guests will stay in your room for the week. You will have to move into your sister's room." Barging in on our time: "I need mama's helper to baby-sit your little brother today." Barging in on our bodies: "Come and sit on my lap, pretty girl." There was always someone barging in on our privacy with demands to help in the kitchen or to fix our little sister's hair. Our brother wasn't "on call" like we were. There were long stretches of time when he had nothing to do except what he wanted to do. His time was his own. Our time belonged to others. We were required to be helpful at the expense of our own healthy need for private time and space. The constant repetition of this childhood commandment censored our natural desire for solitude. Sometimes we felt like screaming "Leave me alone!" Helpful and compliant, we swallowed those words and twisted our natural introversion into a much more acceptable and helper-oriented extroversion.

What specific words, images, experiences, and expectations required the relinquishment of your separate-self and the development of the helpful-self interested in, involved with, and available to others? Did you choose to conform by swallowing your own healthy self-interest and self-involvement and by abdicating the solitude necessary to engage these capacities? Was your natural introversion twisted into a more acceptable and helper-oriented extroversion? Were you unprepared for the meditation challenges of the 1990s—certain something was wrong with you because of your inability to shed the external orientation of a lifetime and enter into silence and solitude? Or did you refuse to twist yourself out of shape in childhood by maintaining a relationship to your separate-self and your desire for solitude? What were the gifts and challenges of your choices?

THE GIRL-CHILD IS FULL OF HERSELF

In the very beginning, the girl-child wants to be seen and acknowledged. She feels good around people who look her in the eye, who ask her questions about her life, and who listen to her answers. She can tell when someone really sees and hears and likes her. To be around someone like that feels like eating her favorite flavor of ice cream. She smiles from her head to her toes. The girl-child can tell when someone doesn't see and hear and like her. To be around someone like that feels like eating lima beans. Lima beans are a pretty color and shape and lots of grown-ups like them, but she doesn't. Just like it's OK that she doesn't like certain foods, its OK that she doesn't like EVERYBODY. The girl-child only shows her projects to the special people in her life, the ones who make her smile. She tells them about her special dreams, except the very private ones, and lets them know about most of her special adventures. She loves it when they say:

"WOW, you're fantastic!"

"That's a colorful picture you drew. I like to look at it."

"Your body is so very strong."

"I'm so glad you are in my life!"

Their words feel warm like the sun calling her out to play on a summer day. Their words say what she knows is true. She is a special girl: fantastic and strong and the maker of color-filled pictures and fun to be around. The radiance of the universe pulsates through her. She is full of herself.

Pause to remember your healthy desire for acknowledgment and recognition: the time when you hung all of your second grade paintings on the living room wall and sent invitations to the neighbors to come to your first art showing; the time when you asked all the Thanksgiving guests to listen to the stories you had written and to clap after each one; or the time you called your mother's best friend because you knew she'd listen to your ideas with the same interest she showed to adults.

If you do not remember your childhood, recall the healthy desire for acknowledgment and recognition expressed by your pre-adolescent daughter, granddaughter, or niece: the time she asked if the family could have a weekly "show and tell" time so everybody could be applauded; or the time when she wrote to the president about how to help homeless people through the cold winter and called the White House because she didn't get a response soon enough to suit her. Allow your daughter, granddaughter, or niece to awaken memories of a time when you were full of yourself . . . in the very beginning of life.

A Reversal of Value: *The Development of the Humble Self*

Our desire for acknowledgment was judged as conceited, big-headed, self-inflated, and pompous by our families. Daily, we walked through a minefield of warnings and admonitions to be humble about our projects, dreams, accomplishments, and adventures, to be humble and quiet about ourselves at the expense of our own healthy self-celebration:

Don't be so egotistical and full of yourself. Don't blow your own horn. Don't brag. Pretend you don't know what you know so you won't hurt his ego. Do well quietly so others won't feel intimidated by you. Don't be so obvious with your talents. Don't hurt other people's feelings by being so good at everything. You're too big for your britches. Stop showing off. Who do you think you are? Pride goeth before a fall.

The constant repetition of these childhood commandments censored our natural desire for acknowledgment and recognition. We were required to be quiet about ourselves, to pretend that our ideas, projects, dreams, and talents were small and inconsequential so we wouldn't hurt other people's feelings and so we would be liked. Humble, discreet, and considerate, we learned that girls are suppose to applaud for others, especially the boys.

What specific words, images, experiences, and expectations required the relinquishment of your celebratory self and the development of the humble self? Did you choose to conform by becoming quiet about your ideas, projects, dreams, and talents? Were you unprepared for feminism's celebration of women, certain something was wrong with you because of your inability to shed the pseudo-humility of a lifetime? Or did you refuse to twist yourself out of shape in childhood by maintaining a relationship to your celebratory self and your desire for acknowledgment and recognition? What were the gifts and challenges of your choices?

MISSION ACCOMPLISHED

The price tags successfully reversed on our body capacities, we become alienated from our precious woman-bodies. No longer moving, we sat and waited and groomed our nails while our brothers and boyfriends shot hoops or skated by. Or we joined the boys hoping for acceptance into their clubs in spite of the encumbrance of our bodies. No longer shouting, we whispered to our girlfriends as we scrutinized magazine images of models and actresses whose perfection had been defined by a misogynistic culture and whose beauty had been created by lights and make-up. Or we shouted with the boys and watched as they scrutinized the same magazines for kicks. No longer in love with our bodies, we felt uncomfortable in them. The urge to cover, to starve, or to violently alter them began to grow within us. The vibrant and healthy capacities of our bodies were hidden away and forgotten. Instead we spent our time scrutinizing our bodies for flaws. By junior high, we had successfully restrained, ignored, and repressed ourselves. Numb and bored, we waited—in front of a mirror—for a prince to come along and make life worth living again. Or straining to transcend the weakness of our femaleness, we worked hard to hang with the boys—acceptance into their world would be our remedy. *Eve's daughters are in need of a savior.*

The price tags successfully reversed on our expressive capacities, we became alienated from our precious feelings, perceptions, and creativity. Convinced that our lives were not our own, we became alienated from our inner sense of what was true, right, and appropriate for us. We became experts at watching the way others lived and we shaped our lives accordingly. From talk show hosts, to Ann Landers, to our therapists and trainers, to the countless experts we consulted to design our experience, everyone knew better than we did. We have spent a lifetime trying to fit into someone else's idea of what is right for us: assembling our bodies according to society's formula of the perfect woman, forming our thoughts and opinions to suit the audience, limiting our feelings to what's acceptable, and formulating our behavior and actions according to the expectations of others. We have become emotionally crippled as a result of habitually abandoning ourselves into the shapes of others. Each surrender of our feelings, our truth, our originality becomes a mini-abdication of who we are. *Eve's daughters surrender to the specifications of others.*

The price tags successfully reversed on our intra-personal capacities, we became alienated from our precious self-interest, involvement, and celebration. We set aside our own pursuits to become interested and involved in the lives of others, supporting their projects, adventures, and dreams with our blood, sweat, and tears. We relinquished our private time and space to create privacy for others, making sure father had his quiet time at the end of the day to read and write, keeping the kids quiet so the elders of the church could meet without disturbance. We became embarrassed by our own delight in ourselves and our desire for acknowledgment. There are rare moments when we re-member the capacities of the very beginning and words start to form on our tongue in response to the request of a partner, colleague, or friend: "No, I can't help out today. There is a creative idea I want to pursue." And before those precious words have a chance to escape, we hear the commandment of old whispered across the centuries, "Share, selfish one, share." and we say instead "Sure I'll be right over." *Eve's daughters are secondary and supportive.*

WOMEN'S STORIES
WALKING THROUGH THEIR PERSONAL PASTS

PIECING TOGETHER THE PUZZLE   *Mani Feniger*

I was a vivacious child, excited about being alive. I was affectionate and had a passion for singing and dancing around the house when no one else was around. I grew tall very quickly, and could easily pretend to be older than my years. By the time I was in second grade, I stood at the end of the line in school.

One night when I was eight, I started to tell my mother about a problem I was having with one of the kids at school. "If you only knew how little your problems are compared to mine," she told me. The message was clear: My feelings were not important. I gave her a hug and patted her arm gently to show her I understood, but inside I was confused. I hid my own feelings in a secret place because I thought they had no place in our family.

My father had died suddenly the year before and I knew my mother was sad and lonely. She had already experienced too many losses, having left Germany in the early thirties, sixteen and both her parents dead. She had never talked about her family and I wasn't aware of the history that had shaped her perspective.

Mixed in with her genuine love for me, my mother passed on the messages that hardened her edges and made her bones brittle with arthritis. She taught me that life takes away what was meant to be yours, that people let you down when you need them. Her pain became as familiar to me as the air I breathed. After a while I couldn't distinguish her feelings from mine.

I became self-conscious and tentative, anticipating life's dangers and losses. I read books considered too serious for someone my age and often felt separate from the playfulness of other kids. I hunched my shoulders and hung my head. No terrible abuse or intentional neglect marred my childhood, but something in me was set aside: a child—exuberant, innocent, trusting, playful, pleased to be herself.

Piecing together the puzzle of my family history made visible the myths and beliefs I had taken to be reality. I began to see that I had embraced a view of life that was not based on my personal experience, or who I was. It was the inevitable result of a sensitive, intuitive human being sensing her parent's reality. I thought I had failed, because I was unable to see that I had assumed responsibility for a world that failed my mother. This realization has set me free.

TOO BIG   *Erin Louise Stewart*

I was harassed throughout childhood because of my size. I reached 6' 2" and wore a size 11 shoe by the ninth grade. I would literally walk the back routes to school to avoid any potential harassment. I hid behind buildings to escape the attention of classmates and bypassed the main areas of town and campus where groups of kids hung out. I never went to athletic games or to social events, like dances. I never joined any clubs or participated in extra-curricular activities. My tall body was a target everywhere I went. I was assaulted daily by the negative comments of adults as well as children. I have spent my whole life trying to dodge or ignore hurtful words directed at my bigness.

I tried to understand what was so horribly wrong with me that it provoked such strong reaction. I went home after school and looked into the mirror to see what they saw. I scrutinized every feature of my face and body and still could not understand what caused such a response. I finally got the message that I was different and "abnormal" because of my size, that it was OK for guys to be big, but it was not OK for me to be big. I broke a basic rule by growing too tall as a girl. They could only deal with the intimidation of my height by labeling me as a lesbian, a boy in drag, or some sort of freak of nature. They held me responsible for their own discomfort.

My shaky self-esteem was weakened by not having the clothes and shoes to support my size. I had to wear "old lady" shoes, like hush puppies, or men's shoes. Nothing really fit me or was appropriate for a young girl growing up in very large body. No resources were available to help me feel comfortable in my own body.

As I heal into the present, I am refusing to be defined by others. I am a tall woman. My height and strength are gifts, not flaws. I lift weights to develop my strength. I wear clothes that are comfortable and fit me. I no longer hide behind buildings or avoid contact with people. I am surrounded by friends who celebrate every aspect of my expansiveness. And as I have embraced an inner strength and bigness that matches my physical size, I am stepping out, consciously claiming the power to influence people that was mine even as a child. I am taking responsibility for my capacity to bring about transformation in people's attitudes and lives. My very presence in the world challenges and overturns the basic sexist assumptions that women are always weaker, smaller, and more fragile than men.

THE BALANCING BEAM   *Jane Sterrett*

Introduction

My mother died at 88, in 1992. She and my father were missionaries for over forty years. I didn't know her because I had never spent much time with her. At her funeral, no tears came, only anger, and the memory of desperate, lonely tears from years of separation. I was sent away to a missionary boarding school at six. I saw her during three months of vacation each year. By the time I was twelve, I had written her off. Her life was a bore, her work drudgery. When she asked me to do the simplest tasks, I cried out "Why do you want me to sit in the house and get fat? Let the servants do it." I was an angry, resentful child who'd rather stand among the wood shavings and watch her father turn candlesticks on the lathe.

As I began to write the stories of my childhood, I had to force myself to write about her. As I began to write, and to cry into the keyboard, she came back to me as a vital spirit, a sad and maybe even angry woman who gave birth eleven times, whose husband loved her dearly but didn't really see her or listen to her, who came to the States at the end of the war so worn the doctors told her to take a complete rest, and she with nine living children, and used to servants. I am still working on the stories, and I am learning how family stories repeat themselves generation after generation, and I am talking to my children, asking their forgiveness.

An Excerpt From "The Balancing Beam"

"You remind me of myself," Mama said. "I had to stop being a tomboy when I turned fourteen and was confirmed. And I hated it."

"You were a tomboy?" Alice asked, amazed.

"Yes," her mother said, "I remember those awful high-button shoes. They were hot and tight, and I couldn't climb trees in them."

"I'm sure glad I don't have to wear high-button shoes," Alice said. "They sound like prison."

"They were," her mother said. "They were part of what you had to do to become a lady. No one asked me if I wanted to be a lady. Why would I want to be a lady like my mother? She looked unhappy all the time. I thought it was because she had so much to do, and so many children. So I decided I would never get married. I would become a deaconess and make a vow not to marry. Then I would work only for the Lord."

Alice had heard this story before, and it always hurt her a little. Her mother had not wanted any children, and here were all these children, far too many for one family. It was no wonder to Alice that her mother was always frowning, like her grandmother.

But now Mama laughed at her childish dream as if it had been ridiculous. Mama's merry laughter was famous in the mission. Everyone thought she was a happy and funny person. Other girls wished she was their mother, but Alice knew the truth, and that was that her mother laughed when company came to the house and frowned when they left. This time Mama laughed with Alice.

"Yes," Mama said. "I was so foolish. I didn't ever want to be a lady. I longed to go on climbing trees with the native boys, to feed them raw sweet potatoes from the bin and play hide and seek with them in the yard, over by the Joseph's coat bushes. I didn't want to be a lady, but there I was, the oldest daughter and doomed to become a wife some day, and so I must try to restrain my running and shouting and foolishness."

When Mama talked about her girlhood, Alice thought of the picture her grandfather had taken on Mama's confirmation day in 1918, Mama's beautiful light hair shining in the sun, a big bow at the back of her head, Mama's funny little smile, as if she were about to cry. Oh Mama, Alice thought, I wish we could have been friends then. I wish you were my big sister.

What had conspired against Mama would conspire against Alice. The mission tried to bind her soul like the feet of Chinese women. They were partly successful. Alice learned to laugh with company and frown when company went away.

Mama raised her daughters in a bondage like her own, much as she wished she could do otherwise. They didn't have to wear trusses and petticoats. They didn't have to force their feet into buttoned shoes. But they had to learn to keep their children quiet so men could think important thoughts, to receive guests of men's choosing with a smile as open as it was hidden, to mend stockings with a careful weaving pattern when their hearts were worn beyond mending. They needed to know these things, as surely as God chose to be incarnated as a man. She wanted them to survive in a world that is not kind to women.

Alice remembered the day when she was nine, and living most of the time across the road at the American Missionary Children's Boarding School and Home, how she had decided that she'd never grow older than twelve. After twelve, the world changed for girls. She watched the big girls grow fat and slow, and spend their time talking in closed rooms, embroidering pillowcases and napkins. She couldn't bear to think of becoming like that.

But the years turned and turned, and Alice was unable to stop the flow of time or blood.

THE RED NIGHTGOWN   *Cody Douglas Oreck*

I grieve now for the red nylon nightgown with ruffles and red lace. I was in the first grade. It had been carefully laid out next to my stocking on Christmas morning and it caught the lights from the tree in deep luxurious ruby glints. My sisters had gowns to match and somewhere there is a studio portrait of the three of us, cheeks scrubbed like shiny apples as red as the gowns, smiling with our baby teeth. We saved them for special occasions so that summer, when we went to visit our other grandmother, the gowns were folded neatly into Mom's old white leather suitcase along with our play clothes.

Our other grandmother, Nanny, was living in St. Louis that year. We didn't see her much. She moved a lot. But Dad said she'd settled for a bit in this apartment and wanted us to come. Mom looked at Dad and said, "It'll be fine." Dad titled all our vacations but this one was the first I remembered. "The Great Midwest: The Farms and Cities of the Plains." We drove for days and sang and played "I Spy." I remember the bleeps and whine of the radio as Dad adjusted the dial to find new stations along the way. He was always amazed to find classical music. "Way out here, Kath!"

I looked out of the car window to see endless unchanging fields undulating in the same strong warm wind that whipped my pony tail across my cheeks. Then St. Louis was suddenly dark and grimy and colorless. We each carried something heavy as we climbed a long staircase to Nanny's apartment. She was thrilled and fussed lovingly over each of us. She introduced us to her boyfriend, Harry, and plopped into a chair so she could see me eye to eye and find out who I really was. I liked the smell of her smoky breath and perfume as she hugged me over and over again. Then she bustled us in for a bubble bath where she laughed and laughed with her big white teeth. I admired them as she pulled the red nightgown over my head and she explained to me about the glamour of dentures. "But wait now, let me see!" Nanny stood back in awe as I twirled in my gown, the red lace floating dreamily around me. "Speaking of glamour!" she exclaimed. I stood very proud and loved her with my eyes.

Nanny had her very own television and she set us up to watch Gunsmoke while she and Mom and Dad went into the kitchen to visit. The boyfriend, Harry, stayed with us to watch and I remember how reluctantly I dragged my eyes from the screen to watch him in the bluish light as he gestured that I should come to sit on his lap. Swishing my red gown like Miss Kitty, I stepped over my sisters—who never blinked—and climbed dutifully up on his knees. We didn't have a TV at home and I was quickly reabsorbed in Matt Dillon. But the picture went away when Harry slipped his hand under the red lace and began to stroke beneath my panties. The darkness of the room suddenly ebbed and breathed with his breath and the lurid moving lights from the screen. "Doesn't that feel good?" His whisper in my ear felt hot and sweaty. I marshaled all my good girl training to always be polite, but could only whisper back, "It's okay," distinctly wincing at my own insincerity. For it was not okay, this strange grown-up tapping and rubbing my softest, safest part. And somehow, most fearful of all was that I was lying to a grown-up and might displease the grown-up. My heart thumped with anxiety until I mustered almost brightly, "At least it doesn't hurt!" to his face so close to mine, but he wasn't listening. His eyes were fixed and glazed and as he shuddered, I shuddered too, in horror and then slid cautiously from his relaxed grip.

Soon the room was bright again and I was helping Mom and Nanny make a pallet where we were to sleep on the floor when I heard strange wild sobs and found myself frantically trying to bury my head in my mother's stomach. "What's wrong? What is it?" She bent over me and hugged me. "She's never like this!" "What's the matter? Why is she crying?" Everyone was talking at once and Harry's voice seemed to be loudest of all. I was grateful for the blind wet darkness of tears in my mother's skirt so I couldn't see his face or watch him plucking nervously at my father's sleeve. "What's the matter with her? What's wrong with your little girl?" Nanny must have watched him though. Even today I pray that she did not yet suspect what he'd done, but ordered him to leave because of the way he fed the confusion and seemed to be finally fairly shouting in my father's ear while my sisters joined me, wailing in bewilderment.

Only in the wan morning light in a room alone with Mom and Dad could I finally tell them what had happened. I told them with my whole heart, the words rushing out in a childish jumble of shame and Gunsmoke and new, clean tears of relief. But somehow more shocking than Harry's probing sweaty fingers and hoarse whispers and lidless eyes was the stricken silence of my beloved parents as I stopped talking, and my mother's first words. "Are you telling the truth?" I watched her lips move in slow motion. Her voice was heavy and strange and tolled in my head like a deep, dark bell, a death knell. I reeled and believed I was dying. I wanted to die. But what died instead was just one vision of the world that I had believed in up to that summer after the first grade. There have been many, many deaths since then. But I have never searched the dusty boxes in my mother's attic for the portrait of my sisters and me. I never wanted to see the red nightgown again.

A WALK THROUGH THE PAST
TELLING YOUR OWN STORIES

1. Find a movement, image, or sound to express the phrases you marked while reading Chapter 5. Draw, dance, express the whole range of emotion you experienced.

2. Gather your Chapter 5 writings about your daughters and granddaughters into a poetic tribute, celebrating their presence in your life and how they inspire you to bite into your own life and the fullness of its possibility.

3. What fragments of your own story were touched while reading Chapter 5? Using "The Balancing Beam" as your guide, write your story in the form of a scripture passage or a fictionalized short story, describing your experience in the third person.

After writing your story, read it aloud as if you were reading the Scripture text at a Sabbath service or a short story on public radio. Invite a friend to listen and take note of the phrases of significance that moved her, touched sensation in her body, or cause her heart to smile or to tremble. Ask her to write a sermon, essay, or poem expressing the outrage or delight she experienced as you heard your story.

Tape your third person narrative or have a friend read it to you. As you listen, imagine that your story is being read aloud in church as the scriptural text for the day. Write a sermon, essay, or poem expressing the outrage or delight you experience as you hear the story, *your* story.

A WALK THROUGH THE PAST
Parenting Inventory

I. Acknowledge the gifts and the challenges of your childhood experience by filling out "the other side of the report card." Grade your parents' performance based on each of the eight natural capacities presented in Chapter 5. Use the following grading system or develop your own:

S - My parents were skilled at nurturing this capacity.

U - My parents were unskilled at nurturing this capacity.
   It was neglected in our household.

R - My parents actively reversed the value on this capacity.

After grading your parents, write them a note of appreciation for the areas in which they did well and an expression of anger, frustration, or disappointment for the reversals of value.

II. Acknowledge the gifts and the challenges of your parenting by grading yourself based on each of the eight natural capacities. Use the following grading system or develop your own:

S - I am skilled at nurturing this capacity.

U - I am unskilled at nurturing this capacity.
   It has been neglected in our household

R - I actively reverse(d) the value on this capacity.

Write a note to yourself, appreciating the areas in which you've done well and acknowledging the areas in which you need support.

Capacity	Grade
1. The Girl-Child is Body-Centered.	
2. The Girl-Child Expresses Her Needs.	
3. The Girl-Child is Sexually Autonomous.	
4. The Girl-Child Expresses Her Feelings.	
5. The Girl-Child Tells the Truth.	
6. The Girl-Child is Creative.	
7. The Girl-Child is Interested In and Involved With Herself.	
8. The Girl-Child is Full of Herself.	

6

HEALING TASKS:
ASSUMING
PERSONAL RESPONSIBILITY

*The strongest reason for giving woman all the opportunities
for higher education, for the full development of her faculties,
her forces of mind and body; for giving her the most enlarged freedom
of thought and action; a complete emancipation from all forms
of bondage, of custom, dependence, superstition;
from all the crippling influences of fear—is the solitude and
personal responsibility of her own individual life.*

—ELIZABETH CADY STANTON,
"The Solitude of Self," 1892

In Chapter 4 we re-membered the time in the very beginning of human history when "full of themselves" goddesses were spun from the imaginations of our ancestors, and we incorporated the images and understandings of that time into our unfolding spirituality. Here, we will remember the time in the very beginning of our personal history when we were full of ourselves and reclaim the entire range of our human capacity. The journey from self-criticism to self-celebration leads us home to ourselves: to our bodies, their needs and sensations; to our feelings, thoughts, and creativity; and to our self-interest, involvement, and celebration.

Women are assuming personal responsibility for their lives by reclaiming the eight natural capacities that are their birthright as children of life.

They are reinstating the price tags to their original positions by reversing the question "what's wrong with me." The natural and essential-self is once again embraced as they discard the facades and personas of a lifetime. Originality and truth are once again celebrated as they shed the conformity and lies of many lifetimes. No longer content with self-improvement schemes or feminist platforms that merely require a rearrangement of their outer lives, women are experiencing a transformation of their inner worlds, a complete reversal of everything they were taught to believe about themselves. They are choosing to heal into the present—full of themselves!

TRANSFORMATIVE RESOURCES

I have a developed a series of summer retreats at which women experience the woman-affirming processes I offer regularly in Northern California. Women begin their journey from self-criticism to self-celebration at the "A God Who Looks Like Me" retreat. We travel paths one and two together, covering much of the material you encountered in Parts I and II of this book. The "Be Full of Yourself!" retreat escorts women on the third path of their journey as they assume personal responsibility for their lives and reclaim the eight natural capacities introduced in Chapter 5. I weave four transformational resources into each retreat experience:

The *"Home is Always Waiting"* Meditation

The *"Essential Connection"* Expressive Arts Flow

The *"Imagine into Being"* Guided Reflection

The *"Vow of Faithfulness to One's Own Life"* Commitment Ceremony

These resources have evolved over time and are based on a set of personal convictions rooted in my own journey home to myself. I will outline the evolution of each resource and its specific application at the "Be Full of Yourself!" retreat. You will then be invited into eight experiences designed to facilitate the reclamation of your natural capacities. Come let us take the next step on our journey from self-criticism to self-celebration.

"HOME IS ALWAYS WAITING" MEDITATION

My life as I had known it fell apart at Princeton Seminary. Religious fundamentalism had been the organizing focus of my time and energy, and

God the father and the Bible had shaped my every thought, feeling, and action since childhood.[70] Having assumed theological equality while at Princeton, I was slowly dismantling the throne of God and the infallibility of the scripture. I was being drawn inward to re-establish a relationship to myself and my own inner wisdom yet I had forgotten the way home. I needed an escort.

Jean Hauser, skillful therapist and guide, was my first escort into the rich resources of my inner life. I arrived at her office ready to talk about my past. There was a certain safety in my attempts to understand the complexities of childhood with words. She patiently listened to my stories and then asked if I was willing to try a relaxation exercise. In the silence, she gently invited me to turn inward and descend into my inner life. At times I couldn't handle the discomfort of the silence, so I retreated into the safety of words again. Over time I became fascinated with what was emerging from the deep places within me. I'd walk into Jean's office and announce, "No talking today. Take me down!"

Jean did not seek to influence my experience. She used a simple relaxation technique to support my descent. Then she left me alone while I traveled through a magical forest, discovering paths and clearings, encountering snakes and trees, and befriending the richness of my own inner life. Jean sat in the silence as a compassionate witness to the tears and laughter, screams and moans, movements and stillness that accompanied my transformative journey. Each session became a sacred drama of sorts performed deep within the forest of my being. Sometimes it seemed important to tell her about my adventures. Most of the time it was enough that I had experienced them. During our two years together, I learned to trust my inner life, to discern its intricate design, and to listen to its healing truth. I discovered that the deepest impulse of my being was to heal into the present. As I descended into my own life, I reconnected to this impulse and tapped a reservoir of transformative resources.

I believe a woman discovers the way home to herself in a quiet descent into the richness of her own life, not in the rat-race for equal pay and position, in the adoption of a traditional or feminist persona, or in the ability to articulate the intricacies of her childhood. In the descent, she reverses the tendency to look outside of herself for salvation. In the "deep places," she reunites with her essential self and reclaims her natural capacities. Based on this conviction, I include the "Home Is Always Waiting" meditation in each workshop, retreat, support group, or private session I facilitate. You will read excerpts of it throughout Chapter 6. It begins with these words, *"Home is always waiting. It is as near as a conscious breath, conscious contact with your woman-body, and a descent into the rich resources of your inner life."*

A Conscious Breath

During adolescence, my favorite hymn was a prayer to the Holy Spirit: "Breathe on me, Breath of God. Fill me with life anew." The Spirit seemed like an energy, pervading all of life and giving me a sense of my connectedness to all living things. Years later, I discovered that "spiritus" means breath. While preparing a sermon at Princeton, I was reminded of one of Jesus' final encounters with his disciples. He breathed on them and said, "Receive the Holy Spirit." His final gift to them was the breath of life, not an explanation, theory, or theology.

In the Catholic church of my childhood, I heard the Latin chant, "Veni Sancte Spiritus," meaning "Come, Holy Spirit, come." Inspired by our earliest ancestors for whom prayer and movement were inextricably bound, we begin the workshop with a movement prayer, invoking the "Holy Breath" accompanied by the music of the chant. Our movements acknowledge the breath rising from the depths of us, moving out and beyond us, and then returning again as we chant, "Come, Holy Breath, Come." With each circular movement, our awareness of the breath of life awakens.

After we have invoked the breath through movement, we sit and begin our descent. The breath is a faithful escort toward the "deep places." I invite women to turn their attention inward and pay attention to each breath. With each inhalation, they gather their attention, thoughts, and feelings from the far reaches of their lives. With each exhalation, they let go of the accumulation of the day or of a lifetime.

As women turn their attention inward, they remember the very beginning of their lives when self-interest and self-involvement were as natural as the breath. On a cellular level, they are reversing the life-long habit of focusing outside of themselves. And as they gather themselves and what is nourishing, and then release the critical words of others and what is depleting, they are participating in an organic rhythm that supports health on every level of their being.

Come home to your breath. Turn your attention inward by taking a few deep breaths. Savor the breath of life as it flows in and through and around you. As you inhale, gather all of yourself from the far reaches of your life. Bring your energy and attention "home." As you exhale, release the accumulation of your day. Allow sighs, sounds, and yawns to ride on the back of each exhalation to support your letting go. Weave an affirmation into each breath: I come home to my breath. Home is always waiting.

Gradually, I invite women to notice the depth of their breath. In the very beginning of our lives, we breathed deeply into the belly. A healthy breath begins in the abdomen and moves upward toward the chest and then is released downward toward the belly. Each time a natural capacity was exposed, scrutinized, and judged in our childhood homes, this deep belly breath was reversed and we developed the habit of shallow breathing into the upper chest while chronically tightening our abdominal muscles. We inherited this "fight or flight" survival breath from our earliest ancestors. Our socialization sets us up either to "fight" against the natural self by banishing it to a subterranean basement of our being, holding it in and back lest an unscrutinized need, uncensored feeling, or spontaneous thought slip out—or to take "flight" from the natural self by participating in countless distractions. A shallow breath is evidence of our alienation from the deepest parts of ourselves.

Notice the depth of your breath. Place your hands on your upper chest. Inhale, expanding your chest with the breath. And exhale. Breathe into your upper chest for two more breaths. Now place your hands on the sides of your rib cage—the middle chest. Inhale deeply, pushing the breath against your ribs. Exhale. Continue to fill your rib cavity for two more breaths, deepening your capacity to hold the nourishing breath of life. Now place your hands on your abdomen. Inhale deeply into the abdomen, imagining the breath as a great wave filling your belly. Allow your belly to swell. This is a deep breath. And exhale as the wave retreats, leaving nourishment and fulfillment in its wake. Continue to breathe deeply into your belly for two more breaths. To breathe consciously and deeply into the belly is to participate fully in your life.

As women return home to the deep breath they knew in the very beginning, they reclaim the natural and organic capacities introduced in Chapter 5. With each deep breath, they take personal responsibility for the "shape" of their thoughts, feelings, and creative impulses; for the solitude necessary to nourish their self-interest and involvement; and for the cultivation of self-celebration. On a physiological level, their original body centeredness is re-established as they breathe consciously and deeply. With each breath, they actively nourish the body, balance its systems, listen to the wisdom of its sensations, and participate fully in every body-centered activity. I invite women to consider the following benefits of deep breathing:

1. Conscious breathing treats the body to a banquet feast of nourishment. A deep inhalation nourishes a larger quantity of blood cells than a shallow breath. A full exhalation releases the accumulation of carbon monoxide. A shallow breath leaves residues of this waste product within our systems and supplies our bodies with only enough nourishment to function at a minimal level.

2. Conscious breathing balances all of the systems of the body. It lowers the blood pressure, massages the internal organs, supports the digestive processes, and aids in the body's eliminatory functions. A shallow breath is only capable of supporting the body's processes on a superficial level.

3. Conscious breathing supports us to pause in the midst of our busy lives to pay attention to our bodily sensations. They are the voice of our organic needs for food, rest, orgasm, exercise, elimination, and touch. With each deep breath, we become more skillful at discerning the intention and wisdom of each sensation. And as we step into self-responsibility, we meet the needs of our bodies with tenderness and grace.

4. Conscious breathing is our opportunity to participate with the body in each of its adventures. As we become more attuned to the flow of the breath, we develop our capacity to direct it into any part of the body to enhance sexual sensations or to relieve painful ones:

> Conscious breathing transforms our relationship to physical pain, a sensation we've been taught to "fight." As we turn toward the pain and "breathe with" it rather than tightening the muscles around it, we release our body's own healing resources and the pain subsides. Pain is no longer viewed as an enemy to be conquered. It is honored as a faithful reminder of our disconnection from our bodies. Deep breathing reestablishes the connection.

> Conscious breathing re-introduces us to the rich reservoir of sexual energy we tapped in childhood. As we turn toward the sensations of tingling, warmth, and aliveness by "breathing with" them, they are enhanced and spread throughout the body. With each deep breath, our capacity to experience the fullness of our erotic potential deepens. We learn to savor every sensation as it rises, and then to let it go with a blessing as it passes. To breathe deeply is to participate fully in all aspects of our lives.

Until our work together, most women were aware of the breath only as it related to their concern about "bad" breath. In a writing exercise, a retreat participant's first free-association with the word breath was "Tic Tac." Months later, these same women acknowledge with gratitude this most precious natural resource:

> *I am learning how to breathe for the first time in my forty years. I am becoming one with my breath through a regular practice of meditation. Through it, I can reach into and touch the core of myself, the center where my Deeper Wisdom dwells. The breath teaches me to trust my inner resources.*
> —Jen Elson

> *I have learned that to breathe slowly and deeply is not an invocation of death but an enhancement of Life. To breathe is to let go and to live fully. The breath is a newly found treasure, offering me a surprising lightness. The breath gives me permission to live each small increment of time to its*

fullest truth. The breath supports me to set healthy limits. My spirit soars with the breath.
— *Erin Stewart*

A few years ago, I was sobbing in despair over a relationship. I tried to calm myself using all my god-concepts and nothing worked because my sense of hopelessness was so deep. Then I focused on my breathing. I breathed in and out over and over again and affirmed, "As I breathe, I am one with all other living beings. As I breathe, I am assured of the presence of the spirit of life within me. I am not alone." This profound revelation continues to support me in challenging moments. — *Colleen West*

Conscious Contact with Your Woman-Body

A woman's body is an essential resource on the way home to herself. As she becomes conscious of the breath, it reminds her that she lives in a woman-body. I invite women to continue their descent by making conscious contact with their bodies. Each woman takes a gentle walk over and around her body through tender self-touch or massage, through movement or stretch, or in the quietness of her healing imagination, directing the breath to reach into each part of her body. At her own pace, beginning at the top of her head or the bottom of her feet, she slowly moves, touches, or imagines each part of her body, creating a "Meditation of Acknowledgment."

Come home to your body. Turn your attention inward again by taking a few deep breaths into your belly. Savor the breath of life as it flows in and through and around you. As you breathe deeply, turn your attention toward your body for five minutes. Move or stretch it, touch or massage it, or imagine the breath reaching into each part of your body while you affirm: "I come home to my body. Home is always waiting."

Initially women are uncomfortable turning toward their bodies with tenderness and conscious, prolonged attention. Their discomfort makes great sense. Our bodies have borne the brunt of our self-criticism. In response to the critical words, images, experiences, and expectations discussed in Chapters 1, 3, and 5, most women scrutinize every detail of their bodies under an unmerciful magnifying glass. They inspect their bodies, searching for flaws: too big, too small; too much, too little; too round, too flat; too tall, too short. Over time, we develop a chronic resentment toward our bodies because they are always falling short of perfection as defined by the culture, our families, a current lover, and ourselves. They are never quite good enough no matter what we do to them. I invite women to notice their discomfort without judgment, and then to imagine the discomfort riding on the back of the breath to be released with each exhalation.

Turn your attention toward your body again by taking a few deep breaths. Turn a merciful eye toward your body. Look upon it with lovingkindness. What feelings rise as you turn toward your body with tenderness: discomfort . . . sadness . . . fear . . . despair . . . excitement . . .? Meet each feeling with the breath. Acknowledge it on the inhalation, then let go of it on the exhalation.

As we turn a merciful eye toward our bodies, we begin to reverse our harsh scrutiny and chronic resentment of them. We come home to our bodies as they are and in the company of women, we commit the forbidden act, the essential political act, of loving our bodies as we did in the very beginning of our lives. A woman who is full of herself honors her body as the sacred temple of the spirit of life. She embraces it as a community of support within her, a harmonious partnership of cells, tissues, organs, and systems. She enters into a partnership with her body, improving conscious contact with it through meditation, and consulting it through each season of her life. She pays attention to its sensations as faithful reminders of the way home. She celebrates her body as an exquisite resource, a faithful ally, and a trustworthy companion.

A Descent into the Rich Resources of Your Inner Life

In the very beginning of life, many of us developed an intimate connection with the natural world in the form of our favorite tree, rock, or creek. Women write of their early adventures in meadows and forests, referring to the natural world as their friend, refuge, and hiding place. For many, their earliest sense of the divine was felt in the starry night sky, in the bird's nest found in the neighbor's tree, and in the comforting quiet of the forest. Their original at-home-ness evaporated by adolescence and was replaced by a growing alienation from their natural capacities and spontaneous impulses and by a fear of the natural world that had once been their friend.

As I descended into the rich mythology of my inner life, I encountered my own fear of the forest. The forest was a familiar place, it was clear I had been there before, and yet I was afraid to enter it. In an attempt to unravel my fear, I consulted an index of forest literature and discovered these listings: forbidden forest; wife and child abducted in the forest; woman abducted in forest; witch lives in the forest; woman lured into forest and captured. I remembered the stories and fairy tales of my childhood, as well as the ones I read to my baby-sitting charges in adolescence and later, to my students. My fear, our fear is not surprising given the forest images imprinted upon our imaginations in our formative years. For the boy-child, the forest is a place of adventure and conquest. For the girl-child, it is a wild, dangerous, and unpredictable place. Eventually, the forest becomes off limits to her.

The breath and body support us as we continue our descent toward the rich resources of our inner lives. Imagine yourself as a leaf let go of by an autumn tree . . . a leaf slowly and gradually descending toward the ground . . . its descent cushioned by the breath of life . . . a leaf touching the ground in the forest deep within your being.

Everything breathes in the forest. Savor the breath of life flowing in and through and around you. Inhale deeply as the breath rises up from the rich earth beneath you. Release the breath into the cool and moist air around you. You are as grounded, as connected to Mother Earth as a tree is. You are held, supported, and nourished by her. Acknowledge the firm ground that holds you, as you breathe deeply.

As women descend into the deep places, their fears of the forest and of the unexplored terrain of their inner lives are triggered. Our inner lives are often in disarray due to the inattention of years. The accumulation of a lifetime frightens us: unused capacities, unexpressed needs, and unexplored sexual potential; discarded thoughts, disregarded feelings, and untapped creative impulses; unexpressed longings for both solitude and acknowledgment swirl within us. The journey from self-criticism to self-celebration requires that we descend into the complexity of our inner lives. There we will discover a forest of inner treasures. Every capacity, need, and unexplored potential; every thought, feeling, impulse, and unexpressed longing we have feared is actually a disowned aspect of ourselves waiting to be reclaimed.

As women befriend the forest within them and reclaim their own natural resources, they reverse the fears of a lifetime. They redirect their energy away from self-critical patterns toward adventures of self-discovery. Recognizing each self-critical thought as an indication of disconnection from self, they learn to pause, notice the disconnection without judgment, and then return home, making conscious contact with their breath, woman-body, and inner life. Thus they re-establish the connection. No longer denying any aspect of themselves, these women are tapping into their own self-healing capacities as deeper layers of inner truth and wisdom become available to them.

"ESSENTIAL CONNECTION" EXPRESSIVE ARTS FLOW

In 1986, I dreamt that I was being processed into a prison. I had to wait for an execution in order to secure a bed. Finally, I was issued a bed. A few days later, I was given a pass to go outside the prison for an appointment.

No one accompanied me yet I was reminded of my "prisoner" status by the crossing guards at each corner. I would be required to return. I arrived at a lovely house and asked the four sisters sitting in their kitchen, "Where is Ms. _____, the dance teacher?' (She was Jewish but I cannot remember her name.) They scorned my disheveled appearance and reluctantly pointed out her room.

I don't remember what happened in her room. In the next scene however, I was free and sitting outside of a beautiful yellow Victorian house with a group of women, including one of the four sisters I met earlier. It was our house! We were celebrating a performance we had just completed. Two of the "haughty" sisters approached our celebratory group. They thanked us for our dance performance, and then thanked me for helping their sister to heal through movement and dance. In gratitude, they handed me a check.

Several months after the dream, I attended a week-long movement retreat. Each movement, dance, and sacred drama experience escorted me into the deep places of my being and invited the memories and emotions of childhood to be released. As the facilitator, Carla De Sola, and I moved together in a womb dance, I re-experienced the trauma of the turbulent nine months in my mother's womb, tossed to and fro by my parents' troubled relationship. I also re-experienced my deep ambivalence about entering the world. As we moved in synch, emotionally and in dance, my body groaned with the pain of a lifetime. With her support, I was able to push beyond my ambivalence and choose life. With the group's support as my labor coaches, the womb of the mother thrust me out of hiding toward visibility.

As Carla and I continued to experience a healing connection through movement, I was reminded of the dance teacher in the dream. I was puzzled because "De Sola" did not seem to be a Jewish name. When I asked her about it, she told me her family was indeed Jewish! As a result of our sacred drama experience, my creativity began to unthaw. In the subsequent months, I danced, painted, and wrote the creativity of a lifetime. I decided to enroll in the Expressive Arts Therapy Program at Lesley College in Cambridge. Imagine my amazement as I arrived to register at the school and found myself standing outside an exact replica of the yellow Victorian in my dream.

It is essential for a woman to give expression to the movements, sounds, and images that emerge from the deep places within her. In the development of a expressive arts vocabulary, she reverses the historic tendency to hide all that is essentially true for her. And in the use of sound and movement; ritual, play, and drama; paint, clay, and collage, she gives voice to the originality of her own feelings, thoughts, and creativity. Based on this conviction, I developed the "Essential Connection Expressive-Arts Flow."

It honors the essential connection between meditation through which women descend and discover the richness of their inner lives and the expressive arts through which they emerge and express that richness.

Create a sacred space in which to experiment with the expressive exercises in this chapter. Bring a tape deck and your favorite quiet/meditative and rowdy/playful music into the space. Gradually gather paints and crayons of all colors, sponges and tongue depressors of all shapes, and a large sheet of paper tacked up on a wall or taped to a large table. Create an entry ritual: light a candle, bless yourself from a bowl of "holy water," and come home to your breath.

Movement and Sound

Following the "Home is Always Waiting" meditation, we enter into the expressive arts flow, beginning with sound and movement. We begin with these two essential natural resources because they require no special materials or trained experts to access them. Our acquaintance with sound and movement begins in the womb. The fetus is not motionless. It engages in its own rhythmic pulsations choreographed by the movement of the mother's digestive processes, and by her breathing and bodily motions. The fetus' response to sound can be felt in its movements.

In the very beginning, no separation existed between us and our movements and our sounds. We were finely-tuned expressive instruments through which our responses to life flowed as naturally as the breath. Over time, these responses became imprisoned within our muscles, joints, and throats. They make themselves known indirectly through troubling symptoms and the ever-present reality of many women's lives—depression. Initially, our work together facilitates the release of the unexpressed movements and sounds of a lifetime. Eventually, women incorporate movement and sound into their daily lives to express the whole range of emotion and response passing through them on any given day.

We begin with a birthing dance, "In the Very Beginning was the Mother," awakening each woman's deep connection to the mystery and meaning of life and to her fundamental relationship to all humanity. The simple dance rekindles her understanding of the movement and sound vocabulary she once knew. It includes archetypal movements, transcending the particularities of race, culture, and class: expansion-contraction, reaching-crouching, lengthening-shrinking, opening-closing, advancing-retreating, passivity-activity, balance-imbalance, holding-releasing, and containing-thrusting. The dance invites the expression of universal sounds, transcending the particularities of language: crying, giggling, laughing, moaning, purring, and whimpering; cackling, clucking, groaning, grunting, and howling; bellowing, roaring, screaming, screeching, shouting, and shrieking. The instructions for the birthing dance are included at the end of the chapter.

After our communal birthing dance, we explore the primary emotions, using movement and sound. The exploration and expression of a full range of human emotion is essential to physical and psychological health. Our immune systems are strengthened by an appropriate circulation of emotions on a daily basis. Most of us confuse our thoughts with our feelings. We are much more adept at conceptualizing our emotions ("I *think* I'm afraid of my boss.") than we are at noticing, and then expressing the bodily sensations that reveal our emotions to us: "I notice a tightness in my abdomen whenever I'm around my boss." And we aren't able to distinguish between emotions given the reversals of value we discussed in Chapter 5. It is more acceptable for women to be sad than angry. Consequently, our sadness often conceals our anger. Our bodies are faithful: as we return home to them and pay attention to their sensations and impulses, we reclaim the skillfulness we knew in the very beginning of our lives when our feelings danced through us as gracefully as the breath.

I invite women to move and sound each of the core emotions while remembering a time when they felt the sensations of sadness, anger, fear, arousal, and joy in their bodies. The dance of sadness usually includes protective and vulnerable movements centered around the heart and upper chest accompanied by sobbing, whimpering, moaning, and wailing sounds. The dance of anger elicits strong leg (stomping) and shoulder (punching) movements, accompanied by loud, strong sounds. The dance of fear is expressed in the tightening of the abdomen, the holding of the breath, and in crouching and contracting movements, as well as in shivering sounds. The dance of arousal is expressed with fiery movements of excitement and panting orgasmic sounds centered at the genitals and lower belly. The dance of joy is seen in the openness of the upper chest and in the brightness of the eyes, and leads to an energetic and expansive dance accompanied by the sounds of laughter and exuberance.

In the privacy of your sacred space, create a dance for each of the core emotions. Become sadness, anger, fear, arousal, and joy—what sounds do each of them make, what movements give them full expression?

To conclude the movement and sound portion of the expressive arts flow, I invite women to create their own movement and sound meditation by engaging in "Inner Listening." There are four simple steps to this process. Experiment with them in your sacred space:

1. Turn Inward - Close your eyes and turn your attention inward. Listen to the breath as it journeys in and through and around you. Allow the breath to escort you into the deep places.

2. Notice the Impulse - Listen to your inner experience for impulses to move or to make a sound. An impulse may be as simple as the "urge" to move your little finger or as complex as the "whim" to get down on the floor in a fetal position. An impulse may be as playful as the desire to try out the walking, flying, and swimming movements of the birthing dance or as cathartic as the release of a strong sound triggered as you read through the dance. Pay attention as the impulse builds inside of you.

3. Express the Impulse - Allow the impulse to take form in a movement and/or a sound that expresses it fully. Notice when the impulse subsides and your expression is complete. Notice when your impulse shifts to another movement or sound.

4. Return Home - If your attention moves away from your body and breath toward an external distraction, notice the distraction without judgment and practice returning home. Breathe again into this moment and listen for the impulses of your inner experience. If your attention moves away from the expression of your natural impulses toward intellectual attempts to figure them out, reverse your tendency to interrupt pure expression by breathing again into this moment, reestablishing conscious contact with your inner experience. Home is always waiting.

I am honored to witness the dances that emerge from each woman's "inner listening." Some movements and sounds are barely perceptible. Other dances are loud and blatant. The energetic quality of the dance doesn't matter as women relearn the expressive languages they knew in the very beginning of life. They are refusing to ask the question "what's wrong with me" as they engage in adventures of self-discovery using the language of the soul. Across a respectful distance, I witness women visibly transformed as they circulate the impulses, sensations, and feelings of a lifetime or of the moment, reversing the immobilization of repression; women freed of dependency at a deeper level of their beings as they trust their own natural resources, reversing the inertia of mistrust; women engaging in spontaneous activity as they move and sound from the inside out, reversing the inhibition of an imposed "performance-orientation;" women absolutely present in the moment as they pay attention to themselves with tenderness, reversing the paralysis of self-criticism; women healing into the present, one sound and movement at a time.

Image-Making and Writing

When the participants feel ready to transition to image-making, they turn toward the canvasses set up throughout our communal space. Initially, I do not include paint brushes at their art spaces. Sadly, the paint brush represents the performance and perfect-product orientation used to crush the creative wonder we knew as children. A six year old standing in front of a table of paints, brushes, tongue depressors, and sponges does not ask, "What should I do?" With no more than a moment's hesitation to take in the possibilities before her, she reaches for a sponge, dips it into the paint, and makes a line across the canvas. Brightly colored paints, tongue depressors, sponges, and a paper plate on which to mix and experiment with color await each woman.

Prepare your creative space. Use an indoor or outdoor wall or a table top as your canvass. Tape newspaper onto the surface and over it, a large sheet of paper (18 x 24 or larger). Gather luscious paints, tongue depressors, sponges, and a paper plate on which to mix and experiment with color. Enact your entry-ritual and then enter into the "Inner Listening" process.

Using the inner listening technique, they now express the images emerging from the deep places. For many women, a series of images have already formed. They are ready to release them in color, shape, and form.

1. Turn Inward - Close your eyes and turn your attention inward. Listen to the breath as it journeys in and through and around you. Allow the breath to escort you into the deep places.

2. Notice the Image - Scan your inner landscape for images. An inner image may appear as a simple line of color or as a complex image of a woman giving birth. An inner image may be a playful impulse to paint stars across the canvass or a cathartic release of a terror-filled image aroused during your movement meditation. Pay attention as the image forms within you.

3. Express the Image - Allow the image to take form on the canvass. Express the image or series of images fully. Notice when the impulse to form images subsides and your expression is complete. Notice when your impulse shifts to another image.

4. Return Home - If your attention moves away from your inner experience toward an external distraction, notice the distraction without judgment and practice returning home. Breathe again into this moment and scan for the images of your inner experience. If your attention moves away from the expression of your images toward performance-oriented attempts to paint the perfect representation of an image, reverse your self-critical tendencies to interrupt spontaneous expression by breathing again into this moment, reestablishing conscious contact with your inner experience. Home is always waiting.

Some women engage in a playful exercise of acquainting themselves with color and shape, allowing each impulse to lead to the next without thought of a destination. Others discern very clear images on their inner landscape and attempt to express them on the canvass. I invite them to meet each feeling that accompanies the process, whether frustration, delight, or the fear of "blankness," with the breath and then to express it on the canvass, in sound, or through a movement. Throughout the expressive arts flow, we practice the *non-verbal expression* of whatever arises, trusting that we have everything we need to successfully negotiate our own life-process. There is no conversation among participants.

As participants experience a sense of completion, they step back from their painting and view it across a distance, asking "What words dance with the images?" and "What message does the image convey to me?" Allowing the right brain's originality, authenticity, expressiveness, process-orientation, wildness, novelty, and ambiguity full reign, women create word-collages to accompany their paintings. They allow words to spill onto the page without censorship, correction, or editorial constraints.

Again, I am honored to witness the images and word-collages that emerge from each woman's inner landscape. Some expressions are playful and light. Others are dark and intense. Some are representational; others are symbolic. Just as with movement and sound, the energetic quality of the image and word-collage doesn't matter as women relearn the symbolic and intuitive languages they knew in the very beginning of life. They are reversing the question "what's wrong with me" by descending into the richness of their inner lives and then by expressing the treasures they discover there. We conclude the expressive arts flow by gathering at each woman's art center. We honor her images in silence, and then acknowledge her with an affirmation, "Blessed is the fruit of your creative womb."

Honor your images in the silence of your sacred space. Acknowledge yourself with an affirmation, "Blessed is the fruit of my creative womb." Descend often into the richness of your inner life and express the treasures you discover there.

"IMAGINE INTO BEING" GUIDED REFLECTION

There were times when my childhood imagination soared as I imagined another childhood—one with loving parents. While in the orphanage, I became a popular tour guide on Saturday and Sunday afternoons. Kind-hearted Catholic families from northern New Jersey stopped by to tour the spacious complex and to meet the "orphans." Besides making lots of money, prompting the nuns to instate a restriction on the amount I could keep, I was examining each family for new qualities to add to my "loving family" fantasy. I watched the way the parents looked at their children: were their eyes filled with gentleness or harshness? I listened to the tone of voice they used in conversation with their children: were their voices patient or irritable? I paid special attention to how they touched their children: were the exchanges affectionate or rough? By the end of an afternoon, I knew who the kindest families were and hoped they would ask for permission to take me home for a week-end . . . or a lifetime. And most of them did ask. I spent many week-ends with kind families who nourished my imaginative fantasies of the family I wanted—one that kept its children. Throughout my life, I have adopted families, chosen-families who have looked at me with gentleness, who have spoken to me with respect, and who have touched me with affection. One by one, I have "imagined into being" the powerful visions I developed in reaction and response to childhood realities.

My childhood fantasizing was not a unique experience. Women write detailed accounts of comforting childhood fantasies. Some women imagined into being whole new worlds inhabited by families who loved, respected, and protected their children. Other women, discontent with only a few aspects of their family life, imagined into being "rehabilitated" family members. In the solitude of their imaginations, whether creating new families or rehabilitating the familiar cast of characters, they developed intricate dialogs and interactions between family members.

Their dialogs reflect three longings that appear repeatedly in women's writings: the longing to be acknowledged, listened to, and taken seriously; the longing to be free of household responsibility; and the longing for their parents to love each other. For some, their flights of fancy were inspired and nourished by the unconditional love of a grandmother or by non-argumentative dinners at a best friend's house. Each child-friendly fantasy and experience settled into the ground of our being as a seed of promise, reminding us that things could be different and that our fantasies were not vain imaginings. In the fullness of time, the seeds of promise bear fruit in a healthy life in the present.

To heal into the present, a woman must enlist the transformational capacities of her imagination. Based on this conviction, I have developed a series of eight "healthy family fantasies." The fantasies re-awaken and inspire each woman's imagination:

1. Refusing to settle for a life that condones the "reversals of value" she experienced in childhood, she "imagines into being" a life that fosters the deepening of her capacity to love her body, its needs and sensations; to express her truth and perceptions, her feelings and creative potential; to cultivate her solitude; and to celebrate herself.

2. Refusing to settle for partners, colleagues, and friends whose critical voices and attitudes resemble those of her parents, she "imagines into being" a

community of advocates—a chosen family available to nurture her deepening connection to herself and to applaud her fullness.

3. Refusing to turn toward her own children with the same critical words and conformity-based expectations once offered to her, she "imagines into being" an environment in which her children's natural capacities are supported to develop and flourish.

The "Imagine into Being" Guided Reflection begins with a meditation, escorting women home to their breath, body, and inner experience. The meditation is followed by eight "healthy family fantasies," supporting women to heal into the present and challenging them to design a woman-affirming life and home.

Meditation

Come home to your breath and your woman-body. Turn your attention inward by taking a few deep breaths. Savor the breath of life as it flows in and through and around you. As you inhale, gather all of yourself from the far reaches of your life. Bring your energy and attention "home." As you exhale, release the accumulation of your day.

Allow sighs, sounds, and yawns to ride on the back of each exhalation to support your letting go. Weave an affirmation into each breath. As you inhale, "I come home to my breath." As you exhale, "Home is always waiting."

As you breathe deeply, turn your attention toward your body. Move or stretch it, touch or massage it, or imagine the breath reaching into each part of your body while you affirm: "I come home to my body. Home is always waiting."

The breath and body support us as we continue our descent toward the rich resources of our inner lives. Imagine being a leaf let go of by an autumn tree . . . a leaf slowly and gradually descending toward the ground . . . its descent cushioned by the breath of life . . . a leaf touching the ground in the forest deep within your being.

Everything breathes in the forest. Savor the breath of life flowing in and through and around you. Inhale deeply as the breath rises up from the rich earth beneath you. Release the breath into the cool and moist air around you. You are as grounded, as connected to Mother Earth as a tree is. You are held, supported, and nourished by her. Acknowledge the firm ground that holds you, as you breathe deeply.

Your attention moves upward and you notice the trees reaching arm in arm for the sky. You become a tree. Your feet grow roots extending deep into the ground. Your arms become branches stretching high into the sky.

You sway with the breeze. The birds of the forest dance with you as they leap from branch to branch. You see many things from your new height. A nearby stream calls to you, "Come and play." In a moment, you are at the stream, splashing in its bouncing waters. As you are drying off in the warm sunlight pouring through the forest canopy, a path opens up before you and invites you to follow it to a special place. You accept the invitation and follow the path.

The path leads you deep into the forest to the edge of a clearing . . . a magical open space surrounded by a ring of ancient redwoods, forming the outer circle, and by a sparkling stream, forming the inner circle. As you peek through the stately redwood circle, a group of women greet you. They know your name. "Daughter of Woman, to enter the clearing you must cross the stream of living water. You must shed the robes hiding your body and the veil covering your head. You must wash in its clear waters."

"Yes, I will step into the stream. Yes, I will shed the coverings. Yes, I will wash in its clear waters." You are startled and delighted by the clarity and strength of your "Yes." A beautiful young woman approaches you, "I am Alexandra. I will guide across the stream." Slowly, you enter the stream following the one who has gone before you. As you cross, the coverings of a lifetime fall one by one from your body and your eyes—until you are, as you once were, transparent and free.

Alexandra is waiting for you on the far bank. She reaches for your hand as you step out of the stream. "The Mother is waiting. She has a story to tell you. Come let us meet her in the center of the clearing where she dwells." You see her at a distance. She is radiant. Darkness and light dance together within her translucent being. You approach her with your arms at your sides, your body uncovered, and your eyes unveiled, yet you feel no shame in her presence. Her eyes meet yours and in her gaze, you are recognized . . . shaken . . . and relieved. She embraces you, and in her touch you are as you once were . . . fully present in your body.

"Come Daughter of Woman, gaze into my Well and see glimpses of a childhood hoped for." You look into the well and see visions of yourself as a child . . . a child who is looked upon with gentleness, who is spoken to with respect, and who is touched with affection. Enter into each vision through play, movement, touch, or in the quietness of your healing imagination. Trust your own impulses to sit quietly or to enact the fantasy in your sacred space. Enter into a childhood hoped for . . .

LOVE YOUR BODY

*"Come Daughter of Woman, gaze into my Well
and see glimpses of a childhood hoped for."*

Every Sunday night when everyone else is out of the house and you and your mother are home alone, you read together from the *Book of Woman*—a special book kept in a special place brought out in special moments sometimes by your mother, sometimes by your father. A sacred book that tells the story of woman. Your mother begins: *"You are enough, my dear daughter. You are blessed. Hold nothing in. Allow your body to take its shape. Love the shape of your body."* And then you read to your mother, *"You are enough, my dear mother. You are blessed. Hold nothing in. Allow your body to take its shape. Love the shape of your body."*

Beginning at the top of your heads, you and your mother begin your weekly dance in celebration of your bodies in front of a big mirror. Sometimes you giggle together all the way through the ritual. Sometimes you cry.

Let us acknowledge our round heads.
　We nod them to say YES. We shake them to say NO.
　We massage our heads so that our thoughts will take a nap.
Let us love our hair. We touch it. Stroke it. Twirl it.
　We bless its curls, its straightness, its color, its texture.
　I comb your hair. You comb mine.
Let us love our eyes. We open and close them.
　We honor our unique view of the world.
　I see you. You see me.
Let us love our ears. We trace their shape and size.
　We love our unique reception of the world.
　I hear you. You hear me.
Let us love our noses. We bless their shape and size.
　We breathe in and out slowly.
　We honor the Breath of Life as it passes through us.
Let us love our mouths and lips. We trace the shape of our lips.
　We love the sounds of our mouth. We make sounds.
　Loud sounds. Quiet sounds. Funny sounds.
Let us love our necks. We hold them up high pretending to be giraffes.
　We roll our heads around on top of our neck.
　We massage our necks to thank them for carrying our heads around.
Let us love our shoulders. We raise them to our ears.
　And then let them fall again. Up and down. Up and down.
　I massage your shoulders. You massage mine.
Let us love our arms. We bend them at the elbows. We bend them at the wrist.
　We clap our hands together. We are applauding ourselves!
　I kiss your hands. You kiss mine.

Let us love our breasts. Firm, sagging, full, flat, beautiful as they are.
  We trace the shape of our breasts.
  I drink from yours. You drink from mine.
Let us love our stomachs. We fill them with the breath.
  We honor our round bellies, growing like a balloon.
  We release the breath. We honor our flattening bellies.
  I peek in your belly button. You peek in mine.
Let us love our genitals.
  We trace our pubic triangle as it is now or as it will be in a few years.
  We name the parts of our woman-body, looking at them in the mirror:
  Pubic Mound. Hood. Inner Lips. Outer Lips. Clitoris. Hymen.
  Opening to Urethra. Opening to Vagina. Anus.
Let us love our bottoms - our gluteus maximus. The biggest muscle in the body!
  We trace the shape of our bottom.
  We massage it, grateful that it's a comfortable cushion to sit on.
Let us love our legs. We bend our legs at the knee.
  The top of the leg is the thigh. We feel our strong thighs.
  The bottom of the leg is the calf. I massage your calf. You massage mine.
Let us love our feet. We bend them at the ankle.
  We spread our toes out wide. We bend our toes backward and forward.
  We count each toe. This little piggy went to market; this piggy stayed home.
  We have dancing feet.

You and your mother put on your favorite dance music and move every part of your body in a joyful celebration of your lively and strong bodies!

The images of a childhood hoped for vanish and the well is clear again. The Mother of All Living speaks:

"Dance, Daughter of Woman, dance. Dance the sadness of a lifetime for what could never be. And when your sadness is quieted, dance with her partner, gladness. For as deep a cavern as sorrow has carved within you that shall be your capacity for joy. Dance your gladness for what is now and will be forevermore.

And when there are no more movements wanting release and your dance feels complete, you notice the clearing is filled with joyful women skipping, running, and dancing; throwing, dribbling, and bouncing balls; jumping rope and climbing heights. Women full of energy, movement, and sound. Women body-centered and exuberant. Women full of themselves.

Daughter of Woman, Run free like the wind. Jump high like a horse. Climb a tree. Cross a creek. Wrestle a friend to the ground. Tumble down a hill. Let your voice bellow and be heard by the whole wide world. Dance to the music of your own life in love with your body. It is your teacher, your healer, and your challenge. It is your faithful companion for the length of your days. You body is good. It is very good. Be full of yourself."

BEFRIEND YOUR BODY'S NEEDS

*"Come Daughter of Woman, gaze into my well
and see glimpses of a childhood hoped for."*

Sometimes your father reads to you from the *Book of Woman*. One school night after you finish your homework, he offers to read a story to you. You ask him to read your favorite story "Patty's Best Friend." He begins:

Patty is one big bundle of needs. Everything alive has needs. The plants in the Patty's kitchen need water and sunlight to live. Patty's cat needs food to eat. Patty's apartment building needs to be taken care of or it will slowly run down. People need to be taken care of too or they will slowly run down, fall down, or get sick.

Patty's needs are different than Patty's wants. She wants a new computer but she won't die without one. Patty needs food, air, and water, coming into her body to feed it. And then she needs the food, air, and water her body doesn't need to leave. Patty needs sleep to give her body "quiet time" to get rested for the next adventure. She needs touch from those who love her. Touch is food for her skin, muscles, and heart. Patty needs a roof over her head. Even little girls who do not have an apartment to live in must find a shelter under a tree, bridge, or bench; in a doorway, garage, or abandoned car to protect them from the rain and snow and storms.

Patty's body is her best friend. It's been telling her what she needs since she was a baby when others took care of all of her needs. Her body let her know what it needed and then she let the adults know by fussing and crying. When her body was cold, she cried and someone wrapped her up. When her body was hungry, she cried and someone fed her. When her diaper was wet, she cried and someone changed her diaper.

Now that she can talk and walk, and doesn't wear a diaper, things have changed. Sometimes she uses words to let her family know what her body needs. When Patty's ears tell her that the music blaring from her sister's room is too loud, she asks her sister to please turn the music down or to wear her head phones. Sometimes no words are needed. She crawls onto her grandmother's lap when she needs to be held.

Most times Patty take care of her own needs because she listens to her best friend. When she is tired, she falls asleep wherever she may be—in someone's arms . . . or on the department store floor. And when she doesn't get enough sleep, her body is a big blob all day and she can't do all the fun things she wants to because she feels like going back to sleep. On those days she needs a nap.

When Patty's body lets her know its hungry, she goes into the kitchen and gets a snack. When her body tells her that it's time to get rid of the stuff it doesn't need, she finds her way to the nearest bathroom. When Patty's body is satisfied at the end of a meal it burps to say "Thank-you." And when her sister says, "Well, Excuse You," Patty says, "Its my body's way of saying thank-you for a good meal." And when her stomach isn't happy about the food she's eaten—

like when she eats a turkey burger and then cantaloupe for dessert, it farts. If she tries to be "polite" by holding the fart in, her stomach hurts really bad.

Patty's body tells her everything she needs to know. It even tells her when she likes someone and when she doesn't. Whenever her grandmother is coming over to visit, Patty's heart feels warm and her breath goes all the way down into her belly. One day her mother brought over a new friend of hers. As soon as he walked into their apartment, Patty's stomach got really tight so there was no room for her breath and said, "I don't like him." She whispered, "Thanks for telling me, Stomach." And then after the man left, Patty told her mother what her stomach said. And lo and behold, her mother's stomach said the same thing. And they never invited that man over again.

Patty and her grandmother play a secret game together whenever she visits her "Nana" in Connecticut. It's called "Listen to your Best Friend!" They sit on the couch with their eyes closed. It is quiet, very quiet.

"Listen and tell me what you hear," Nana says.
"My stomach made a sound and the sound skipped up to my belly button," Patty answers.

"Listen and tell me what you hear," Patty says to her Nana.
"My breath is filling my belly and it is growing bigger and rounder like a balloon filled with air," Nana answers.

Patty and her Nana go back and forth listening and telling until their bodies want to get up and move around. When they are all finished, Patty always says to her Nana, "You are my second favorite best friend in the whole world." And Nana always asks, "Who's your first favorite best friend?" "I am my first favorite person in the whole wide world and my body is my best friend." And Nana always hugs Patty and says, "May it always be so, dear one."

The images of a childhood hoped for vanish and the well is clear again. The Mother of All Living speaks:

"Listen, Daughter of Woman, listen. Listen to the sounds and sensations of a lifetime. You body is the bearer of deep wisdom. What does it tell you of the quality of your life, of the shape and pace of your days, of those who dance into and out of your presence, of the food you eat, of the sleep you embrace, and of your response to the experiences of life? Listen to what you hear and meet your body's needs with tenderness and grace. The organic needs of the universe pulsate through you. Be full of yourself!"

EMBRACE YOUR SEXUAL AUTONOMY

*"Come Daughter of Woman, gaze into my well
and see glimpses of a childhood hoped for."*

On a special night near your twelfth birthday, your father and mother meet you at the altar in your room. On the altar are pictures of those you love, a container with the ashes of your grandmother's body, a red candle and scarf, and the special *Book of Woman* given to you by your parents when you were very young. Your mother reads as you and your father listen.

A Reading From The *Book of Woman*
I am Woman. I stride the earth in nakedness.
No robes hide the beauty of my fertile womb, rounded belly, and full breasts.
I am She Who is Complete in Herself.
I live in my body. I embrace its desires as my own.

Daughter of Woman, the Goddesses loved themselves to their edges.
Self-possessed, they strode the earth. Women full of themselves.
Embracing their sexuality as their own. Delighting in pleasuring themselves.
Experiencing all of their erotic feelings and sensations without shame.

Daughter of Woman, own yourself completely.
Embark on an intimate journey into yourself.
Connect with the whole and complete center within you.
Experience fullness, self-possession, and satisfaction.
Delight in your freedom to be alone.
To meet your own needs. To give yourself pleasure.

Daughter of Woman, your body is your own. It is no one else's.
Live in your body. Trusts its natural instincts.
Experience the pleasure of your body's sensuality.
Feel its smoothness and its curves. Touch its lips. Enter its openings.
Taste its juiciness. Delight in its natural fragrances.
Explore the edges of your sensuality.

Daughter of Woman, feel the fire awaken within you.
Fire rising from the depths. Lover uncoiling to meet lover.
Height calling to depth. Earth moving toward heaven.
Celebrate the sensations in your genitals.
They are calling you to your edges.

Daughter of Woman, all the feelings in your body are good.
The tingling. The pulsations of pleasure. The swelling to overflowing.
Honor all that has been demeaned. Receive all that has been cast aside.

Your mother asks you questions: "Have you ever felt the fiery warmth rise in your body? Where did these feelings begin? Where did they end? Have you ever felt a tingling sensations in your genitals? Did these feelings scare or excite you?" Your mother and father answer the questions too.

And then your mother says to you, "It is so very good for you to touch your own body. To explore its smoothness and curves. To open its lips. To enter its openings. Anyone else—other than you—must ask your permission to touch, hug, or hold you. Your NO must be respected as highly as your YES."

After you finish the conversation, you trace each other's bodies on big pieces of newsprint or butcher paper. And then you each draw the fiery warmth and the tingling sensations you feel in special places on your own bodies, using red, yellow, and orange paint and all different colors of glitter. Afterward you talk about your drawings.

The images of a childhood hoped for vanish and the well is clear again. The Mother of All Living speaks:

"Say YES, Daughter of Woman, say YES to life as it pulsates through you. Feel the YES in your curiosity about your body's sensations and in your exploration of its fascinating nooks and crannies, openings and operations. Feel the YES in your heart, your joy, and even in your tears. Allow it to touch every area of your life. The erotic potential of the universe pulsates through you. Be full of yourself."

EXPRESS THE FULL RANGE OF HUMAN EMOTION

*"Come Daughter of Woman, gaze into my well
and see glimpses of a childhood hoped for."*

You return home after saying good-bye to your best friend Amy whose family has just moved away to a new neighborhood in another state. You are crying because she was your very best friend and you will miss her. You spent every waking hour together, making things and inventing new projects to do with the kids in the neighborhood. Your mom and dad invite you to sit between them on the couch in the living room. They each take a hand and in the silence, you cry. Your father says, "Your tears are so lovely. Your sadness touches my heart." Your mother squeezes your hand gently. You look up and there are tears in both their eyes as you sit together in the comforting silence. You cry until the tears stop all by themselves and until the sadness doesn't hurt so much in your heart.

"Does your sadness have anything to say?" your father asks.

"No, there is nothing to say right now."

"Does your sadness want to dance?" asks your mother.
   "No it is quiet now. Maybe later."
"Does your sadness have a color?"
   "Yes let's draw. You draw too. Remember a time when you
   were very sad and draw with me."

Together you gather the special markers, the ones like paint brushes used only to express feelings, and you each draw your sadness. Afterward you talk about your drawing: "My picture is the color blue. Amy's favorite color. She wore it all the time. The blue is going away to the other neighborhood. And there is a little bit of blue left behind in everyone's heart. There's blue in my heart because that's where she will stay."

Your dad and mom drew their sadness because they will miss Amy too. Dad remembered all the times Amy spent the night. He could hear you and Amy whispering until very late. And he would smile, so very happy you had a special friend who loved you. Mom always set a place for her at dinner whether she was with us or not. "Can we still do it, Mom?" "Sure," she says.

And so it happens—every day for many months an extra place is set at the table for Amy until the wonderful day in June when she comes to visit for a week and sits at your table as she once did. Everyone smiles.

The images of a childhood hoped for vanish and the well is clear again. The Mother of All Living speaks:

"Daughter of Woman, there is no separation between your feelings and your body. They are one within you. Feel your sadness forming as an ache in your heart and as the tear flowing from your eyes. Feel your anger rise up within you to be released in loud sounds and strong movements. Feel your fear in the shortness of your breath and in the fluttering sensation in your tummy. Feel your erotic energy in the tingling warmth of your genitals. Feels your joy in the warmth of your face, the smile in your eyes, and in the giggle inside of you. The feelings of the universe pulsate through you as naturally as the breath. Be full of yourself."

SPEAK YOUR TRUTH

*"Come Daughter of Woman, gaze into my well
and see glimpses of a childhood hoped for."*

Your mother calls you and your sisters together for a family meeting. She begins with a reading from the *Book of Woman::*

"For Mother God so loved the world that she sent into its midst the Divine Girl-Child. Whosoever believes in Her goodness, listens to Her wisdom, and celebrates Her power will be awakened to the abundance of gifts within them."

"I have called this meeting to discuss a new job I have been offered. Whatever decision is made will affect all of us so I want to lay out the situation and hear your concerns." She then lists the benefits of the new job: Weekends off. Better health benefits. Paid two week vacation. And then she lays out the challenges of the job: After-school care until 6pm every day. Less time with her during the week. Long days for everyone from Monday to Friday.

Each of the children has a turn to express her opinion about the changes. You respond: "The kids are wild after school and I don't like to be around them for three hours. The child-care people are not as good with kids as the teachers. I'd rather go to Aunt Lucy's than stay at school." Your mother asks you how many days you can handle staying at school. "Three days," you say, "because there is drama class after school on Monday-Wednesday-Friday and I like drama." "OK," Mom responds, " we'll call Aunt Lucy and see if she can pick you up on Tuesdays and Thursdays."

"I have two more problems. First off, I get really hungry after school and the snack is not enough." Your mother asks, "Would it work for you to make two lunches for yourself on Monday-Wednesday-Friday and eat one after school?"

"Good idea. My other problem is that I want to be sure that we really do get to do fun things on the weekend when you are off. Not just laundry and stuff to clean up around the house." "OK," your mom responds, "Let's plan a date for every Saturday evening. We'll go roller-skating or we'll rent a movie. No chores or busyness on Saturday from 5 PM on. How's that?"

"Now that we've worked through all that stuff, I vote yes to your new job." Your mom thanks you for being so clear about what doesn't work for you. "It's fun to co-create solutions with you. You have great ideas and I can always count on you to tell me the truth about things even if it's a hard truth. Thank-you!"

The images of a childhood hoped for vanish and the well is clear again. The Mother of All Living turns toward you with these words:

"Speak, Daughter of Woman, speak. Be sassy and loud. Question. Argue. Debate. Communicate from your heart. Voice your truth. Share your vision. When you don't like your food, spit it out. When you're exhausted from tagging along in someone else's life, refuse to take another step. When you don't like someone and tighten in their presence, make your discomfort known. Tell the untold truths of a lifetime to your parents, lovers, and colleagues, and to your children and grandchildren. The truth of the universe pulsates through you. Be full of yourself!

OWN YOUR ORIGINAL CREATIVITY

*"Come Daughter of Woman, gaze into my well
and see glimpses of a childhood hoped for."*

Sometimes your sister reads to you from the *Book of Woman*. One school night after you finish your homework, she offers to read a story to you. You ask her to read "Patty's Favorite Room."

For as long as Patty can remember, there has been a whole room in the apartments and houses she's lived in filled with paint, crayons, glitter, and construction paper of all colors; glue, tape, stickers, and scissors of all kinds; sponges, brushes, and tongue depressors of all shapes; piles of old magazines, paper plates, and material scraps; containers of leaves and acorns, and other "Found Objects" from family walks and trips to the junk yard; a big table to work on; and large sheets of paper tacked up on all the walls, ready for the next adventure. Even when she lived in a very small apartment, her mom said, "What do we need a dining room for? We'll use it for our "Play Womb" and eat in the kitchen. To create is the food of the soul."

"Play Womb" is what Patty's mother calls the room because she believes that everyone can give birth to images, sounds, movements, and ideas—everyone, she said, even boys, have a "creative womb." Her father calls it the "Family Studio" because the room belongs to everyone in the family and "studio" sounded official to him—"we are all artists and everywhere we go, we will have a studio," he is always saying. And Patty calls it "Play Room" because she has so much fun whenever she is in there.

A big sign is over the doorway. It says, "Be Full of Yourself!" A bowl of glitter is attached to the wall like the holy water containers in the Catholic Church. "This is our family church," her mom is always saying, "it is a holy place so we'll bless ourselves with glitter before entering." So Patty reaches into the bowl and sprinkles herself with glitter every time she enters. There are only three rules in the playroom and they are easy to follow:
1. Cover the paints.
2. Be sure everything you use finds its way home to a pile, container, or shelf before you leave.
3. Move your painting to the "Drying Wall." Return for it within an hour. Hang it in the family gallery for public display or in your bedroom gallery for private display.

There is a sign-up sheet outside the 'Play Room" so everyone in the family can spend private time in there each week. Patty always signs up for the after school hours because she has lots to say after a long day, and she can't find the words to say it all—so she paints instead.

One day after school, Patty was very upset when she entered her special room. She painted rows and rows of girls and boys, and put a big X through each of them while saying, "**Go away.**" She painted 25 Xs and said 25 "**Go** aways" because there are 25 children plus her in the class. She was tired of them all, talking, yelling, fighting, and spilling—she wished she could be the only person in her class. After she painted the 25th X and said the 25th "**Go away**," Patty felt a lot better. She covered the paints, washed her hands, and then went into the kitchen to say "Hi" to her father. No one in the family bothers Patty until she finishes her afternoon time in the Play Room. They know she'll be in a much better mood after spending time in there!

The images of a childhood hoped for vanish and the well is clear again. The Mother of All Living speaks:

"Daughter of Woman, trust your vision of the world and express it. With wonder and delight, paint a picture, create a dance, and make up a song. To give expression to your creative impulses is as natural as your breathing. Create in your own language, imagery, and movement. Follow no script. Be not bound by the customary way things have been expressed. Your creative intuition is original. Gather all of life into your inner crucible, mix it with your unique vision and experience, and produce an original creation.

Daughter of Woman, love the sounds, movements, ideas, images, and words emerging from inside of you. If the creative impulse leads you to share your dance, song, or picture; your design, quilt, or collage; your business, workshop, or sermon, be full of yourself as you "perform" before audiences large and small. If you do not want to share your creative expression with anyone, read to yourself, create an art showing in the privacy of your bedroom, or dance with your beloved stuffed bears as your audience. The originality of the universe pulsates through you. Be full of yourself."

HONOR YOUR SEPARATE-SELF

*"Come Daughter of Woman, gaze into my well
and see glimpses of a childhood hoped for."*

Your mother calls your family together for the weekly family meeting. She begins by asking you to read the "Family Code of Responsibility:"

Part I. The Responsibilities of All Family Members

1. We are a family made up of four members: two parents, one sister, and one brother. Each member is responsible to support the family to run smoothly and to help each other out when there are problems.

2. The two parents are responsible to bring in the money to pay for the basic functioning of our family:

Rent to keep a roof over our heads.

Food to keep us alive.

Utilities to keep the water, heat, and electricity flowing.

Gasoline, maintenance, and insurance to keep the car working.

Fees for garbage pick-up.

Basic supplies necessary to keep a family going: from house-cleaning and personal hygiene supplies to furniture and yard equipment.

3. The two children are responsible to attend school to develop their minds and abilities. They will:

Prepare their school clothes.

Make their lunches.

Do their homework.

Plan transportation to and from any extra-curricular events, clubs, and activities before 7pm Monday - Friday.

4. All four family members share the responsibility for house and yard chores.

Everyone is responsible for their own room and bathroom.

There are no girl/boy-chores, no mommy/daddy-chores.

Each family member picks one daily, weekly, and extra chore to do.

If the children agree to do any chores over and above these basic responsibilities, they will be paid at a rate of $5 per hour.

5. The "Parent Chores" include:

Monday - Friday Breakfast Preparation
On Saturday, everyone fixes their own.
On Sunday, the family goes out for Brunch
Sunday - Thursday Dinner Preparation
On Friday, the family orders pizza.
On Saturday, everyone fixes their own with leftovers.
Weekly Kitchen Cleaning
Weekly Shopping
Chauffeur for School Events
Plant and Yard Care

6. The "Child Chores" include:

Daily Breakfast & Dinner Clean-up
Daily Garbage Take-Out
Weekly Vacuuming & Dusting of Living Room
Weekly Cleaning of Family Bathroom
Shopping Assistant (Unload, carry, and put away groceries.)
Yard Assistant (Rake, shovel, plant, depending on the season.)

II. The Privacy of All Family Members

1. Each family member has weekly private time. We will not barge in on another family member's privacy. We will guard and protect their private time as they will protect ours. All questions and concerns for them must wait until their private time is over.

2. Each family member is entitled to the privacy of their thoughts and feelings.

3. Each family member is entitled to the privacy of their own room.

4. Each family member is entitled to the privacy of their own body.

5. We respect each family member's YESes and NOs.

III. The Family Commitment

We are a family. Together, we will find our way through each challenge we face. Together, we will find a middle space between our differences. Together, we will find a meeting place beyond right or wrong. Together, we will find a comfortable way to live together that brings us all joy. May our family blossom like a garden, one day at a time.

The images of a childhood hoped for vanish and the well is clear again. The Mother of All Living speaks:

"Daughter of Woman, be interested in yourself. Delight in your own adventures. Explore everything in your world with wonder and awe. Gaze at the redness of an apple. Watch the water flow over the rocks in a stream. Listen to the rain dance. Count the peas on your plate. Ordinary life will be your teacher, your challenge, and your delight. Enjoy the privacy of quiet times, under the cover times, alone times to savor the events and experiences of your life.

Daughter of Woman, this is your virgin time. Touch the depths of your uniqueness. Love your mind. Express your feelings. Cherish your reflection in the mirror. Use your time, energy, and attention in service of your own life. Remember yourself. Exist for yourself. Be desirable to yourself. Your life begins anew each moment. Change your life if you want it changed. Do not wait for one to come. The solitude of the universe pulsates through you. Be full of yourself."

BE FULL OF YOURSELF!

*"Come Daughter of Woman, gaze into my well
and see glimpses of a childhood hoped for."*

Sometimes your mother reads to you from the *Book of Woman*. One school night after you finish your homework, she offers to read a story to you. You ask her to read "Patty's Voice" so she does.

One Saturday night a month all of Patty's friends and the friends of her parents are invited over for "Show and Tell." Patty's mother is usually the Queen of Ceremonies because she always wanted to be a comedienne but her parents wanted her to learn to type until she got married. She didn't learn to type until Patty taught her on the family computer, and she is the official comedienne of the family, the neighborhood, and the PTA. She starts off with the same words and actions every month:

*"Be full of yourself.
Brag, boast, and show-off.
Be pompous and big-headed.
Blow your own horn." (She blows a horn and passes it around!)*

*"Be loud about what you can do.
Be too big for your britches.
Have your cake and eat it too."
(She cuts the cake and passes it around!)*

"Everyone gets a standing ovation because it takes courage to show and tell in front of an audience. Sometimes it takes more courage for us grown-ups to sing and dance, to share our ideas, and to read our words, but we do it and we get a standing ovation too. Let's practice the ovation before we begin." (Up and down until she thinks they've got it!)

One Saturday night, Patty was ready to sing her favorite country western song. She had been practicing all week even though she knew the words by heart since she was four years old. She was the first one introduced by her mother and stepped onto the stage as her sister started the tape. At just the right moment she began to sing (with Nancy Griffith's help) "Love at The Five and Dime." Patty invited every one to join in at the chorus.

Dance a little closer to me. Dance a little closer now. Dance a little closer tonight cuz it's closing time and love's on sale at Ivy's five and dime.

Patty got a standing ovation. At school they tell Patty that she "doesn't have a voice." She knows this isn't true. She does to have a voice and she hears herself use it everyday. And Patty loves to sing. It makes her smile deep inside. So she doesn't listen to the people at school who tell her those things about her voice. She listens to her friends and family. She loves it when they say, "WOW,

you're fantastic!" or "That's a great song you taught us. I sang it all week." or
"Your face sparkles when you sing." or 'I'm so glad you are in my life!" Their
words feel warm like the sun calling her out to play on a summer day. Their
words say what she knows is true. She is a special girl with a special voice and
she'll keep singing because it makes her smile!

*The images of a childhood hoped for vanish and the well is clear again.
The Mother of All Living speaks:*

*Daughter of Woman, imagine into being a life that fosters the deepening
of your capacity to love your body, its needs and sensations; to express
your truth and perceptions, your feelings and creative potential; to cultivate your solitude; and to celebrate yourself.*

*Daughter of Woman, imagine into being a community of advocates—a
chosen family available to nurture your deepening connection to yourself
and to applaud your fullness.*

*Daughter of Woman, refuse to turn toward your own children with the
words once spoken to you. Imagine into being an environment in which
their natural capacities are supported to develop and flourish.*

*Daughter of woman, the clearing is not your home. Return to your
own folk and spread the good news that it is right and good that you
are Woman. The radiance of the universe pulsates through you. Be full
of yourself!*

A Vow of Faithfulness to One's Own Life

As I descended into my own inner life and began to reclaim every capacity, need, and unexplored potential, and every thought, feeling, impulse,
and unexpressed longing, I became aware of a disturbing pattern. I was
unable to sustain interest in my own life and creativity for more than three
to five months. I would then create a distraction, usually in the form of a
new and exciting relationship. While in the relationship, I would lose
touch with myself again. Exhausted by this pattern, I wanted a break from
intimate relationships. I wanted to give the fragile relationship with myself
a chance to root deeply within the ground of my being. I needed (and
wanted) to "marry myself," to vow faithfulness to my own life.

Supported by a circle of women, I chose to abstain from sexually intimate relationships for two years. Although initially uncomfortable, the two
year abstinence turned out to be the most valuable gift I have ever given
myself. By the end of the two years, I was certain that I would never again
abandon myself or my creativity. The words of Rainer Maria Rilke, Anne
Marrow Lindbergh, and Elizabeth Cady Stanton sustained me:

"We are solitary. We may delude ourselves and act as though it were not so. But how much better it is to realize that we are so, yes, even to begin by assuming it. Naturally, we will turn giddy." (Rainer Rilke)

"Instead of planting our solitude with our own dream blossoms, we choke the space with continuous music, chatter, and companionship. When the noise stops, there is no inner music to take its place. We must relearn to be alone." (Anne Morrow Lindbergh, *Gifts From the Sea*)

"No matter how much women prefer to lean, to be protected and support- ed, nor how much men desire to have them do so, they must make the voyage of life alone, and for safety in an emergency, they must know something of the laws of navigation. To guide our own craft, we must be captain, pilot, engineer; with chart and compass to stand at the wheel; to watch the winds and waves, and know when to take in the sail, and to read the signs in the firmament over all. It matters not whether the soli- tary voyager is man or woman; nature, having endowed them equally, leaves them to their own skill and judgment in the hour of danger, and, if not equal to the occasion, alike they perish." (Elizabeth Cady Stanton, *"The Solitude of Self"*)

It is essential for women to befriend the solitude of their own lives. A woman's choice to be alone, whether for an hour a day, a weekend a month, or for a full season of life deepens her vow of faithfulness to herself. In her abstinence, she reclaims her abundant inner resources, nurtures her origi- nal creative spirit, reconnects with her own spontaneity and joy, and remembers her personal dreams and goals. Based on this conviction, the focal point of the "Be Full of Yourself" retreat is the writing of vows of faith- fulness to our own lives. At the end of each healthy family fantasy session, the participants incorporate new insights and commitments into their evolving vows. The week culminates in a commitment ceremony.[71]

In preparation, each woman completes her vow and chooses a symbol- ic item such as a ring, earring, stone, feather, or scarf, as a reminder of her vow. The item is blessed by the community and returned to her dur- ing the ceremony.

Vows of Faithfulness

Allow the vows of women who have attended the "Be Full of Yourself" retreat to inspire your own. Use a marker to highlight the phrases that res- onate with your experience. Gather the phrases together, add your own, and compose your first draft of a vow of faithfulness to yourself.

I, Mary Bolling, vow
     to speak in a voice clear and strong;

to look upon myself with a merciful eye;
to notice and accept the feelings my body gives me as trustworthy infor-
    mation, to breathe into them, and then to choose how I will respond;
to state clearly when something does not work for me and to
    create or co-create an acceptable alternative;
to look with lovingkindness upon my shame about my body-
    curiosity and exploration while growing up;
to set aside thirty minutes three times a week for soul-play.

I , Olivia Lara, vow to
Engage in creative expression three times a week.
Establish "creative spaces" in my home to inspire and
    exhibit my expressions.
Increase my sensory awareness and attentiveness
    through sight, sound, touch, taste, and smell.
Structure and experience regular periods of solitude,
    including meditation, reflection, and expressive activities, and rest.
Assertively state what I think and feel.
Observe and gracefully release conditioned thoughts,
    feelings, and sensations.
Treat myself to facials and pedicures monthly.
Trust my sexuality and savor my sensuality.
Accept and appreciate my femininity.
Love myself powerfully!

I, Maria Elena, vow to let go of the notion that I am inferior and that I cannot
do anything of value, no matter how hard I try and no matter what I achieve.
    I vow to love, accept, and esteem my whole being and then let my beauty,
        creative expression, and bright light shine.
    I vow to be true to myself and share my gifts through the avenue of joy.

Before the Mother of All Living and my sacred sisters, I, Annette LaPorte, vow:
    to embrace my life and be faithful to that which matters to me.
    to simply accept, trust, honor, love, and express all that arises
        and flows from every part of my being.
    So be it.

I, Gretchen Blais, vow
    To begin my day from Home. To wake up and breathe in
        Universal Goodness.
    To know God is with me, to welcome the day and be grateful
        for the opportunity to do Her work.
    To dedicate my day to guidance from the Goddess within.
    To allow myself to be touched by the lessons of the East and
        West, North and South.
    To return Home during the day, to take a few moments to remind myself

that Home is always waiting, ever so gentle and loving to welcome me
and provide me sustenance and comfort. Home is always a breath away.
To remember that all that I need is a moment of willingness for
illumination to grow.
To renew my commitment on the new moon as a reminder
that little effort is needed to be at Home.
To send a postcard or e-mail on the new moon to myself or someone
else as an external process to re-affirm my Vow of Faithfulness.

I, Nancy Smith, promise to befriend my body, to lovingly provide the nourishment, rest, and exercise it needs. I will refrain from stuffing it with more
food than it can possibly use up; if I am full of myself, I will not need to be so
full of food. I will ask my body often, "Is this working for you?" and listen
carefully for its answer. I will attempt to find a physical activity that I truly
enjoy to support the well being of my body, mind, and spirit.

I promise to experiment with expressive media—verbal, visual, and
movement—to find a medium for creative expression that works for me.
I promise to emerge from my precious solitude to nurture a dependable
social network to support my need for human interaction and belonging. I will start by calling my friend Karen—no later than Wednesday
of next week, asking her to have dinner, and then asking her to
commit to getting together on a regular basis that works for us both.

*I, Donna Strachan-Ledbetter, vow the following in order to celebrate the
fullness of who I am:*
to tell myself each day "I love you" and know in the depths of
my soul that I have been wanted from the beginning of time;
to practice letting go of the incessant critical voices of myself
and of others;
to make space for the peaceful quiet of just being;
and, before this year draws to a close, begin again to learn and play the
piano, so that the light and the dark may dance together to my music.

*I, Robbie Lilith Lottero, make these vows with a clear understanding of the
power and capacities I invoke. I vow to:*
Honor my own physical, spiritual, and emotional needs.
Honor and respect my judgment and estimation of how I live my life.
Honor that I am a whole being, capable of feeling and expressing
a full spectrum of human emotion.
Allow myself to do or to not do simply because it feels right and true to me.
Allow myself unqualified, unnegotiated time.
Honor my body by what I choose to ingest and how I choose to be touched.
Let go of the rules.
Allow others the choice to express their own needs.
Let go of others with love.
Allow myself creative expression, without wondering if it's the

right way, the wrong way, or anyone else's way
Allow myself the joy of sharing my accomplishments with
    trusted family and friends.
Allow space for the unknown.
Let go of the violence that permeated my life, and invades
    both my images and language.
Reclaim and nurture all that I have neglected or tried to
    destroy in me for the comfort of others.
Finally, to heal and nurture Lilith all the days of my life.

A Commitment Ceremony

Imagine sitting in a redwood circle deep within the forest as you read through the commitment ceremony. Continue to write your own Vow of Faithfulness as you read.[73]

A Call To Gather

Open your eyes and look around you.
    We have chosen the forest as our cathedral.
    We have invited the tall ancient redwoods as honored guests.
    We have invited the inhabitants of the forest to be among us.
    We have invited the moist, green growing things to bless us.
    We have gathered to witness each woman's vow of faithfulness to herself.
Be present *in this place.*

Open your heart and look within you.
    Breathe into this moment and release all distractions,
    Excursions into the past, projections into the future.
    Breathing in, receive the fullness of this moment.
    Breathing out, open your heart to the gift and challenge of this moment.
    We are gathered to witness each woman's vow of faithfulness to herself.
Be present *here and now.*

An Invocation of Spirit

We invoke the presence of the Source of All Life.
    Everything in the forest comes from and returns to the Mother.
    You are as grounded, as connected to Her as the trees are.
    You are held, supported, and nourished by Her.
    Acknowledge the firm ground of the Mother, holding you.
    Mother, we welcome you here.

We invoke the spirit of life, the breath.
    Everything breathes in the forest.
    Savor the breath of life, flowing in, through, and around you.

Inhale deeply as the breath rises from the rich earth beneath you.
Release the breath into the cool moist air around you.
Breath, we welcome you here.

We invoke the wisdom of the body.
Notice the ancient trees around you. You are one with the forest.
Feel your feet grow roots extending deep into the ground.
Feel your arms become branches stretching high in the sky.
Sway with the breeze. Settle into your woman-body.
Wise body, we welcome you here.

We invoke the accumulation of our years and experience.
Notice the forest-dance of life and death and rebirth.
Reach down and touch the forest floor layered with seasons passed.
Look up and view the forest canopy woven from time's evolving.
Acknowledge the seasons of your life. Invoke the richness of your years.
Accumulation of years and experience, we welcome you here.

Musical Interlude

A Commitment

Daughter of Woman, in response to the truth, in love with yourself, full of boldness and grace, express your commitment with the words "I Will."

Daughter of Woman, love your body. Run free like the wind. Jump high like a horse. Climb a tree. Cross a creek. Wrestle a friend to the ground. Tumble down a hill. Let your voice bellow and be heard by the whole wide world. Dance to the music of your own life in love with your body. It is your teacher, your healer, and your challenge. It is your faithful companion for the length of your days. You body is good. It is very good. Be full of yourself!

Will you love your body all the days of your life?
Will you touch it with tenderness and support it with strength?
Will you honor its rhythms and cycles as an exquisite resource?
Will you honor the body of the goddess in your changing body?

Daughter of Woman, meet your organic needs. Listen to the sounds and sensations of a lifetime. You body is the bearer of deep wisdom. What does it tell you of the quality of your life, of the shape and pace of your days, of those who dance into and out of your presence; of the food you eat, of the sleep you embrace, of your response to the experiences of life? Listen to what you hear and meet your body's needs with tenderness and grace. The organic needs of the universe pulsate through you. Be full of yourself!

Will you listen to the deep wisdom of your body all the days of your life?
Will you meet its needs with tenderness and grace?
Will you design the shape of your days in accordance with its feedback?
Will you eat foods that support its vitality, drink water to moisten its
capacities, and sleep well to renew its life energy?

Daughter of Woman, embrace your erotic potential. Say YES to life as it pulsates through you. Feel the YES in your curiosity about your body's sensations and in your exploration of its fascinating nooks and crannies, openings and operations. Feel the YES in your heart, your joy, and even in your tears. Allow it to touch every area of your life. The erotic potential of the universe pulsates through you. Be full of yourself!

Will you embrace your sexuality as your own all the days of your life?
Will you delight in pleasuring yourself?
Will you explore the edges of your sensuality?
Will you trust your body's clear YES and NO in the choice of lovers?

Daughter of Woman, express your feelings. There is no separation between your feelings and your body. Feel your sadness forming as an ache in your heart. Feel your anger rise up within you to be released in loud sounds and strong movements. Feel your fear in the fluttering sensation in your tummy. Feel your erotic energy in the tingling warmth of your genitals. Feel your joy in the warmth of your face. The feelings of the universe pulsate through you as naturally as the breath. Be full of yourself!

Will you honor the whole range of human emotion all the days of your life?
Will you circulate your feelings daily using sound, movement, and image,
allowing them to pass through you as gracefully as the breath?
Will you take responsibility for meeting your own emotional needs,
enlisting the support of respectful friends and chosen family?

Daughter of Woman, assume intellectual equality. Be sassy and loud. Question. Argue. Debate. Communicate from your heart. Voice your truth. Share your vision. When you don't like your food, spit it out. When you're exhausted from tagging along in someone else's life, refuse to take another step. When you don't like someone and tighten in their presence, make your discomfort known. Tell the untold truths of a lifetime to your parents, lovers, and colleagues, and to your children and grandchildren. The truth of the universe pulsates through you. Be full of yourself!

Will you speak your truth all the days of your life?
Will you tell the untold truths of a lifetime to your parents, lovers, and
colleagues, and to your children and grandchildren?

Will you assume intellectual equality by refusing to defer to the thoughts and perceptions of others?

Daughter of Woman, reclaim your original creativity. Trust your vision of the world and express it. With wonder and delight, paint a picture, create a dance, and make up a song. To give expression to your creative impulses is as natural as your breathing. Create in your own language, imagery, and movement. Follow no script. Your creative intuition is original. Gather all of life into your inner crucible, mix it with your unique vision and experience, and produce an original creation. The originality of the universe pulsates through you. Be full of yourself!

Will you love your creative impulses all the days of your life?
Will you give expression daily to the words, shapes, images, and movements that emerge from within you?
Will you celebrate your unique vision and experience, producing original creations and refusing to color inside someone else's lines?

Daughter of Woman, deepen your self-involvement. Be interested in yourself. Delight in your own adventures. Explore everything in your world with wonder and awe. Gaze at the redness of an apple. Watch the water flow over the rocks in a stream. Listen to the rain dance. Count the peas on your plate. Ordinary life will be your teacher, your challenge, and your delight. Enjoy the privacy of quiet times to savor the events and experiences of your life. The solitude of the universe pulsates through you. Be full of yourself!

Will you sustain interest in yourself all the days of your life?
Will you embrace your own life as teacher, healer, and challenge?
Will you value its lessons above the prescriptions of experts?
Will you befriend the solitude of your own life?

Daughter of Woman, practice self-celebration. Imagine into being a life that fosters the deepening of your capacity to love your body, its needs and sensations; to express your truth and perceptions, your feelings and creative potential; to cultivate your solitude; and to celebrate yourself. Imagine into being a community of advocates—a chosen family available to nurture your deepening connection to yourself and to applaud your fullness. The radiance of the universe pulsates through you. Be full of yourself!

Will you choose to be full of yourself all the days of your life?
Will you honor your desire for acknowledgment and recognition?
Will you surround yourself with friends who applaud your fullness?

Musical Interlude

Reading of The Vows

To be said before the women speak:
Let us witness each woman's vow of faithfulness.
Let us review our commitment to ourselves as we listen.
Each woman speaks her vow.

Blessing of The Symbols

To bless the symbols:
With holy water from the womb of the Mother, we bless each symbol.
May it be a reminder of your vow when you forget yourself.
May it escort you home when you wander away from yourself.
May it bring a smile to your soul all the days of your life.

To be said as call and response after all women have received their symbols:
As a sign of my love and respect for myself, (Women repeat.)
I give myself this ___ with a pledge to honor my vow (Repeat.)
In tender times and turbulent times. (Repeat.)
In graceful moments and in awkward situations. (Repeat.)
In flowing times and in seasons of stagnation (Repeat.)
In fullness and in emptiness. (Repeat.)
In fear and in courage. (Repeat.)
In trouble and in beauty. (Repeat.)
With all that I am and all I shall become (Repeat.)
For the rest of my life. (Repeat.)

To be said by the gathered community: *So be it.*

A Pronouncement of Loving Partnership

Inasmuch as you have grown in knowledge and love of yourself, and have vowed faithfulness to your own life and capacities, I now joyfully proclaim that it is right and good that you are woman. You are full of yourself!

A Blessing

To be said by all participants in unison:

No More Waiting
This is it. This is my life.
Nothing to wait for.
Nowhere else to go.
No one to make it all different.
What a relief to have finally landed
Here . . . now.
Blessed be my life!

WOMEN'S STORIES
ASSUMING PERSONAL RESPONSIBILITY

LIGHTENING THE LOAD
Valerie Bowman

During the "Home is Always Waiting" meditation, my load was lightened . . .

I see myself descending a set of stairs built into the side of a hill. The steps are grassy and wide and as I gently descend, I feel myself relaxing further with each step. I am in a deep forest, with shafts of sunlight pouring through the redwood trees.

As I reach the bottom, I see a clearing with a stream running through it. I go to the stream and settle even deeper into my inner self as I watch the water rushing over smooth rocks. As the sun moves higher, I feel a weight on my shoulders.

I take off a red wool coat with gold buttons that I recognize as my mother's. I drop the coat into the stream and as it floats away, I let go of my mother's perfectionism and her demands of me. I see those are not my burdens to carry. As I lovingly let them go, I bless my mother and see her taking care of herself.

Next I remove a Navy jacket of my brother's. As I let it go and the water pulls it effortlessly downstream, I release my brother's depression, addictions, and moodiness. I see that I no longer have to carry them on my shoulders. I bless him and see him taking care of himself in whatever way he chooses.

There is still a weight on me, and I remove a leather jacket belonging to my daughter. I drop it into the stream and watch as it floats down the stream over the rocks. I let go of my daughter's worries about school and her future as I know that she has inner resources of her own to see her through. I see that I cannot live her life for her and I feel a freedom as I bless her and release her.

I take off a dark gray suit jacket and let it go in the rushing water. It represents my father and his criticism of me. I see that his loneliness is his concern and let it go.

With the release of this last coat, I am wearing a flowing white cotton dress that blows in the breeze and feels light and joyful. I lie down next to the stream, free of the burdens that weren't mine to carry. I make a commitment to myself to shake off the old material I have been lugging around. I breathe deeply with a new sense of freedom and knowing that I can come back to this place anytime I want, with a simple breath.

SO MUCH MORE   *Carol Marshall*

It wasn't until the fourth day of the Women's Spirituality Retreat that I understood my obsession with removing the paint from my hands. On that day as I smeared paint liberally on the paper canvas and on my hands, fingers, and wrists, I heard my mother's well-intentioned words in the depths of my being: "Be sweet, Carol, be sweet. People will love you if you are sweet." The daily painting sessions from that point on became the setting for my transformation as I accepted myself as a whole and holy, complex and complicated woman. No longer would I allow my mother's words to shape my response to life. When the time came to pick up my journal, my pen fairly flew across the page:

Yes, I am sweet. And I am so much more . . .
I have the marks of the Goddess on my body and canvass. I see the risings and the fallings. I see the anguish, despair, and abandonment. I see the desperation, turmoil, confusion, chaos, anger, and rage. Lines of black and deep purple criss-cross my canvass. Red, red, blood red. Lots of orange. Is that the color for hope, for wholeness, for healing? My painted canvass is beautiful. My painted hands are beautiful. The paint feels at home on my hands.

I can hear Mother saying: "Goodness gracious! Is all that in you? All that stuff? Negativity? Confusion? Chaos? Mess?"
And I say: "Yes, Mother, it is all in me. And it was all in you, too. Some of that in me was given to me by you."
"No, no," you say. "I only gave you beautiful, lovely things."

Oh, Momma, I know that's what you meant to give me. And I also heard your gut screaming in the night. I heard your tamped, cramped, cement-and-steel enclosed colon screaming in the dark of the night.

Momma, I love you. I honor you. I am healing for you and for me . . . maybe for your mother and her mother and her mother and her mother, paving the way, putting up the sign-posts and road markers for the women to come. For Ryann and her daughter and her daughter and her daughter and her daughter and her daughter . . .

I know you wanted me to be sweet.

I am sweet, Momma, and so much more.

MY CEREMONY
Amy Fishbach

While at the East coast "Be Full of Yourself" retreat, I was inspired to write a Jewish wedding ceremony for myself. From early childhood, my one all-consuming fantasy has been of standing under the "chupah" (wedding canopy) with my beloved. Tired of this fantasy and the romance and relationship addiction it inspired, I included the chupah in my own private ceremony, witnessed by the other retreat participants. Here is the outline of the ceremony:

1. Light the Shabbat candles and chant the blessing in Hebrew, including G-d's name as female and as "Queen of the Universe." At the end of the prayer, change the word "shabbat" to "ha yom," making the blessing for "Today."

2. Four women hold the corners of the chupah, the wedding canopy, over my head.

3. I recite the following:

> I, Amy Stern Fishbach, vow that:
>
> As I so love the moon,
> Shall I so love myself.
>
> And as I so love the sound of running creek water,
> Shall I so love myself and the sound of my Inner Voice.
>
> And as I so love special stones
>   and a certain way sun falls through the leaves,
> Shall I so love what makes me special to myself.
>
> I will remember that by myself
> I have everything I need and
> I am enough.

4. Walk around photographs of myself three times.

5. Recite the Hebrew prayer I invented for myself, addressed to G-d: "Anachu ovdeem b'yah-chad." ("We work together.") Ask the women: "Nachon?" (Right?") All the women reply: "Nachon!" (Right!")

6. With my foot, smash the tree-bark, representing the broken years of my life. L'chaim! ("To life!")

HEALING INTO THE PRESENT:
"HOME IS ALWAYS WAITING" MEDITATION

Softly and tenderly. Wisdom is calling.
Calling for you and for me.
Come home. Come home. All who are weary come home.
Softly and tenderly. Wisdom is calling.
Calling, O woman, come home.

Self-critical thoughts are a signal that you have become disconnected from yourself. When you notice one, thank it for the reminder and use the "Home is Always Waiting" meditation to re-establish connection with your breath, body, and inner life. Below you will find an abbreviated version of the original meditation.[72] Personalize it to suit your own needs. Some women choose to sit quietly, following a traditional meditation model. Others choose to journal; draw or paint; dance, move, or stretch as the spirit moves them. Over time, you will discover the essential connection between meditation and self-celebration. You have everything you need within the rich resources of your own life.

Home is always waiting. It is as near as a conscious breath, conscious contact with your woman-body, and a descent into the rich resources of your inner life.

A Conscious Breath

Making Conscious Contact

Let us begin by making conscious contact with the breath. Turn your attention inward. Become conscious of the breath and its faithful rhythm, supporting you the length of your days.

If you are particularly distracted, you may find it helpful to count each inhalation and exhalation. The breath will escort you into this moment. Pay attention to the coming and going of the breath for at least ten inhalations and exhalations. Breathe into this moment with each inhalation. Release anything that is not of this moment with each exhalation. (Pause.)

Allow sighs, sounds, and yawns to ride on the back of your breath, releasing the accumulation of your day, of a lifetime. Life becomes simpler, clearer, and lighter as you come into this moment, paying attention to your breath and letting go of all distraction. Weave an affirmation into each breath: *I am enough. Just as I am. I am enough. Without doing anything.* (Pause.)

A Deep Breath

Notice the depth of your breath.

Place your hands on your upper chest. Inhale, expanding your chest with the breath. And exhale, slowly letting go of all burdens that are not yours to carry. Continue to breathe into your upper chest for two more breaths. (Pause.)

Now place your hands on the sides of your rib cage. Inhale deeply, pushing the breath against your ribs. Exhale. Continue to fill your rib cavity for 2 more breaths, deepening your capacity to hold the nourishing breath of life. (Pause.)

Place your hands on your abdomen. Inhale deeply, imagining the breath as a great wave filling your belly. Allow your belly to swell. This is a deep breath. And exhale as the wave retreats, leaving nourishment and fulfillment in its wake. Continue to breathe deeply into your belly for two more breaths. (Pause.)

Now place your hands on your lower back. Breathe into your lower back, the location of your kidneys, the well of life-giving energy within you. Breathe deeply into the well within you. Allow this deep breath to nourish you, to enrich you, to fill you. Continue to breathe deeply into your lower back for two more breaths.(Pause.)

Bring your arms to your sides and continue to breathe deeply. Inhale, as the full swell moves upward from your abdomen, into your rib cavity, and then into the upper chest. And exhale, as the wave retreats downward from your chest, your rib cavity, and your abdomen, leaving in its wake serenity. Continue this deep breathing for two more breaths.(Pause.)

Noticing Distraction

If your attention moves away from home, away from your breath, away from this moment, notice the distraction without judgment, and then practice returning home. There will always be distractions. Our life-practice is to return. Home is always waiting. It is as near as a conscious breath. (Pause.)

Conscious Contact With Your Woman-Body

Make Conscious Contact

Imagine that you are in an ancient forest. You have roots like the trees surrounding you. You are as grounded, as connected to Mother Earth as a tree is. You are held, supported, and nourished by Her. Acknowledge the firm ground that holds.

Everything breathes in the forest. Breathe deeply and savor the breath of life that flows in and through and around you. As you inhale, imagine the breath rising up from the rich earth beneath you. And as you exhale, imagine releasing the breath into the cool and moist air around you. Weave an affirmation into each breath: *My body is enough. Just as it is. My body is good. There is no blemish.* (Pause.)

Make conscious contact with your woman-body by taking a gentle walk over and around it—using tender self-touch or massage, gentle movement or stretch, or the quietness of your imagination, inviting your breath to reach toward each part of your body.

At your own pace, create a Meditation of Acknowledgment. Beginning at the top of your head or the bottom of your feet, slowly move, touch, or imagine each part of your body, personalizing the affirmation: *"My nose is good just as it is. There is no blemish." "My breasts are good just as they are. There is no blemish."* Bless your woman-body in the silence. (Pause.)

To complete your Meditation of Acknowledgment, turn a merciful eye toward your body. Look upon it with lovingkindness as you pay special attention to the areas it has been difficult to acknowledge—a scar, a place trespassed by another, a layer of protective fat, an untouchable part. Are you ashamed of certain parts of your body? Proud of others? Notice what is true for you without judgment. Meet each response and feeling with the breath. Acknowledge your response on the inhalation, then let go of it on the exhalation. Affirm: *My woman-body is holy. Just as it is. There is no blemish.* (Pause.)

A Descent Into the Rich Resources of Your Inner Life

Imagine yourself as a leaf let go of by an autumn tree . . .
a leaf slowly and gradually descending toward the ground . . .
its descent cushioned by the breath of life . . .
a leaf touching the ground in the forest deep within your being.
You rise from the ground, thanking the leaf for transporting you so gently.

Everything is breathing in the forest. Savor the breath of life flowing in and around you. Inhale deeply as the breath rises from the rich earth beneath you. Release the breath into the cool and moist air around you. Weave an affirmation into each breath:
Breathing in . . . I come home to rich resources of my inner life.
  Breathing out . . . Home is always waiting.

Your attention moves upward and you notice the trees reaching arm in arm for the sky. You become a tree. Your feet grow roots extending deep into the ground. Your arms become branches stretching high into the sky. You sway with the breeze. The birds of the forest dance with you as they leap from branch to branch. You see many things from your new height.
Breathing in . . . I am rooted and grounded in the earth.
  Breathing out . . . I come home to the ground of my being.
Breathing in . . . I am expansive and fill the universe.

Breathing out . . . I come home to the spaciousness of my being.

A nearby stream calls to you, "Come and play." In a moment, you are at the stream, splashing in its bouncing waters. As you are drying off in the warm sunlight pouring through the forest canopy, a path opens up before you and invites you to follow it to a special place. You accept the invitation and follow the path.

Breathing in . . . I am escorted on the path of life.

Breathing out . . . I come home to my inner guidance.

The path leads you deep within the forest to the edge of a clearing . . . a magical open space surrounded by a ring of ancient redwoods, forming the outer circle, and by a sparkling stream, forming the inner circle. As you peek through the stately redwood circle, you recognize the clearing as the home you once knew in the very beginning of your life. You cross the stream. You enter the clearing. You are home.

Breathing in . . . I return home.

Breathing out . . . Home is always waiting.

For the final moments of this meditation, in the quietness of your healing imagination or in your journal-sketchpad, reflect on the images that surface while you linger in the clearing. Draw them. Dance them. Write them. Breathe into them. Come home to the rich resources of your inner life. (Pause.)

Home is always waiting.
In tender times and turbulent times.
In graceful moments and in awkward situations.
In flowing times and in seasons of stagnation.
In fullness and in emptiness.
In fear and in courage.
In trouble and in beauty.

Home is always waiting.
It is as near as a conscious breath,
conscious contact with your woman-body,
and a descent into the rich resources of your inner life.

HEALING INTO THE PRESENT
A Birthing Dance

You were introduced to the words of "In the Very Beginning was the Mother" in Chapter 4. Reacquaint yourself with the poem before you begin. When you are ready, experiment with the movements and sounds of the birthing dance. If helpful, tape the following instructions and listen to them while learning the simple dance.

In the very beginning was the Mother.
Find a "Big Mama" stance, bringing your awareness to your pelvis and thighs.
Feel the strength of your lower body.
Place your hands on your belly.

On the first day, she gave birth . . .
Spread your legs and bend your knees.
Bring your hands from your belly through to the space between your legs.
Push life from you with sound and movement: groan, grunt, purr, and
    whimper unto life.
Birth is not a quiet event!

. . . to light and darkness.
Find movements to express light, visibility, openness, and expansion.
Find movements to express darkness, invisibility, closedness, and contraction.

They danced together.
Allow your light and your darkness to dance together.
Do not elevate or despise either one.
Both are essential movements in the dance of life.

On the second day . . .
Back to the "Big Mama" stance.

she gave birth . . .
Spread your legs and bend your knees.
Bring your hands from your belly through to the space between your legs.
Push life from you with sound and movement: cry, giggle, cackle, and
    cluck unto life.

to land and water.
Find movements to express land, groundedness, being settled.
Find movements to express water, fluidity, being flexible.

They touched.
Allow your land-groundedness and your water-fluidity to touch.
Do not elevate or despise either one.
Both are essential movements in the dance of life.

On the third day . . .
Back to the "Big Mama" stance.

she gave birth . . .
Push life from you with sound and movement: laugh, moan, howl, and
  bellow unto life.

to green growing things.
Emerge as a green growing thing: a plant, tree, or flower.
Find movements to express growth outward and upward from the ground,
  the center, the womb.

They rooted and took a deep breath.
Find a "rooting" movement.
Together, let us take a deep breath in with an expansive movement,
  opening as the breath rises.
Belly swelling, chest expanding, head back, arms open wide.
And then a complete exhalation, contracting downward as the breath falls.
Arms inward, head down, chest and belly contracting.

On the fourth day . . .
Back to the "Big Mama" stance.

she gave birth . . .
Push life from you with sound and movement: roar, scream, screech, and
  shout unto life.

to land, sea, and air creatures.
Point to the earth, outline waves in the air, and point to the sky.

They walked, and swam, and flew.
Walk . . . Swim . . . Fly . . .

On the fifth day,
Face a partner. Take her hands.

her creation learned balance . . .
Lean backward gently, finding the place where tension and balance meet in
  your hands and bodies.

. . . and cooperation.
Move toward each other, your hands reaching to chin level.
Gaze into the eyes of your partner.

She thanked her partner for coaching her labor.
Bow in gratitude for those who coach our labor unto life and health.

On the sixth day,
Back to the "Big Mama" stance.

she celebrated the creativity of all living things.
Make all of those sounds and movements quieted in childhood: the precious
    expressions of a child full of life.
Honor all that has been despised. Receive all that has been cast aside.
Your sounds and movements are good. They are very good.

On the seventh day,
Back to the "Big Mama" stance.

she left space for the unknown.
Open your arms, leaving a space for the unknown.
Dance with your own personal space for mystery, for what is beyond words,
    beyond form, beyond "figuring out."

PART FOUR

Self-Celebration:
A Transformed
Perspective

7

THE LANGUAGE
OF
SELF-CELEBRATION

Maybe the most authentic celebration
begins with rejoicing in that
which is breaking up from down under.

—NELLE MORTON,
"The Dilemma of Celebration"

The transformation of our self-critical perspective to one of self-celebration was possible only as we traveled the historical, religious, and personal paths of Parts One, Two, and Three. It was necessary to dismantle the hierarchically-based intellectual systems that provided legitimacy to our self-critical voice, to exorcise the sin-based words and images of religion which gave authority to our self-critical voice, and to reverse the critical messages we heard from our parents and teachers that taught us the language of self-criticism.

Two essential tasks must be accomplished before our shared journey is complete. In this chapter we'll learn the language of self-celebration to express our inner transformation and we'll incorporate it into our conversations and relationships, and into our daily meditation practice. And in Chapter 8, we'll gather the woman-support necessary to maintain our commitment to self-celebration and to the manifestation of our fullness in the world.

A HISTORICAL PERSPECTIVE

Sixteen years ago I read Walt Whitman's *Leaves of Grass* in a secret corner of the Princeton Seminary library. I drank in his blasphemous words. They quenched my lifelong thirst for a language with which to celebrate myself without conditions, apologies, or disclaimers. Having just begun the journey through my intellectual, religious, and personal past, I wasn't ready to allow his words to form on my lips yet they remained within me and inspired my journey.

Years later, my three-fold journey completed, Whitman's words from "Song of Myself" became my first self-celebration. And throughout the years, they've inspired many of the rituals, meditations, and affirmations I've composed to support the development of a language of self-celebration. *Speak his words aloud. Celebrate yourself without conditions, apologies, or disclaimers:*

I celebrate myself,
And what I assume you shall assume,
For every atom belonging to me as good belongs to you.

I call to (hu)mankind, Be not curious about God,
For I who am curious about each am not curious about God.

I hear and behold God in every object, yet I understand God not in the least,
Nor do I understand who there can be more wonderful than myself.

Why should I wish to see God better than this day?
I see something of God each hour of the twenty four, and each moment then,
In the faces of men and women I see God, and in my own face in the glass . .

I am larger, better than I thought. I did not know I held so much goodness.[74]

I invite women to incorporate Whitman's words into their daily meditation practice. For many women, the repetition of these words is their first opportunity to practice the language of self-celebration. We continue our practice with a simple guided meditation, supporting us to move beyond Whitman's words to develop our own personalized "Song of Myself:"

Imagine Eve, the Mother of All Living approaching you, bearing a multi-colored jewel in her hands. She carries it into the stunning darkness of your heart of hearts. The jewel illuminates the many facets of your goodness and giftedness as a child of life. Imagine her saying to you: "Open to the depths of goodness within you—you are good. Celebrate your goodness—you are very good. Live out of the abundance of who you are as a Child of Life—you have everything you need." Acknowledge the goodness and giftedness she illuminates—in word, image, movement, or sound.

Here's a sampling of women's first attempts to engage in self-celebration. Allow their words to inspire your own self-celebration.

I celebrate my anger and strength. I will no longer look to men to express my assertiveness.

I celebrate my intensity of feeling and consciousness, energizing every task I set out to accomplish.

I celebrate my powerful perception, bringing clarity to my introverted adventures and to my extroverted interactions.

I celebrate my spirit of adventure, supporting me to explore new paths, to try alternative ways of thinking and doing, and to challenge existing life-styles and cultural patterns.

I celebrate my generosity, my delight in song and dance, my ability to listen deeply to my children, my sparkling intuition, my capacity to just "be" in someone's presence, my love of my body when I see its reflection in the mirror, and my enjoyment of my spirit when I spend time alone.

I celebrate my courage to heal into the present by rewriting the "myths" of my family history to more closely conform to my memories, by altering ineffective behaviors, by leaving disrespectful relationships, by learning to speak my truth, and by listening to and acting on my intuition.

I celebrate my ability to stay in the present moment, observing my feelings, thoughts, impulses, and behaviors, without judgment; my sense of humor; my strong desire to live a peaceful and compassionate life; my accountability for what I say and do; and my growing willingness to be vulnerable.

I celebrate the intensity of my intelligence, vitality, strength, sensitivity, and sensuality. Her acceptance of my intensity replaced the self-critical mantra "I am too intense." I now celebrate my intensity as a gift of life and its expression in word, image, dance, and erotic interaction as the gift I offer back to life.

SIX WOMAN-AFFIRMING PERSPECTIVES:
THE LANGUAGE OF SELF-CELEBRATION

Although the practice of self-celebration begins with direct statements of personal celebration, its ramifications touch the breadth and depth of our use of language. My life and ministry are based on six woman-affirming perspectives that explore these ramifications. Throughout the years I have utilized the perspectives to appraise the merit of religious teachings, therapeutic models, and recovery principles; and to evaluate the quality and mutuality of relationships to friends and lovers, teachers and therapists, and religious leaders. They inform every word you've read in this book.

I invite women to consider these perspectives as we sit together in workshops, classes, and support groups. Their initial reactions range from fear to ecstasy. For a woman to reject cultural and religious dogmas is a forbidden act. One woman exclaimed, "These feel like dangerous and heretical words. I'm afraid to say them out loud." For a woman to affirm her goodness, power, courage, and self-possession; her body, natural processes, and erotic potential; her willfulness, voice, wholeness, and wisdom without shame or hesitation is a forbidden act. Another woman responded, "What a relief to be in a circle that celebrates women so deeply!"

Using the six perspectives as our starting place, let's explore the personal, interpersonal, and systemic ramifications of the language of self-celebration and learn the vocabularies of goodness, equality, reverence, self-possession, willfulness, and connection. The chapter includes sample letters, conversations, and affirmations. As you read, highlight the insights and vocabulary relevant to your current personal, interpersonal, or systemic challenges.

The Vocabulary of Goodness

WE REJECT the dominance of a creation myth that portrays women as the instigators of evil. We reject the historical, theological, societal, and familial messages that stressed our wrongs, our defects, and our insufficiencies and that required the relinquishment of our natural capacities.

WE EMBRACE a woman-affirming perspective that reminds us of the original goodness and sanctity of all life, that it is right and good that we are women. In circles of women, we recover ancient beliefs, affirming that all of creation is good; that we are originally blessed, not cursed; and that there is strength, goodness, and creativity within each of us. We reclaim Eve as our champion and join women from every age who have committed the forbidden act of stepping outside of systems of thought and belief that denied their very existence. Women who refuse to ask "what's wrong with me." Women who make a powerful statement with every thought they share, every feeling they express, and every action they take on their own behalf. Women full of themselves.

THE VOCABULARY OF GOODNESS replaces the sin-based vocabulary we learned in childhood and the habitual "pathologizing" we engage in as adults. It's based on the dual premise that our natural impulses are toward health and wholeness and that self-celebration involves the acceptance of personal responsibility for our actions, choices, and lives.

Personal Ramifications

1. We speak to ourselves with kindness, incorporating self-celebratory affirmations into our inner dialogs:

> *"It is right and good that I am woman. I believe in my goodness. I celebrate my goodness. I will live out of the abundance of who I am as a child of life. I will affirm the original goodness of my children and my children's children until the stories of old hold no sway in their hearts. I am full of myself."*

2. We refuse to pathologize our behaviors. Instead we reflect on the organic explanations for a response or behavior:

Recently a woman was criticizing the dormancy of this season of her life: "I'm not doing anything productive, just laying around, eating and sleeping." She practiced shifting her understanding to a self-celebratory one: "After years of people-pleasing and care-taking, of twisting myself into the expectations of others, of lying in order to fit into a script that didn't work for me, I'm exhausted. Nestled in my precious little cottage, living alone for the first time in 40 years, it's OK for me to "do nothing" while on some deep level of my being I'm shedding the personas of a lifetime and reconnecting to my truest self. I'm in a mid-life cocoon and will emerge again in the fullness of my time."

At a support group, a woman began to criticize the length of the first chapter of her dissertation. She went on for 10 minutes listing all the pathological reasons why she wrote such a "ridiculously long chapter:" she was "too intense;" she was trying to please her dead father; she was sabotaging her career. Midstream, she got tired of the same old words and practiced self-celebration: "I have so many great ideas about my dissertation topic that the first chapter is chock full of them. In the fullness of time, I'll craft my ideas into chapters of readable length. For now though I'll allow the ideas to flow in all their abundance without censorship."

Inter-Personal Ramifications

1. We eliminate the words "I'm sorry" from our vocabulary. Instead we take responsibility for our actions, clearly and directly. Notice the difference in tone and quality between the superficial "I'm sorry" and the responsible alternatives below.

To a friend: "I acknowledge that I'm ten minutes late. I'm available to hear your feelings and responses triggered by my chronic lateness. I'm restructuring my life to allow for more roominess between commitments so this won't happen again."

To office-mates: "I didn't eat lunch on time. As a result, my irritability affected our office atmosphere again. I'll alter my morning work-load to guarantee ample time for lunch so this won't happen again."

2. We refuse to be splattered by someone else's judgments whether expressed directly or indirectly. Instead, we take responsibility for setting contacts-limits with those who gossip and those who tend to "shame and blame."

To a co-worker: "I'm aware that you do not like me or the choices I've made in my life. But it is my life and my life is none of your business. Stop gossiping about me to our co-workers. If you have something to say about the quality of my work as it affects you, speak to me directly and I'll listen."

To an ex-lover: "I take full responsibility for my desire to end our relationship. I know my decision has caused you great pain. I too have experienced the full range of emotion. Yet I made the decision out of respect for myself. I had no choice but to act in accordance with my deepest wisdom. I am no longer available to hear your judgmental tirades about my decision."

3. We support each other to shift from self-criticism to self celebration by reframing self-critical statements into self-celebratory ones.

During a phone conversation, a friend began to batter herself with self-critical language: "I did nothing today. I wasted the whole day vegetating." We decided to explore the meaning of "vegetate." Consulting our dictionaries, we discovered two meanings: to grow in the manner of a plant; to lead a dull inert life. Clearly the second meaning reflects an androcentric bias. Reclaiming the word from years of misuse, my friend reframed her initial criticism into a self-celebration: "During the previous week I have been very creative, gathering images and ideas. They are now vegetating within me. My process is deeply wise and always allows for the essential under-the-ground womb time. A product will come if it is meant to—in the fullness of time."

A woman spoke during the discussion period at a Boulder book event: "I look around the room and see women and men genuinely moved, provoked, and affirmed by this experience. I enjoyed the evening but it didn't affect me the way it affected others. I wonder, what's wrong with me? Will you comment on that?"

I invited her to reframe her perspective: "Consider for a moment that nothing is wrong with you or your response to the evening. Let's explore two alternatives to your self-critical conclusion. First of all, are you Jewish? "Yes," she replied. Well, my work and creativity flow from my own experience which is clearly rooted within the Judeo-Christian tradition. Jewish women find the work interesting but they don't identify as deeply as Catholics and Protestant women do. Secondly, let's consider the "lima bean factor." Lima beans are a pretty color and shape and lots of people like them, but I don't. They do nothing for me. We aren't energetically compatible. Just like it's OK that we don't like certain foods, its OK that we don't like everybody or enjoy every experience. Perhaps it's as simple as your experience was what it was: interesting but not earth shattering. When you stepped outside of your experience to compare it with others, the self-critical question emerged. I support you to stay within your experience and honor it."

Systemic Ramifications

1. We refuse to embrace any set of principles based on the belief in our fundamental sinfulness and defectiveness, or on the necessity of ego-deflation, humiliation, or the surrender of our natural impulses. Instead, we reframe them to reflect our commitment to self-celebration. For example, women are rewriting the Twelve Steps based on their belief in original goodness. Each step now answers the question, "What's good and right about us?" and affirms our natural impulse toward healing and wholeness.

Step 1 as written: We admitted we were powerless over alcohol—that our lives had become unmanageable.

As rewritten: I do not have all the resources I need to deal with my alcoholism. I have reached out for help to AA. This was a brave action on my own behalf. I celebrate my courage today.

Step 8 as written: Made a list of all persons we had harmed, and become willing to make amends to them all.

As rewritten: I will make a list of all persons I have hurt in my life and all persons I have helped. I will take responsibility for my ineffective behaviors that have hurt others. I will celebrate my life-affirming behaviors that have supported others even in the most overwhelming moments of my addiction.

2. We refuse to participate in a pathology-based therapeutic process. When choosing an advocate to support us through life's challenges, we interview therapists carefully to determine if they're willing to co-create woman-affirming solutions and strategies.

She/he recognizes the historical, political, intellectual, and religious context within which women's lives are shaped, and acknowledges these systemic realities while addressing the current challenge.

She/he moves beyond insight and information to facilitate a woman's reconnection to her body and breath, and to her rich inner resources of creativity and wisdom.

She/he supports a woman's journey from passive dependence on experts to trust in her own inner wisdom, from over-responsibility for the lives of others to action on her own behalf, from self-criticism to self-celebration, and from personal recovery to healing action in the world.

THE VOCABULARY OF EQUALITY

WE REJECT the dominance of cultural and religious myths and rituals that excluded the Mother from the creation of the world and the girl-child from the divine. We reject the hierarchically-based messages that convinced us of our inferiority and secondary status in the "natural order," barring us from full participation in the affairs of family, church, community, and world.

WE EMBRACE a woman-affirming perspective, reminding us of our original equality and celebrating the Mother's intimate involvement in the origins of life. In circles of women, we learn of ancient women who didn't apologize for their fertile wombs, pregnant bellies, and full breasts. Women who celebrated themselves as the embodiment of the Mother of All Living. We learn of ancient times when it was from the mother, the giver of life, that the line of the generations was traced. A time when all children born of the mother were legitimate and respectable, and were given her name and social status. We learn of ancient women who did not apologize for their girl-children. Mothers and daughters, full of themselves!

THE VOCABULARY OF EQUALITY has replaced the hierarchically-based vocabulary we learned in childhood and the exclusive language that continues to be used in every arena of life. Through our use of the language of equality, we step into our rightful place beside men. We assume equality in our personal and professional relationships, and in the church, home, and world.

Personal Ramifications

1. We speak to ourselves with self-respect, incorporating self-celebratory affirmations into our inner dialogs:

> *"I celebrate the birth of my daughters, granddaughters, and nieces as I celebrate my own. I believe in their goodness as I believe in my own. I nurture their wisdom as I nurture my own. I cultivate their power as I cultivate my own. We are mothers and daughters, nieces and aunts, girls and women full of ourselves!"*

2. We step into our rightful place in the human community.

> *"I now know it is possible to have healthy and mutual relationships with men. And this is not because the male-dominance of the world is changing. My vision of what is possible is transforming as I develop a loving and respectful relationship with myself. I no longer hate myself. I no longer believe that I am inferior. I walk into every encounter as a whole person expecting respect and mutual-enhancement."*

Inter-Personal Ramifications

1. We are no longer available for relationships based on a one-up, one-down mentality in which men's interests take priority. We assume mutuality. We speak our mind and expect our intimate partners, friends, and associates to listen and acknowledge our thoughts, ideas, and concerns. We express our feelings and expect others to witness them without invalidating how we feel. We bring the fullness of our years, experience, and wisdom into each relationship and expect others to be touched, challenged, and changed by who we are.

> *"I have a full life today that includes special friends, personal projects, and compelling interests. I don't have time to elevate anyone to god status."*

> *"I'm an active participant in work situations. I celebrate the talents and skills I bring to the workplace. I work with men as partners. I'm no longer intimidated by their presence and intelligence."*

> *"I refuse to diminish my life so that others will feel better. I expect peer relationships in which we bring 100 percent of who we are to each exchange. We allow our lives to be enlarged by each other's gifts."*

> *"Today I enjoy the quality of my life, thoughts, and interests. I bring this enjoyment of myself into mixed groups. I expect to be heard with respect and for others to be enlarged as a result of encountering me."*

> *"Arguments are no longer my style of communication. Arguments involve a winner and a loser. I engage in healthy interactions today. We each present our concerns or issues. Then our challenge is to discover a way in which we both win for the greater good of the relationship."*

> *"My own life is most important today. I expect men to take care of their own emotional and spiritual needs in the company of other men. I no longer service them. I expect them to bring fullness rather than emptiness to our relationship. I am drawn to men who have learned to take care of their own practical needs and aren't looking for a mother replacement. And I don't expect a man to be the primary caretaker of my needs. I take responsibility for my own life today. I'm the primary caretaker of myself."*

2. Using Simone de Beauvoir's challenge, we evaluate our relationships to our children and partners.[75] We articulate our commitment to the essential task of designing relationships of equality within our families:

We will bring up our daughters from the first with the same demands and rewards, the same severity and the same freedom, as their brothers, taking part in the same studies, the same games, and promised the same future.

As partners, we will assume on the same basis the material and moral responsibility of our children. The mother will enjoy the same lasting respect, responsibility, economic freedom, and prestige as the father.

We will orient our daughters toward their power and courage, authorizing them to test their powers in work and sports. We will instill into our sons a sense of equality, not superiority. They will be encouraged by the example of their father to look up to women with as much respect as to men.

We will surround our children with women and men who are undoubted equals. They will perceive around them a world of equality in which both women and men have access to the full range of their human capacities.

We will surround our children with images of strong women so our daughters will be proud of themselves and our sons will learn to respect a woman's wholeness. We will surround our children with art, music, poetry, and books by and about women. They will hear of men's accomplishments in the wider world. In our home, women's voices and stories will be heard and respected.

Systemic Ramifications

1. We challenge exclusive language whenever it is spoken and wherever it is written. We choose to alleviate the persistent imbalance of voices, bombarding us daily in newspapers, magazines, and textbooks; sermons and lectures; and in the "official" opinions and perspectives of our Western culture.

Women are rewriting the Twelve Steps to reflect a spirituality of equality.

Step 11 as written: Sought through prayer and meditation to improve our conscious contact with God as we understood him, praying only for knowledge of his will for us and the power to carry that out.

As rewritten: Sought through prayer and meditation to improve our conscious contact with ourselves, praying only for knowledge of our own deep wisdom and the willfulness to carry it out.

Women and men are writing letters to magazines and newspapers to express their outrage at the continued use of exclusive language.

A Letter To The Editor Concerning: "Who Is God" (Life Magazine, December 1990). Written by Patricia Lynn Reilly:

In the introduction to your article, you assign the Supreme Being a gender through the use of that ever-present male pronoun, along with your choice of a picture of god as an old white man with a beard. This image has dominated the imaginations and self-concepts of men and women for centuries. Our imaginations have been held hostage by god the father. The "grandest of human imagination" will most certainly come up with a plurality of faces to inhabit the heavens, and with names that move us beyond the limitations of an exclusively white male god.

A Letter To The Editor Concerning: "The Ultimate Approval Rating" (New York Times Magazine, December 15, 1996). Written by Nick Molinari:

At first, I enjoyed the article. Then, I looked at the list of historians who served as jurors in this ranking of our Presidents. I became aware of a double paradox: All our Presidents have been men; one of the 32 jurors is a woman.

I think I can understand the failure of our society to evolve sufficiently so as to sponsor and elect a woman as President. After all, those who hold power are exceedingly reluctant to surrender it, even among male politicians. Compound that with the tradition of male-Presidents and the resistance to a woman-President becomes hysterical!

But, what is especially disturbing for me, is the second-half of the paradox! By my count, only one/thirty-second of the panel of jurors/historians is a woman.

Any other modern survey purporting to be impartial would be laughed off the press! Even those who would claim this survey to be fair and impartial must at some point wonder how a panel comprised of 96.875% men and 3.125% woman is able to yield an unimpeachable result!

I request that you as Editor contact Arthur M. Schlesinger, Jr. for a follow-up on this ranking of Presidents with a view to my complaint!

2. We refuse to participate in hierarchically-based religious communities. We include ourselves by offering alternatives to the exclusive language and imagery used in the liturgy, hymns, and sermons. We reverse the historic neglect of the women's contributions and concerns by telling our stories.

In a letter to each of the ministers, priests, and rabbis in the community: "I am seeking a woman-affirming spiritual community in which my daughter's birth will be welcomed with as much pomp, circumstance, and opportunity as her brother's; where her body and its processes will not exclude her from participation in religious rituals; and where she will be surrounded by images of a god who looks like her in the presence of clergywomen and women priests. Is yours such a community?"

On a sermon response card: "Although I appreciate your congregation's apparent commitment to social justice, I've been disturbed by your sermons. You use quotations extensively to bolster your theme, yet no woman has ever been quoted. You clarify each point by telling a story from everyday life, yet not one story has included a woman, mother, or daughter. It is understandable that you gather experiences, stories, and quotations based on your male view of the world. I invite you, however, to extend your vision to include women in order to more effectively minister to over half of your congregation."

In response to a request to write a review of a male minister's book: "Although I was moved by many of the stories in your new book, I missed the contributions of women-writers, poets, philosophers, and theologians. It makes great sense that the primary contributors to your understanding of the spiritual life have been men. Yet I have chosen to read, review, and recommend books that deepen a woman's connection to the rich resources of woman-inspired thought, theology, and philosophy, resources that must be reclaimed from the margins of history and religion. I will limit my reviews and recommendations to books written by women."

3. We reject the hierarchical paradigm, appointing therapists, gurus, and experts as the "saviors of women." We refuse to participate in the "healer-patient" therapeutic model. When choosing an advocate to support us through life's challenges, we interview therapists carefully to determine if they have developed a collaborative mentality.

"I am contracting your services to support me through a current life challenge. I will participate fully in our sessions to co-create strategies with which to address this challenge. If at any point, our collaboration does not work for either of us, we will reevaluate our contract and dissolve it if necessary."

THE VOCABULARY OF REVERENCE

WE REJECT the dominance of cultural and religious myths, stories, rituals, and taboos, assaulting a woman's body and her natural processes. We reject the shame-based messages, alienating us from the rich natural resources found within our own body's cycles and rhythms, and depositing within us a dread of the aging process.

WE EMBRACE a woman-affirming perspective that reminds us of the original sacredness and wisdom of our bodies in every season of life and that encourages us to fill up the years of our lives without shame. In circles of women, we read of ancient beliefs that a woman's blood was magic, flowing in harmony with the moon. We recall ancient times when the color of royalty was the dark red wine color of our menstrual blood. We learn of ancient women who did not apologize for their bleeding time. We recall ancient societies that celebrated the accumulation of a woman's years and that respected the menopausal retaining of her wise blood. We learn of ancient post-menopausal women who presided at sacred rituals. Women who did not apologize for the fullness of their years and their wisdom. Women full of themselves!

THE VOCABULARY OF REVERENCE replaces the shame-based messages that assault women's bodies on a daily basis. We retrieve our bodies from centuries of male definitions and expectations. We look at them through our own eyes. We develop our own relationship to them. We create rituals to support and celebrate them through each season of life.

Personal Ramifications

1. We speak to ourselves with reverence, incorporating self-celebratory affirmations into our inner dialogs:

> *"My body is the sacred temple of the spirit of life. My body is an exquisite resource, a faithful ally, and a trustworthy companion. My body is enough, just as it is. My body is holy, there is no blemish. I celebrate the rich natural resources found within my body's rhythms and cycles."*

> *"I fill up the years of my life without shame. I bless the wounded years. I celebrate the comfortable years. I refuse to use my precious life energy to disguise the signs of aging in my body and life. I honor the old woman emerging from within me. I honor the face of the Goddess in my changing face."*

2. We shift from a self-critical relationship to our bodies to a self celebratory one by transforming the changes we dread into a celebration of life's rhythms and cycles.

> *"I am learning to honor the changes I am noticing: Wise muscles tell me to go more slowly and thoughtfully through life. Silver strands fall from my hair, reminding me that I have just said something wise. I am awed by their beauty. I keep them in a red box, covered with silver beads. Laughter lines around my eyes remind me of all the funny stories I have heard, and of all the radiant and sunny days I have squinted to enjoy."*

> *"I am learning to honor the changes I am noticing: My extended belly represents the challenges of life that have stretched me beyond the limitations of childhood. My textured legs and pumping veins have supported my weight and the weight of two babies. My defined face has sharpened with experience. My shoulders tighten and signal times to meditate and to release. My bottom is much looser now; I have let go, I am not so tight and guarded."*

3. We refuse to pathologize our body-challenges. Instead we reflect on their organic causes.

> *"I've gained 15 pounds. I wonder what my body is trying to tell me through this weight gain. My body tends to feel comfortable at a higher weight than I have traditionally accepted for myself. Do I need a sense of weightiness as I become more visible with my gifts in the world? Does my body need a cushion as I enter menopause? I trust that if and when my body no longer needs the weight, it will shed."*

Interpersonal Ramifications

1. We refuse to engage in obsessive conversations centered around the fat content of foods, the current diet, or the latest flaw discovered in the

obsessive scrutiny of our bodies. Instead, we practice using the vocabulary of reverence in our exchanges with other women.

> *"I'm learning so much about my body and what supports it to feel fully engaged in life. I've discovered that foods straight from mother earth provide the most energy and satisfaction. If I eat fresh fruit in the morning, it supports my body's digestive processes. If I eat a big dinner after 6:30, I wake up with an upset stomach so now I'm enjoying vegetable soups for dinner. I'm grateful for the wisdom contained within my body. It's directing me in a step by step transformation of the way I eat and therefore live."*

2. We choose relationships with partners who have the depth and the courage to embrace our bodies through every season of life.

> *"My husband loves all of who I am, including my body. He'll put his hands on parts of my body that I find it difficult to honor, like my stomach when it gets really full around my period, and he'll say, "I love this part of you." He supports me to love the parts of myself I've labeled unacceptable. It's very healing to have such loving affirmations come from the man in my life. I'd always assumed that a man could never love me as I aged. Now I know I didn't love myself. Through the support of women, I've begun to honor who I am. As a result, I've drawn a man of depth into my life who loves my changing body without effort."*

Systemic Ramifications

1. We remind the religious community of the truth of women's lives unacknowledged in their principles, theologies, and liturgies. We challenge the religious community to include rituals honoring menarche, pregnancy and childbirth, and menopause.

In a letter to the minister from the women of the church: "It is important to us that our church include rituals supporting our daughters to love their bodies and to appreciate their life-giving capacities. The Women's Forum has created a celebratory ritual with our adolescent daughters, granddaughters, and nieces. We have invited post-menopausal women to preside at the ritual as they did in ancient times and to share with the younger ones the wisdom of a woman's body. We will read the woman-affirming stories of Eve and Lilith. We will wear red, eat red foods, light red candles, and decorate our sacred meeting place with bright red paint and glitter. We want to offer this celebratory ritual in the church twice a year."

2. As a prayer for our daughters, granddaughters, and nieces that they will travel a less turbulent path to self-celebration, we challenge the obsessive focus on body-grooming in the magazines read by them and the irreverence of magazine and newspaper advertisements featuring young women's bodies.

A Letter To The Editor Concerning the November, 1996 issue of "Young and Modern," Written by Patricia Lynn Reilly:

"I was appalled by just about everything in your current issue.

The cover: "Is His Love For Real? 50 Secret Signs; Never Get Dumped Again! We'll Tell You How; Extra: Your Intimate Beauty Horoscope; Banish Fat Days Forever; Mega Makeover."

The ten categories of the Cover Girl Model Search: Beach Babe, Seriously Sexy, Really Romantic, Majorly Mysterious, Classy Cool, Way Dramatic, Fierce Flirt, Nature Girl, So Glamorous, Mega Modern.

The advertisements: "Breast Boost Without Surgery: Silicone pads that look, feel, weigh, and even bounce like real breast. So natural they're undetectable."

Is it any wonder our daughters start asking the question "what's wrong with me" by the time they are 10. Your magazine supports them to resent their own bodies as they scrutinize artificial images of models and actresses whose perfection is defined by a misogynistic culture and whose beauty is created by lights and make-up. Your magazine supports their growing urge to cover, starve, and violently alter their precious bodies. Numb and bored, our young women are waiting, often in front of a mirror, for a prince to come along and make their lives worth living.

For the sake of our daughters, change your message and your image. Support them to know, love, and trust themselves. Support them to develop the full range of their human capacities. Support them to kiss sleeping beauty good-bye and to awaken to their own lives. Include images of strong athletic women, supporting their bodies to grow and develop organically. Include images of intelligent women, refusing to twist their bodies out of shape. Include images of wise women with fully formed lives, refusing to set them aside in order to pursue men."

THE VOCABULARY OF SELF-POSSESSION

WE REJECT the dominance of cultural and religious myths and theologies that exiled self-possessed women and elevated submissive women who relinquished the ownership of their bodies, the authorship of their lives, and the naming of their experience. We reject the dependency-based messages that emphasized our inability to control our own destinies and to function independently in our own lives.

WE EMBRACE a woman-affirming perspective, reminding us of our original self-possession. In circles of women, we recall ancient times when virginity meant a woman who was "one in herself," owned by no man, author of her own life, and creator of her own destiny. We learn of ancient women who did not apologize for their self-possession. Women who refused to surrender the ownership of their bodies except to their natural rhythms and cycles. Women who refused to surrender the authorship of their lives except to their deepest wisdom. Women who refused to surrender the naming of their experience except to their inner truth. Women full of themselves!

THE VOCABULARY OF SELF-POSSESSION has replaced the dependency-based vocabulary of our socialization and our chronic tendency to abdicate our lives to the design and specifications of others. From a self-possessed center, we simply acknowledge our thoughts, feelings, experience, reality, and truth as they pertain to our own responses and responsibilities in daily life.

Personal Ramifications

1. We speak to ourselves with strength, incorporating self-celebratory affirmations into our inner dialogs:

> "My body is my own. *I will not allow the standards of others to twist it out of shape.* My thoughts are my own. *I will not allow them to be molded by others.* My feelings are my own. *I will not allow them to be expressed by others.* My life is my own. *I will allow it to be shaped by the expectations of others. I refuse to surrender my self-possession to the dictates and specifications of others. I will live in harmony with my natural rhythms and cycles, my deepest wisdom, and my truest self. I am full of myself!*"

2. Having reclaimed our inner natural resources, our first question when faced with a life challenge is "What inner resources do I have to address this challenge?" We begin by consulting our own feelings, thoughts, intuition, and bodily sensations. They will escort us on the journey toward a creative solution.

> "*I notice that I become irritated in the presence of a colleague. Clearly the irritation is mine. I'll take responsibility for it and get to know it before I dump it on her. I'll begin by paying attention to the feelings and thoughts that pass through me when I'm in her office next week.*"

> "*I notice a growing sexual attraction to my daughter's teacher. It's my attraction and I wonder what it's telling me about myself. I'll take responsibility for it by paying special attention to my body and its sexual needs this week.*"

Inter-Personal Ramifications

With courage and respect for our own lives, we no longer hide our truth within convoluted narratives and indirect explanations. We make direct statements in response to the requests of others, set clear limits in our interactions with others, and offer respectful solutions to the interpersonal challenges, confronting us daily. Initially, our use of the vocabulary of self-possession is awkward. Eventually, our responses become graceful and effective. Highlight the phrases relevant to your current interpersonal challenges.

To a spouse who disapproves of his/her partner's dress, music, or friends: "I'll be considerate of your preferences when appropriate but I'm unwilling to eliminate those things that bring me joy and pleasure."

To a daughter who will not deal directly with her father: "I am no longer available as the go-between in conflicts with your father. I support you to speak to your father directly."

To a mother who gives unsolicited advice: "I appreciate your concern for me, Mom, but I need to find my own way through this problem and would prefer you help by just listening."

To a sibling who is irritable in response to a change in the ground rules: "I am unwilling to give you advice anymore. I understand how uncomfortable this change is for you, yet it has been crucial to my emotional health to back off and allow you and others to find your own way without my interference."

To a partner who complains daily about his job: "I can't do anything to change your situation and it makes me crazy to hear you repeat this litany over and over again. Only you have the power to change your situation. Please limit what you tell me about it."

To the family at the end of a day filled with intense interactions: "I need time alone to read and write for the rest of the evening. I'm unavailable to anyone from this point on."

To a neighbor who asks for a ride: "It won't work for me to give you a ride because my time is limited today."

To a friend: "I don't enjoy our interactions. They are no longer supportive to me. I need some time away from the friendship. Let's touch base in a month to see if things have shifted for me."

In response to an invitation: "Thank-you for the invitation but that particular event doesn't interest me. I enjoy your company so let's find an activity of interest to both of us."

In response to an employer's request: "I'm unwilling to take on any more projects without additional compensation and the readjustment of my basic job description."

In response to a friend's request to participate in her/his project:

"Thanks for thinking of me, but I don't have the time to work with you now. My own projects demand all of my energy and attention."

In response to a request to become a member of the board of directors: "Thank you for asking me, but I don't want to commit to a long-term and time-consuming job. Please keep me in mind for short-term projects."

In response to a request to shift to a committed relationship: "I'm attracted to you and would like to date occasionally. I also want to date others so a committed relationship is not possible at this time."

THE VOCABULARY OF WILLFULNESS

WE REJECT the dominance of cultural and religious myths and theologies that exiled willful women, portraying us as powerless victims incapable of independent thought and action, of self-determining choice, and of the successful implementation of our desires in the world. We reject the passivity-based messages that required the surrender of our wills to the dictates of others.

WE EMBRACE a woman-affirming perspective that reminds us of our original willfulness. In circles of women, we remember ancient women who valued their willfulness and who encouraged their daughters to know their own will and to believe it was valid and achievable in the world. We remember ancient ways that taught women to refuse submission and subordination and applauded women for their assertiveness. Women who exerted, initiated, and moved in their own behalf without shame or guilt and in harmony with their own deep wisdom. Women full of themselves!

THE VOCABULARY OF WILLFULNESS has replaced the passivity-based vocabulary fed to us since childhood. No longer waiting for a deliverer to come, we take responsibility to implement our desires in the world. No longer accepting spectator status, we choose to participate fully in our lives. No longer asking "what's wrong with me," we change what isn't working and celebrate what is.

Personal Ramifications

Supported by our willfulness, we take action in our own behalf by acknowledging what works for us and going after it, and by acknowledging what doesn't work for us and changing it.

1. We speak to ourselves with courage, incorporating self-celebratory affirmations into our inner dialogs:

> *"I no longer look outside myself for salvation. I've reclaimed my own willfulness. I am capable of independent thought and action, of self-determining choice, and of the successful implementation of my desires in the world. I exert, initiate, and move in my own behalf."*

2. No longer accepting depression as a fact of our existence, we regularly inventory our lives to notice what's working and what isn't. Calling upon our inner and outer support systems, we change what we can and let go of what we can't.

> *"It's not working for me to eat dinners alone. I will invite my unpartnered friends to share meals with me three times a week, possibly rotating to each other's homes."*

> *"My job is depleting me. I refuse to use my precious life energy complaining about what isn't working. I will speak to my boss and arrange for a four day work week. This will free up an extra day for my creative projects while the kids are in school."*

> *"My apartment is cluttered with the stuff of the past. Every time I walk into it, I cringe. I will spend this week-end sorting and cleaning. I will hire the neighbor kid to help once I've brought some order to the mess. When completed, I will invite my women's group over to bless the apartment's new life."*

Inter-Personal Ramifications

1. No longer settling for relationships that don't work, we regularly evaluate them, express our concerns, and invite participation in the co-creation of solutions that work for us.

> *"I am no longer willing to reach out to you on a regular basis unless you meet me half-way. I am unavailable for relationships that are not mutual. If you value our time together, please call and make the arrangements for our next get together."*

> *"I am unavailable to hear another litany of complaints about your marriage. If and when you become ready to co-create solutions or to take action in your own behalf, I will gladly listen. Until then, let's talk about other areas of interest for the two of us."*

> *"I am no longer available to support you through your current life challenge. You broke two of our agreements: you did not call me concerning your Al-Anon commitment and you did not call to cancel your Monday session. When you are ready to act with integrity in your own behalf, give me a call."*

"This is the third time you've been late to pick the kids up for the weekend. Out of respect for the children's anticipation of your arrival and in recognition of the importance of my week-end plans, I ask you to redesign your Friday afternoons. Or arrange for a friend or colleague to pick the children up and bring them to your office. If it happens again, we must sit down with the mediator and co-create a solution that works for all of us."

"My life is full at this time. I do not have the time or energy to engage in these daily conversations. It works for me to check in weekly. And I support you to extend your circle of support to include others who can be there for you on a daily basis."

"My financial resources are limited. I'm saving for a house for me and my children. I'm unable to lend you the money you need. I support you to address the underlying concerns which have created your financial vulnerability. Here's a meeting schedule for the Debtors Anonymous groups in the area."

"Given the shifts in my schedule, it no longer works for me to prepare the dinner every evening. I would appreciate sharing that responsibility with you. I can handle it on Tuesday, Thursday, and the weekend. Will you cook the other nights? Or should we hire a cook?"

2. From a place of self-possession and willfulness, women are experimenting with intimate relationships. Their eyes are open. Their senses are engaged. Their choices are wiser because they trust what they see and what they sense. Based on the cumulative wisdom of their lives, they have clarified what works for them and what doesn't in an intimate relationship.

I encourage women to write a self-celebration in which they boldly acknowledge their vision of "A Matching Yes." Here is a sample taken from my own journal. I use it to evaluate potential partners. Yes, full of themselves women have the audacity to pick and choose. Who do they think they are!?!?

Healing into the present: My past remains within me. I have acknowledged it. I have walked through it. I am healing into the present. *I choose partners* who are aware of the past's influence on the present. Who have faithfully walked through the past. Who are aware of historic vulnerabilities and take responsibility for their own stuff.

Being present in the moment: I have worked hard to be able to breathe into this moment without the clutter of an unresolved past and without projection into an unknown future. I love the moment and its unfolding. *I choose partners* who are available in this moment. Who are attentive and aware. Who stay in touch with their feelings, needs, and wants. Who acknowledge what is true for them in the moment.

Feeling in the moment: I delight in feeling a full range of emotions. Without tightning, I breathe into each feeling. They offer me precious information about myself and my responses to the experiences of life. *I choose partners* who have befriended their feelings and are able to articulate them. Partners who do not categorize feelings as good or bad. All feelings will be welcomed in the relationship.

Living a conscious life: I am awake to my life. I pay attention to it. It is my teacher, healer, and challenge. I dance, draw, and write through its challenges, lessons, and healing. *I choose partners* who do not use drugs of any type. Partners who are awake to life and pay attention to it. Who embrace its gifts, lessons, and challenges.

Living a joyful life: I am playful, energetic, and alert. I have reclaimed my original vitality. I am unwilling to use my precious life energy in managing crisis and conflict. Instead, I choose graceful relationships that deepen in satisfaction and contentment without depleting my creativity and joy. *I choose partners* for whom crisis and conflict are not the drugs of choice. Partners who have developed the relationship skills necessary to dance gracefully through challenging moments. Who are committed to a joyful life.

Living an accountable life: I am accountable to certain principles of living I have gathered through my association with the recovery, psychological, Quaker, Unitarian, and women's communities. *I choose partners* who are accountable to a vision that is larger, deeper, and wider than themselves. Partners who consult this vision, whether it is a set of principles, spiritual practices, psychological understandings, or tools for living. Who are not lone rangers.

Significant creative expression: I have reclaimed the well-spring of creativity within me. Daily, it flows through me in song, movement, poetry, essays, letters, workshops, meditations, retreats, and creative relationships. *I choose partners* who are in touch with their own creativity. Partners who welcome and encourage shared creative adventures.

Deepening sexual intimacy: My body has healed. I have reclaimed my original erotic potential. There is nothing to hide. There is nothing to withhold. All will be accepted. *I choose partners* who are willing to explore all levels of sexuality. Partners who say YES to all the rises between us. Who let go into the dance of our affection.

Living a woman-affirming life: I am 47 years old. In circles of women, I have healed of the self-criticism that accompanies a woman's aging. Today, I refuse to spend my precious life energy disguising the signs of aging. Rather, I celebrate the accumulation of my years and wisdom, and the changes in my body and life. I choose relationships with women and men who have the courage and depth to embrace all of who I am and will become in the next decades of my life. *I choose partners* who have acknowledged their own issues around aging. Partners who celebrate the fullness of my years, experience, power, and wisdom.

THE VOCABULARY OF CONNECTION

WE REJECT the dominance of cultural and religious attitudes, fostering rivalry and suspicion among women. We reject the competition-based attitudes, setting women up to compete with each other for the attention of men. We reject the homophobic messages, alienating us from each other and from the organic resources available in women-centered relationships. We refuse to give credence to attitudes and fears designed to keep us separate.

WE EMBRACE a woman-affirming perspective, reminding us of our original connection and solidarity with all women past, present, and future. In circles of women, we recall ancient times when daughters celebrated their essential connection to the mother from whom they came and to whom they returned. We remember ancient women who valued each other and sat in circles to tell their stories and to remind each other of the truth. We remember women who did not apologize for their love of women. Women full of themselves . . . and each other!

THE VOCABULARY OF CONNECTION replaces the competition- and separation-based vocabulary we learn in a society that revolves around men. It supports us to reclaim the right to define our own relationships. It reaffirms our primary connection to women as we embrace our primary connection to ourselves.

Personal Ramifications

1. We speak to ourselves with integrity, incorporating self-celebratory affirmations into our inner dialogs:

> *"I am developing intimate and honest relationships with beautiful, powerful, intelligent, and spiritual women. I no longer see them as a threat. They are a part of me and together we all become beautiful and strong. I am learning to love women as I learn to love myself."*

2. We take responsibility for our competitive attitudes and behaviors by acknowledging the women we have been jealous of, gossiped about, called names or slandered, and competed with for the attention of a man. We become willing to make amends by changing our behaviors.

> *"I will make amends for my competitive attitudes by strengthening my relationships with women and giving them support rather than focusing on receiving the approval of men at work and in other settings. My colleagues and I are struggling to keep from feeling inferior to men so we compete with each other for their attention. I will make amends by learning to express appreciation and support, and by affirming our solidarity as women."*

Interpersonal Ramifications

1. We spend more time in the company of women and less time swirling around men. Women are no longer just fillers in between our relationships. They are the ground of our support.

> *"The community of women abides with me, comforts me, and provides me with a kind of security that a male lover can never do. The point is that I am a woman. The struggles and triumphs that other women experience as they go through life can guide and inform me as only women can."*

> *"As my connections with women have grown, my relationship with my partner occupies a smaller place in my life. My partner no longer dominates my life, thoughts, and feelings. He has diminished in significance and in psychological size. I am clearer. I have my own life. I can do things completely apart from him. I make my own decisions. I know what I think and feel. My relationship has changed so much. It's a new and different organism."*

2. We no longer turn primarily to men to meet our needs or to answer our questions. Many of our emotional, spiritual, and intellectual needs are now met by women.

> *"In the past, I expected my partner to take care of my feelings and to always be present for me. I don't have these expectations any more. He's just one thread in a big tapestry of support that surrounds my life. There are many times when I feel anxious or upset, or when I need to think an issue through with someone, and I don't go to him. I'm happy to go to the women in my life. I share with them my challenges and my celebrations."*

> *"Before being in a women's community I wasn't aware of how strongly my search for truth was influenced by the male images of God. Nor was I aware of how these images invalidated me as a woman. It had never occurred to me to look toward a nurturing, strong, and feminine image of the divine. I've realized AT LAST that what women offer is far more in alignment with what I've been seeking. Now, I'm drawn to articles, books, and films written by women that deal with women's spiritual quests."*

3. We incorporate woman-supporting behaviors into our lives.

We complement our friends' successes and support them to be full of themselves.

In mixed groups focused on men's concerns and accomplishments, we acknowledge the presence of women. We listen to their stories and concerns.

We refuse to be the middle person between friends and colleagues, and those who may have an "issue" with them. Instead, we challenge the complainer to take responsibility for her own feelings and responses by talking to the person directly.

We refuse to participate in the dramas of others. Women who operate out of a "victim" mentality create dramas and then form clubs in defense of their positions. Rather than joining their "club," we invite them to take responsibility for their own feelings and projections by talking to their sponsor or therapist.

4. We choose celebratory and creative relationships with women. If a friend is unwilling to shift from competition to support, we respectfully bring closure to the relationship.

A letter to end a fragile friendship:
"The distance of the last months has been because it no longer felt comfortable to be "full of myself" around you. I was never sure if you would respond with joy or jealousy when I shared my courageous strides to be faithful to my calling in the world. At moments you have offered me precious support and in others, you have withdrawn your support.

I have come to believe that ours is a fragile connection and that I need to be surrounded in my closest, most intimate circle by women who celebrate each other's fullness without reservation. I am in a flowering time, the culmination of many years of transformational work. My life is full of creativity, feeling, health, clarity, and joy. I do not choose to apologize for my life, my feelings, nor my successful work.

During our last encounter, you told me you were angry because I didn't apologize for my life, because I wasn't quiet about my contentment: "Can't you be a little less confident about yourself?" were your parting words. In that moment the distance between us was born . . . out of love and respect for myself. I refuse to diminish my life so you will feel better."

WOMEN'S STORIES
The Language of Self-Celebration

A Red Gift   *Rita Reed*

While making love with a new partner, I mentioned that I had a tampon in. Although he merely nodded, I sensed that my bleeding was an issue for him. I felt disappointed at the thwarting of our sexual rhythm. I felt worried, too. What other revulsions about bodies and women did this imply? But I also felt compassion, and a strong willingness to nurture our relationship, rather than to instruct him or defend myself. We discussed it. He confirmed that he did have negative feelings about blood in general, and menstrual blood in particular. And I told him of the dilemma of vanity and principle it posed for me.

Then I posed the situation to myself as a creative problem: What could I do that would honor both his feelings and my own? How could I respect the fact that in this culture many men are, for complicated human and archetypal reasons, fearful of and revolted by the mystery of women's bodily functions? And how could I respect the fact that as a human woman through whom this mystery pours every month I need to be accepted and, yes, found lovely?

The solution came to me in the computer store. I would ask him to give me a small red present each month. It could be as simple, I explained, as buying a spool of red ribbon and supplying me with a stick on which he could tie a piece of the ribbon each month. He eagerly accepted the idea. I was touched by his willingness to embrace the issue as his own, while simultaneously recognizing its effect on me. He has not yet given me his gift, but I trust that we will use this ritual to further the tenderness and respect between us.

Many Options   *Karen Heide*

There have been many opportunities for me to develop a self-critical response to my choice not to have children. The most frequent self-criticism formed by societal expectations has been: "You're selfish—how could you not want to have children when its our biological destiny as women to give birth? You'll be an incomplete woman." And then comes the voice of family expectations: "All of your siblings have children except for you. It's not like you can't have children, Karen—you're choosing not to, which is an outrageous and unnatural choice! No one in our Michigan community has made that choice except when infertile—and that's always considered a pitiful condition." On a subtler level, the internalized voice of my mother adds, "Look how I sacrificed for you kids all those years, and you're not going to do the same? The lot of a woman's life is to do what's expected even if she wishes to do something different." Compounding the effect of these messages is the lingering image of Mother Mary in my Catholic girl heart—a good and virtuous woman surrenders to her God-given calling. To choose otherwise makes one vulnerable to the wrath of God.

As I sit in circles of women the language of self-criticism is being replaced by an acceptance and celebration of my choice. In Michigan there were no other options offered to women—the mother-script was set from early on. Now I have been introduced to alternatives. I hear the stories of women who are full of themselves—creative, powerful women with rich and satisfying lives who have chosen not to give birth to children. They are not selfish women. Some made their choice based on a commitment to the children already on the planet, needing their nurturance and support. Some have chosen to turn their creative energy toward their work in the world. Others have never had any interest or inclination to have children. Although I love children and chose to be a pediatric nurse, hearing these women's stories helped me to accept the fact that I've never wanted to have my own children.

Today I can state my decision clearly—even in the face of family and societal misunderstandings. I choose to use my available life-energy in service of my own healing journey and spiritual practice, and toward the development of my career. Motherhood is one among many valuable options to tap into our creativity as women—and it's not the way that I choose.

Today I know that any decision brings with it a whole range of emotion. As my biological clock ticks away, there will be times of sadness for possibilities lost just as every mother I know grieves the dreams and aspirations she set aside to carry out her choice. For the first thirty years of my life I didn't know the purpose for my life. For the past seven years, I have become clear that I'm a spiritual being on a spiritual path and that my purpose is to know my essential and true nature. For many women giving birth to and nurturing their children is the spiritual path they choose. Today I honor their choice and my own.

Learning a New Language   *Kate Wolf-Pizor*

I am the daughter of a strong woman. She gained her power from the "old boys' network." Her decision to reject her femaleness in pursuit of professional success brought struggle and sorrow to our relationship. She rejected the "feminine" in favor of the clarity of logic and the hierarchy of the academic ladder. She expected logic and academia to save me also. I fulfilled some of her expectations by getting a B.A. with honors in philosophy. To achieve academic success, I hid my intuitive knowledge by disguising it as research or burying it in the words of an accepted authority. I felt like I was speaking a foreign language. I longed for a native tongue of my own. When I read Simone de Beauvoir's concept of woman as "other," I felt as if the term had been invented from my own experience.

I became a therapist in part to bring my "feminine" self out of hiding and to learn to use my native qualities and language in service of healing and transformation. Fortunately a few other therapists were rejecting the pathology-based medical model when I entered the profession. A female supervisor insisted that I already knew enough and that my challenge was to learn to listen to myself and to my clients.

By the time I read *A God Who Looks Like Me,* I realized that my personal dissatisfaction with speaking the foreign language of patriarchy was a common experience among women. The book inspired me to join a group of women searching for a self-understanding, a language, and a spirituality that resonated with our experience as women. There was no leader to show us the way. The book reminded us of what we already knew. We spoke a common language. We were heard by each other and deeply understood. Sisterhood is a hard-earned luxury in a society that continues to teach women to compete for the attention of men.

As a therapist, my most valuable instrument is not technique but knowledge of and trust in myself. My journey to self-celebration has profoundly affected the way I practice my incredible profession. The trust placed in me by a client carries with it a sacred obligation. I fulfill that obligation by respecting each client's personal authority and by witnessing each client's journey toward self-celebration. The power of transformation is already at work in each client's life and my role as witness is to affirm the faithfulness of that process. I notice. I listen. I believe. My capacity "to witness with respect" flows from the certain knowledge that I am a miracle among miracles and that the valuable processes of human growth need to be witnessed.

PARENTING IN A NEW VOICE   *Erin Louise Stewart*

My children and I are healing into the present and breaking the cycle of violence and dysfunction I inherited from my family of origin. We respectfully share life with each other, honoring the places where we meet and where we separate. We are co-creating a life that works for all three of us. We have chosen a daily pace that supports us to be present with each other, in balance, cooperation, and joy. We have created a tribe—my children are surrounded by affirming and respectful people. Each friend brings a unique richness to their lives. They are made fuller as we sit in circles of full-of-themselves women and men.

Savoi

My son is being gifted with the feminine. Most men are taught to reject the feminine on their way to becoming men. Their lives are out of balance. My son has been surrounded by the feminine to balance the input he gets from the wider world. He will not have as hard a time embracing new ways, being open and flexible, and exploring his own questions. He will not be limited to living in the very small world men find themselves in when they exile the feminine.

He's going to be a gentler soul, a kinder spirit. He's going to operate from a softer place. This will not diminish his strength and power. He has all of that, too. I don't negate his maleness. I give him a full circle way of being that is inclusive of all. There is room for him to design his own limits, to carve out what he wants to do, and to honor his unique vision.

My son faces a big challenge. He is black in a society where young black men are becoming extinct. His father died a violent death at 39. He will need much more than I can ever give him to survive. I'm limited, and yet what I have given him is very powerful. When I speak to him about the challenges he will face, I feel no tightness in my abdomen, where I hold most of my anxiety. I feel confident that I have done my very best. My son's heart is expansive. His vision is clear. His posture toward life is strong and compassionate. I feel very hopeful.

Moizeé

I have such a strong connection with my daughter. She reminds me of the girl child I once was. She is perfect. I look at her and I don't see any flaws. Everything I celebrate in her reminds me of my true nature. As I parent her in the way I wish I had been parented, the child in me is healed.

When I think of my daughter, deep emotion rises. From the depth of my heart, I say to her, "I don't want you to ever be abused. I don't want your power to be squashed." And from the depth of my soul, I stand up loud and strong for her. I tell her, "Be loud and strong. Shout as much as you want. Be full of yourself. Shine as bright as you can. Be quiet and vulnerable. Hide whenever you need to. I celebrate your energy, your challenging spunky nature, your clear YESes, and your very clear NOs. I celebrate your humor, your beauty, and your body."

I don't want my daughter to be set aside as we struggle for the survival of our black men. I don't want her to have to carry the legacy of strong black women who are required to endure against any odds and who believe pain and suffering are the lot of a woman's life. I don't want her to be stronger and harder and more protective than she needs to be. I don't want her to be consumed by fear.

My connection to the women's community isn't what gives my daughter her strength, spunk, voice, and clarity. These are her true essence. What the women's community does is support her so she can hold onto these qualities. Women will be there for her when the pressures start and she's told to shut up her clear voice, to quiet down her vitality, to tone down her colorful expressions. When she's told to care for others at the expense of her own well-being. When she's pressured to follow the script, to have babies, to live a traditional way of life. Through the women's community she's been given another voice that's louder and stronger. A voice surpassing those other voices because it sings the truth. A voice affirming what she already knows and reminding her of what's already there within her.

PRACTICING SELF-CELEBRATION
TRANSFORMING YOUR INNER DIALOG

Self-Criticism: Your Inner Critic

1. What does your inner critic sound like?

"It sounds like a broken record. Its messages are repetitive, shaming, and exhausting. They drain life energy, invite self-doubt, erode self-confidence, and lead to immobilization".

2. How does self-criticism affect the choices you make?

"I signed up for a writing class which has been a life-long dream of mine. The morning of the first class I tried to fight off the critical voice: "Who do you think you are? Do something more productive with your time. Your writing is inferior to your brother's. Don't rock the boat." I wasn't successful. I decided not to go to the class because I developed a stomach ache."

3. Write a story from your own experience. How has your inner critic affected the choices you've made?

Self-Celebration: Your Inner Advocate

1. What does an inner advocate sound like?

"Its voice is energizing and refreshing. Its messages support me to take full responsibility for life; to step across each threshold into unscripted relationships, unfamiliar challenges, and uncharted creative, financial, and vocational adventures; and to feel the fear and show up for life anyway."

2. How does self-celebration support you?

"I signed up for a writing class. The week before the first class I gathered together a group of friends. I told them about my creative adventure. I asked them to support me in the next week by leaving specific messages on my machine: "We believe in your gifts. We support you to follow your dreams and express your gifts. We encourage you to feel all of your feelings while you act on your own behalf." The morning of my first class I called several friends to receive their encouragement and support. I showed up for the class, felt all of my feelings, and began to write the novel that has been percolating in my mind and heart since adolescence."

3. Rework your story from Part I with a different ending. Describe how your inner advocate will support you.

PRACTICING SELF-CELEBRATION
TELLING THE TRUTH

Women, full of themselves, make direct statements in response to the requests of others, set clear limits in their interactions with others, and offer respectful solutions to their interpersonal challenges. With courage and respect for their own lives, they no longer hide their truth within convoluted narratives and indirect explanations.

1. List the interpersonal challenges you are facing. For example:

With Whom	Nature of Challenge
My mother.	She gives me advice. She won't just listen.
My boss.	She disregards our agreements.
My lover.	He calls late at night after my bedtime.

With Whom	Nature of Challenge
_____	_____
_____	_____
_____	_____

2. Re-read the interpersonal ramifications of the vocabulary of self-possession, highlighting the responses relevant to your situation. Gather a truth-telling vocabulary to use in your particular interpersonal challenges.

3. Reread your list of interpersonal challenges. Practice truth-telling with the support of the samples you've read. For example:

Nature of Challenge	Truth-Telling
My mother gives me advice.	#3
My boss disregards our agreements.	#10
My lover calls late at night.	Please don't call me after 10.

Nature of Challenge	Truth-Telling
_____	_____
_____	_____
_____	_____

3. Address one of your interpersonal challenges each week for the next month by writing a letter, making a phone call, or arranging an in-person encounter. Tell the simple truth!

8

A Circle of Women Full of Themselves

I am so perfect so divine so ethereal
I cannot be comprehended
except by my permission
I mean . . . I . . . can fly
like a bird in the sky . . .

—NIKKI GIOVANNI, *ego-tripping*

We've come a long way from the groups described in the introduction in which the self-critical question "what's wrong with me" reigned undisturbed. Having ousted the question from our hearts, minds, bodies, and lives, we no longer second-guess our impulses, we trust them; we no longer pathologize our decisions, we take responsibility for them; we no longer theorize about our feelings, we feel them; we no longer endlessly process our relationships and lives, we participate in them; and we no longer attribute positive achievement to an external force of one sort or another, we celebrate our own stunning capacities as children of life.

Today we begin our circles with a simple meditation, inviting those present to come home to their breath, body, and inner life. We conclude the meditation with these words, "Turn a merciful eye toward yourself. Look upon yourself with loving kindness and notice what it is you delight in and appreciate about yourself today." We then introduce ourselves and share what we noticed in the meditation: we appreciate ourselves out loud! Imagine sitting in a circle where it is not unusual to hear a woman say, "I have no issues to work on. I am deeply satisfied with my life today. I trust my ability to make life-affirming choices. I am grateful to have felt the full range of human emotion today."

The journey from self-criticism to self-celebration was a warrior's journey through the critical words, images, experiences, and expectations that cluttered our historical and personal landscape. The journey transformed our inner worlds. We experienced a complete reversal of everything we were taught to believe about ourselves. The journey has led us home to our own inner resources and capacities.

The journey from self-criticism to self-celebration has been a shared journey. We joined women from every age who have committed the forbidden act of stepping outside of systems of thought and belief that denied their very existence. Inspired by them, we have become intellectually, spiritually, and emotionally arrogant women who trust ourselves and our own experience. We refuse to ask the question "what's wrong with me." We make a powerful statement with every thought we share, every feeling we express, and every action we take in our own behalf.

The journey from self-criticism to self-celebration was an essential journey. Our beloved planet is in desperate need of women full of themselves. We design woman-affirming solutions to address the challenges confronting humankind as it enters the 21st century. We give birth to images of inclusion, poems of truth, rituals of healing, experiences of transformation, relationships of equality, and households of compassion. We are women full of ourselves!

A CIRCLE OF SUPPORT AND CELEBRATION

The final step on the journey from self-criticism to self-celebration is to practice self-celebration in the company of women who are full of themselves. Here in Chapter 8, you are invited to sit in a circle of twenty-six women. Shameless women, who are taking full responsibility for their lives. Powerful women, who have awakened to the truth about themselves. Courageous women, who have assumed their rightful place in the human community. Generous women, who support other women to be full of themselves. Grateful women, who are expanded by the fullness of their sisters. They will celebrate their bodies, their capacity to feel, their rich creativity, their self-defined spirituality and lives, the lessons of their ordinary lives, and their willful presence in the world. At the end of each section, add your poetry, prose, or collage of celebration to theirs. Take this opportunity to practice self-celebration in the privacy of your own home and heart. By the time you finish the chapter, you will be ready to invite your friends and colleagues to join you. Everything needed to start a "Be Full of Yourself!" group is included at the end of the chapter.

CELEBRATING WOMAN

Imagine a woman who believes it is right and good she is woman.

A woman who honors her experience and tells her stories.

Who refuses to carry the sins of others within her body and life.

Imagine a woman who has acknowledged the past's influence on the present.

A woman who has walked through her past.

Who has healed into the present.

Imagine a woman who values the women in her life.

A woman who sits in circles of women.

Who is reminded of the truth about herself when she forgets.

THE PUZZLE

I use to wonder why my period didn't begin
        on the same date every month
Why only boys could be un-cursed,
            and athletic,
                and reliable.
Why I couldn't quite get with it and be regular.
But now I know it wasn't me at all.
It's men's calendar that's irregular—missing the Moon!

I use to wonder why it seemed bad to be so smart.
Why only boys could be mathematicians,
            and generals,
               and composers.
Why I couldn't quite get with it and be a housewife.
But now I know it wasn't me at all.
It's men's history that's ignorant—missing the Women!

I use to wonder why I wasn't happy
        teaching the way I was trained.
Why only boys could be professors,
            and principals,
              and presidents.
Why I couldn't quite get with it and be authoritarian.
But now I know it wasn't me at all.
It's men's educational system that's upside down—missing the Children!

Karla Crescenta

I use to wonder why a scar on the earth made me hurt too.
Why only boys could be architects,
                    and planners,
                            and rearrangers.
Why I couldn't quite get with it and enjoy consuming.
But now I know it wasn't me at all.
It's men's ecology that's out of balance—missing Mother Earth!

I use to wonder why I had to wear a hat to church.
Why only boys could be acolytes,
                    and priests,
                            and gods.
Why I couldn't quite get with it and really believe.
But now I know it wasn't me at all.
It's men's religion that's un-believable—missing the Great Goddess!

I used to wonder a lot why I felt like the misfit piece
                            of some huge puzzle.
But now I know that was all backwards.
I AM THE PUZZLE, searching for the lost pieces
            like the Women
                    and the Children
                            the Mother Earth
                                    the Great Goddess
                                            and the Wondrous Moon.

Karla Crescenta is a Montessorian, Mediator, Artist, Ceremonialist, and Aqua-therapist. In 1981 she published Daughter of the Lady Moon. Slowly she's spinning "South Witch"—the story of Dorothy's Crone-age return to Oz in search of Glinda's previously unmentioned sister. Her vision includes a Wellness/Art/Communication center at her hotspring property, and a circular off-the-grid co-operative home.

THE LESSON PLAN

There comes a time
when the lack
of
education

Becomes
an education
in itself

You see
one starts to understand
deeply
with her
soul and cells
the barricades

My formalized learning
the lessons
in your books and annals

I find them
simply
lacking

Utterly void
of me

This is my first lesson
which I will
smash
with a hammer
the kind they use at
carnivals

Maria D. Ramos

you lift it up
behind your head
   and the weight of it
comes down   hard
DING!

Now I see the fat lady
inside of me
and the two headed wonder

when I look in the mirrors
I'm tall, lanky
short and stubby
wide   oval
it all depends on how you
look at it

Here's how I'm looking at it
I'm going back in time
gonna talk to Harriet Tubman about freedom
and the slave who killed her baby child about resistance
the sterilized mother in Puerto Rico about the Pope
the bride with no dowry about poverty
the maid servant who was raped about power
Sonia Johnson about mormons
Margaret Sanger about birth control

I'm going back in time to talk to the
Virgin of Guadalupe about religion
Sappho about romance
my great great great grandmother about history
the gypsy women about life

I'm gonna ask Cinderella how she feels now
and visit the witch that haunted Hansel and Gretel.

They all have my answers
    or my questions

I'm going to ask Miss Manners
if
I should write thank you cards to
Assata Shakur, Yvonne Wanrow, Lorena Bobbit and Ellie Nestler
for teaching me about what
Darwin might have meant
today
by survival of the fittest

Queen Liliuokalani
can teach me about the conquest

and Roza Robota
    the Jewish woman who helped bomb a gas chamber
    in Auschwitz-Birkenau
    her last words before execution
    "be strong, be brave"
    That's a lesson

and lazy Susan
    I want her secret
    the recipe of the adjective
    of rebellion
    to the kitchen, perhaps
    what did she do with her extra time
    that "lazy Susan"?

I want to meet Necessity
   she's invention's Mother
   I know she has a lot to share

Joan of Arc
once met me for a vision
it was outside in the moonlight
near a burning stake in Rouen
she told me to teach

in your books and annals
I now have a voice
I will question every last word
you wrote
I will re-write
your lessons

educate my masses
until they feel it in their cells
and soul
near a burning stake in Rouen

Maria Diana Ramos, J. D. is a writer, educator, and mediator. As a six-ties baby, she attended protests against the Vietnam War, rallies to "Free Angela Davis" and marches to picket the Miss America Pageant where she witnessed the famous bra burning that launched the Women's Liberation Movement. A graduate of the University of Pennsylvania School of Law, Maria facilitates trainings on domestic violence, sexual harassment, non-profit Board development, and multi-culturalism. She is the Clinical Director of a Community Legal Education program at New College of California School of Law.

Femininity

When I was in elementary school, I was so shy a school psychologist pulled me aside to give me a battery of tests. When he reported to my mother I had checked out OK, he was still puzzled: "Why is she so afraid of people?" My mother replied with a sly, knowing smile: *"Oh . . . she's just feminine."*

Her statement had several layers of meaning, each more insidious and profound in its level of deception and destructiveness. I was being sexually and emotionally abused. I was so ill, my emotions so damaged, that to speak to anyone was too overwhelming. I wasn't shy—I was ill. It never occurred to me that my emotions were the result of mistreatment. I attributed them to some innate defect of my own—as my mother did with her statement.

That statement says a lot. It was not only that sensitive, "ladylike" behavior could be confused with the abuse victim profile, but that powerlessness, in itself, was the hallmark of "femininity." With her tone and attitude she said much more.

My father used to go by my room at night and make a point of saying to me through the slatted French doors which could not be locked and offered no protection: "Good Night, *Missy*!" He said this in a way which turned it into something nasty and evil, as if being a *"miss,"* a female, was something to be despised. He spoke as a vulture who has captured his prey and now just toys with it until he decides to pounce. I felt invaded by his words, the deep hatred and contempt of *"missy"* spewing through the slatted doors and into my very being. *Good Night, Sleep Tight.*

My mother spoke the word "feminine" in this way. There is a horrifying irony that she knew she could get away with this—which to her, was also a justification. She was saying, *"She's just feminine"*—merely, only feminine, female; i.e., despicable, deserves no better, "that's just the way they are, it's not worth bothering about." We punish her because she deserves it; she

Emily Krahn

deserves it because she's female. It's a labyrinth of strange, ironic, macabre twists. The meaning seemingly innocuous, was really quite devious and sinister. It's terrible to think she knew she could say this and get away with it, that people would mistake serious post-traumatic stress for femininity.

"She's just feminine," my mother said, and the life raft rescinded—my hope turned to mud with those words—given with that cruel, sneaky, smile.

You betrayed me so thoroughly with those words and that smile: you had me back in your clutches.

Femininity has nothing to do with being fragile!
Femininity has nothing to do with being afraid!
Femininity has nothing to do with illness, and hurt,
    and the kind of petrified, concave trance I felt.
How dare you tell me that to be feminine is to be ill!
Femininity waves a banner on horseback.
It is brave.
Femininity stands up for what is right—
    and proclaims it with the white blast of a trumpet call!
Femininity feeds the birds and tends the growing,
    tender plants.
It is abundance, and you are a killer of the worst kind.
Femininity is the stillness of a river on a summer's day,
    the call of a lone bird in the forest.
It counts the days and knows from where it comes,
    it knows The History.
Femininity is a smooth, rounded stone.

IT SINGS!

Emily Krahn is a survivor of incest. She is a writer, teacher, and healer. Her current writing project explores the personal, political, and social implications of society's tenacious belief in the inherent weakness of girls and women.

TO BE GOD

A psychic told me once I had chosen to live this life as a woman.

Why would anyone choose that—
to come into a world of
    batterers
    rapists
    clitoridectomies
    glass ceilings
as the battered
    the raped
    the amuputated
    the denied
as a woman.

I never was good at multiple choice.
Give me the essay question every time.
But Judge—I can explain!

Maybe I did it for the freedom
from expectation and responsibility.
I didn't do it for the salary
or for the expectations and responsibilities.

Maybe I did it for the body.
For the breasts alone it would have been worth it.
How can anything be so
    soft and heavy
    fluid and solid
    round and pointy
    silky and hard
    fleshy and electric
all at the same time?

Kris Welch

It was for the options
the possibilities
the range
I did it.
For the sensations of the body.
For the way a feather at the inside of an elbow,
the inside of a thigh,
can reach the inside of the psyche.

That's why I did it—to get inside
A woman is access.
Is integrated.
Is connected.
You can get there from here.

From the outside in.
And from the inside out.

Yes, the body must have had a lot to do with my choice.
And with my body and my choice
I grew a child
(Let's see you try it, bub.)

Well, really, I let my body do its stuff.
I was merely along for the ride.
Yeah! Show me what you can do, your mysteries, your powers,
    your magic!
No anesthesia, please.
It's a girl!
It certainly is.

Not biology as destiny.
Choice is destiny.
Biology as option.

And today is for celebration of the female, biology and all
and if that psychic was right, of my choice of destinies
to be female in the 20th century.

"The feminine powers of intuition and imagination"
You'd need a lot of both to choose to be female.
Don't confuse me with the facts!
the facts of a male-dominated universe
where God is the Father
and sometimes His Son
but the mother is just
    a coincidence
    a convenience
    a vessel
    (or was that a Vestal??? . . .)

The Kabbalah says the vessels broke
they could not contain the magnitude of creation
creativity cannot be contained.

Intuition and imagination will not go back in the bottle either.
Although there may never be a time when they don't frighten
some people into persisting in trying to eliminate them.
    Don't read that story!
    Don't talk about feelings!
    Don't think about ideas!
    Don't question authority!
And they're coming soon to a school and a young mind
near you.

But fear is not our destiny
unless we choose it.
And biology is a mystery.

Her biology puts a woman
here and now and there and then
all at the same time.
In this body are the present and the future
and all the mothers of all the world and all time
whether I choose to give birth or not.

It's living proof of the human spirit.
The word made flesh.
Not God in the sky
    with the pie by 'n' by
but here
    in your ear
    in your face
    in your life
inside.

So—that's why I chose in this life to be a woman.
To be god.

Kris Welch hasn't given up her day job, hosting the Morning Show on KPFA 94.1 FM in Berkeley. Raised in the Methodist Family of the Year in a small town in Illinois in the 1950s, she has lived in Tehran, Rome, Munich, Bristol, Manhattan, and Chicago. She has worked factory assembly line, in the accounts payable department of Hertz Corp., as waitress, receptionist, advertising copywriter, newspaper reporter and editor, smuggler, piano player in a bar, ESL teacher. She's a professional actress and singer, an unprofessional single mom. Wrting has always been the thread to quilt these patches together.

CELEBRATING CREATIVITY

Imagine a woman who loves her sounds, movements, images, and words.

A woman who loves them passionately.

Who blesses the fruit of her creative womb.

Imagine a woman who trusts her experience of the world and expresses it.

A woman who produces original creations.

Who refuses to color inside someone else's lines.

Imagine a woman who savors each step in the creative process.

A woman who allows each step to lead her to the next.

Who embraces destinations as the surprises encountered along the way.

THE DANCE OF HEALING

I AM A DANCER. I celebrate my creativity through the healing, unifying flow of dance. As I harmonize body, soul and spirit, I feel not only connected to my inner self, but to the world I inhabit. I have a vision—that of releasing the sacred springs of dance within many people. It has grown from childhood.

It is in my studio that I find the "still waters" so needed to refresh my own body and soul. It is uncluttered, with a wooden floor and an informal altar. I find peace. Here, my soul gathers strength to fly, and my body recovers from the stresses of traveling and dancing on stone church floors. I enter, giving myself a few minutes before working. With music supportive to my soul, I fold into a prayer position. I trace my impulses, attentive to my soul while luxuriating in the interconnecting movements of the parts of my body. One group of muscles provide the impulse for another to initiate new movements. I am completely absorbed. The process is spiritually nourishing. I experience no inner distractions. I fold and stretch and curl, remaining aware of the flow and minutiae of movement. I am healing myself.

The healing began years ago when as a child I would lie on my bed, my hands in the air, making pictures and stories and abstract movements, or racing down the narrow hallway of our New York City apartment, avoiding the walls. Dance is a vital link to my life's path, and to my self-worth. There is a deep imprint of dance on my earliest consciousness. Dance is my way of knowing who I am. To avoid serious psychic pain in childhood I looked within, and danced as part of an introverted way of creating richness out of myself, lest I be overwhelmed with fear and self-hatred.

Today, I can celebrate my introversion, for I chose life by moving inward. I discovered a rich range of imagery and movement that I was able to express externally, bringing joy to others. For this to happen, I had to meet many challenges, including overcoming shyness and making life-affirming choices. I found I needed the extroverted, shared energy that comes from interacting with people in groups, thus seeing the beauty of movement in bodies different from my own. This enabled me to mingle through dance my own inner and outer worlds with the experiences of others.

Carla DeSola

My vocation took form and focus when I met someone who combined these elements and danced as a way of conversing with God. Together we courageously explored our faith, dancing the scriptures, delving into its mysteries and revelations. Sharing this process, I saw movement honed by the integrity of spirituality, and this led to my working creatively within the context of liturgy.

The roots of dance and prayer are long and underground. Perhaps I have been dancing a personal kind of liturgy from my earliest years, but I didn't know it. As Patricia wrote," . . . who you are today is authentically connected to that little girl who watched the movements of her hands while lying on her bed and who was aware of how she turned corners."

Carla DeSola, MA, is a pioneer in liturgical and sacred dance, currently teaching at the Pacific School of Religion and the Dominican School of Philosophy and Theology, in Berkeley. A graduate of the Juilliard School, she founded the Omega Liturgical Dance Company at the Cathedral of St. John the Divine in New York City, where she continues as consultant and artist-in-residence. Currently, she directs the Omega West Dance Company in Berkeley. The author of numerous articles and books on sacred dance, she has produced two videos, "Danceprayer," and "Dance Meditations to the Songs of Taize," available through Paulist Press.

INTEGRATION

Becoming "full of myself" has meant reclaiming the feminine aspects of my life that I long ago discarded because I felt the feminine was undervalued and would hinder my success. Since girlhood, I knew that traditionally female jobs, such as nurse and secretary, were not accorded the status or pay of traditionally male jobs, such as doctor and executive. Moreover, I knew that housewife was the most devalued of all occupations. I vowed not to fall into the trap of becoming a second-class citizen as my mother and many of her contemporaries had.

As an adult, I have sought success in male-dominated professions, first in investment banking on Wall Street and now as a business professor. Both are environments with few women. I was one of only three women receiving a Ph.D. in a class of twenty-one, and am currently on a faculty that is 90% male. Even in this day and age, many people react with visible surprise when they learn my occupation; indeed, at graduation ceremonies, the parents of my MBA students frequently mistake me for one of their children's fellow students.

While my pursuit of success in traditionally male professions has given me much recognition and self-esteem, it has not been without costs. For years I avoided anything considered feminine and thus denied myself many life experiences. I thought I would remain childless because a baby would detract from my commitment to my job. I avoided women's conversations at parties, gravitating toward the men's instead, even if what the women were discussing was more interesting. And I was embarrassed to admit interest in, or cultivate, "female" hobbies.

I recently stopped denying myself "female" things; the personal costs of splitting myself artificially into masculine and feminine parts, and ignoring the feminine entirely, had been too high. Indeed I was ignoring not so much my feminine side, as basic aspects of my human nature. My task has been to reintegrate "feminine" pursuits into my life and thereby reclaim the full range of life experiences that are rightly mine. My early wounding

Karen Schnietz

from living in a culture that devalues women's work and creativity has healed sufficiently so that I have begun to not only pursue so-called feminine vocations, but even to celebrate them.

Five years ago I began to quilt and join quilting circles. I now proudly display the products of my creativity and love being involved in an activity that women have been pursuing for centuries. An even bigger leap was to accept my desire to experience the ultimate feminine act of creation: In April 1996 I gave birth to my first child, for whom one of my deepest wishes is that she grow up without feeling shame about her interest and gifts, but rather celebrates all of her capacities.

Has "integration" hurt my career progress? I don't know yet, but I'm determined to have a full personal and professional life. Men have been able to have families and careers—to be entirely "full of themselves" and experience all facets of life. Since I've always gone after what men have, it seems natural to pursue a life of wholeness in which I raise my daughter, tend to my quilting, and at least make the attempt to excel in a man's profession.

Karen Schnietz is a professor of business in Houston, Texas. In addition to teaching and conducting research on the political strategies of business, she quilts and collects antique textiles. Before their daughter was born, Karen and her husband, John Faucher, tossed a coin to determine which one of them would give their last name to their child. Sophie Schnietz is the proud owner of one of her mother's quilts, as well as her last name!

THE PROMISE

Ferrel Rao

I will wait for you patiently
until you reach that inevitable state
of just being who you are,
just naturally doing what you naturally do.

I'll wait, holding that which is yours
until the moment comes
when you reclaim yourself
one last time forever.

Ferrel Rao is a full of herself designer of greeting cards, posters, address books, journals, and other stationery and gift products too numerous to mention. She lives in Oakland, California with her beloved dog Jenny.

CELEBRATING ORDINARY LIFE

Imagine a woman who is interested in her own life.

A woman who embraces her life as teacher, healer, and challenge.

Who values its lessons above the prescriptions of experts.

Imagine a woman who is grateful for her own life.

A woman who appreciates the ordinary activities of her day.

Who celebrates the ordinary moments of beauty and grace.

Imagine a woman who participates in her own life.

A woman who meets each challenge with creativity.

Who leaves space for the unknown and unexpected.

A SEPARATE SOLITUDE

KALI VISITED. Disrobed me, right here in the middle of my room. Took off my career, numbed my capable committee hands, exchanged my hiker's legs for washboard calves, addled my brain. Then she gave my spouse a zafu and pointed out a zendo several cities away. Kali said to me, *"Learn to be content."*

Making soup begins at morning market.
From mountains of broccoli stems
I select the most heavily crowned;
I gather bunches of spinach/ wet and green
the color of Earth Mother's gown.
For the cooking I reserve a different morning
(before energy leaves my body),
Clear the crumbs from the counter
Leave plenty of vacant space
Open windows for light and air
Decide: music or silence?

Years ago I cultivated bonsai. My mother said, disgustedly, "You're an isolate, just like your father." *Kali teach me. Teach me how to claim my solitude!*

I open cupboard doors—see gleaming stainless pots.
Which kettle today?
A process evolves—
Largest pot to the counter
lid to the stove
Lay out the vegetables/Arrange them
Add onions   garlic   herbs
Stand back/Relish the vision

My spouse is leaving again. Another vacation, "retreat" she calls it. The spiritual word legitimates. She travels south, along the coast line. *Our* coast line. Our first rendezvous. She packs, gathers food, sings, chatters to the dogs. I cry and don't even try to smile. An old voice clatters through my head: "Oh, don't be so sensitive. You mustn't take things to heart!" *Kali, namo namah!*

Mary Ellen McNelly

Begin: (haven't I yet begun?)
   Break broccoli stems/Separate crowns
   (Protect your fingers from cold: ask her to wash the
      spinach before she leaves)
   Cut the onions (Remember to move your fingers
      away from the knife)
   Mince the garlic
   Crush the basil
   Measure the mustard
   Add broth /Turn on the burner
And sit down in the next room.
Wait.
Smell it simmer   in this room
      every room in the house
      outside the open window

I war with my own peace. *O Kali, teach me!* I frown at my smiling heart, spit at my simplicity. But when I chant in the morning, kissing my juniper tree, dancing in the street, I give thanks for help already on the way. *O Kali, Kali!*

   After hours of cooking
      Separate parts disappear.
   I measure soup
      Freeze it in a single servings.
   Another day, warm it
      Ladle some into my bowl
         into her thermos
   Deliver some down the street
      to a neighbor.

Mary Ellen Mc Nelly, former secondary and college teacher, Fellow and presenter for the Bay Area Writing Project, University of California, Berkeley, member Religious Society of Friends and published poet, has led a quiet life since 1988 when Chronic Fatigue Immune Dysfunction Syndrome surfaced. Now, through friends and neighbors, lessons come to her rather than her traveling into the world. When she accepts present reality, she contentedly loves her partner, garden, various divinities, and people whose hearts allow them to know her simple spirit.

Among Wildflowers

"O my lord . . . " The words floated up into my mind, as if from a supplicant to a king, to a master of life and death. I prayed for the right to exist. Then in a flash, I knew that I have, all my life, begged for permission to live, never convinced of my right to the next breath.

I was on my usual route, walking, two miles each way, through my city neighborhood, from my house to the river bluffs. As I walked, I asked myself, "Who says you have the right to life?" I wondered who this ruler, this master of life and death, could be. My father? God? Myself, or some deep aspect of myself? This question added to my despair, because I had never known who to turn to for this affirmation.

"O my lord, give me your blessing." The words came again.

I had wrestled for the blessing many times. All I had gained from those dark contests was pain, scars. The cold angel challenged me and then set up unbeatable odds, and I never gained the blessing.

At my feet, along the top of the bluff, a wild garden bloomed in the afternoon sun, a radiant zone of blue, white, pink, red, yellow, orange, lavender. I knew the gift of the wildflowers was my gift to them, that we bless each other by being alive. And I remembered, because of their gift, that there is in me a robust, energetic, delighted flower of life. The religion of my childhood did its best to deny the blessing, to wither my spirit, yet on many days I burst with joy.

Who pours out this blessing without my asking? Call her Nature, the Mother, call her Soul.

I listened to her, and she said, "All living beings and all things are blessed. The blessings are a fact of existence."

Jane Sterrett

"But . . . "I wanted to tell her how wrong she was, in my case, how deep the wounds.

She raised her eyebrows and said, "Who are these people who usurp the power of blessings?"

We paused to look out over the warehouses and lumber yards at the foot of the bluff, the ships in dry-dock, the narrow strip of river, and the wooded hills beyond. The fine threads of evening wove through the clouds. The evening star showed faintly. With the low sun in my eyes, I opened my heart to her.

She spoke urgently. "You must find your way among those who do not claim what is not theirs to give or withhold. You must go among those who stand under the stars and feel neither diminished nor enlarged. They will stand beside you and affirm with you what there is to receive. No one owns anyone, nor has the right to control other hearts. There is almost no need to make the effort to share. We all have what is given, and there is enough."

Cars passed by in the street behind me. I turned toward home, tears beginning, defeating the ancient coldness.

Jane Sterrett is a self-employed writer/editor specializing in municipal bond prospectuses. In the seventies she staffed local political campaigns. Her poems have appeared in literary quarterlies, and she is writing a fictionalized account of her girlhood as a missionary's child during World War II, Dost Thou Renounce the Devil? She is a crone with four children and eight grandchildren. She welcomes the stories from other missionaries' daughters, and plans to compile their experiences in another book.

TOMATO

UNCHARACTERISTICALLY, I agree, with less than fifteen hours notice, to go away for a Sunday. I whizz to a hot springs eighty miles north, leaving my desk messy, three letters unwritten, and Proper Rest Before the Week untaken.

Now I'm sitting on the deck with my friend Carla. It's overcast; no possibility of my starting to bleach my leg hairs. We have the get-up-and-go of two plants.

"Did I ever tell you about my theory of anti-epiphany?" asks Carla, her humorous mouth ready for a Carla-story. I shake my head. I've got Carla's bathrobe draped over my shoulders.

"You know *epiphany*, right?"

"Well, yes, I mean, I think so."

"You know, it's when the gods have your address. You know, when they've got you by the neck, and are making you work for them?"

"Ooh yeah." I think of Carla, pinned to her computer, pounding out her metaphysical treatises. I think of myself, raw as the broken end of a rope, collecting my myths.

"Well, this is the thing," says Carla."When they lose your address, the gods, or when you can move quick enough so they can't find you for a while, then you're in *anti-epiphany*. Just ordinary life."

I put down my rice cake. "You know," I say, "I think that's what this marriage thing is doing for me. It's an anti-epiphany."

Carla's gray eyes watch me.

"And it's so ironic," I continue, "because everyone thinks Finding a Partner, Having a Partner is more on the epiphany side of things."

"It's because of capitalism," says Carla. "That's another one of my theories. People dating are caught in a capitalistic mode of human relationship. Everyone trying to get something."

A small wind gusts across the pool and I tighten Carla's bathrobe around me.

"The truth is," Carla says, "I had to stop, because it suddenly dawned on me I didn't have enough love to give. I wasn't really interested in these other people's lives. I just wanted something from them. Something I thought I couldn't get from Gary."

Carolyn McVickar Edwards

She pauses. "Like being taken care of. And then, this week, I actually cried on Gary's shoulder. He said he never hugs me, because I once pushed him away. But I didn't this time."

"That's wonderful," I say. I think of Gary and Carla, housemates for years, figuring this out finally.

I think of my own Wednesday with Dan. Suddenly shrill about how I really couldn't do this relationship thing, I'm too much of a Diana-Artemis-Virgin-type. It's too hard, I'm way too tired, I'm practically ill with trying to stop nagging, I want to change, and I think it's good for me, but I don't think I'm cut out for it. And then another burst. Of sobs, and being held against his chest. "A scene," I call it later in therapy. "Sounds to me," says the therapist, "like just being real and vulnerable."

I blink, then and now, glimpsing a world in which people lean undramatically on each other. Where being needy, discouraged, winded, isn't a catastrophe.

"Yeah," says Carla. "Where you just hang out."

The trees behind us have very slender branches.

"You know?" says Carla "I'm back in a garden again. We rented a house. And I planted tomatoes. I do every year. Not exactly your make-a-mark activity. But . . . "

"Yeah, but pretty vital not so long ago," I interject. "When 'gardening' wasn't a 'hobby' but how you ate—or didn't eat."

"Yeah. Yeah, how you ate," says Carla.

We sit.

"You know, it's that first tomato. When you see it. And pick it. And you're holding right in your hands this work of the sky and the soil. And you know the little part you had in it."

Her gray eyes are beautiful.

"You know that's what every ritual in the world is 'sposed to get you to. And there it is. Right in your hands."

Carolyn McVickar Edwards, author of The Storyteller's Goddess *and* Sun Stories, *makes ritual with individuals and groups; runs an academic tutoring service; and is currently at work on a woman-centered novel based on the patriarchally-formed Hindu epic "The Ramayana."*

CELEBRATING WOMAN-BODY

Imagine a woman who believes she is good.

A woman who trusts and respects herself.

Who listens to her needs and desires, and meets them with tenderness.

Imagine a woman in love with her own body.

A woman who believes her body is enough, just as it is.

Who celebrates her body, its rhythms and cycles as an exquisite resource.

Imagine a woman who honors the face of the Goddess in her changing face.

A woman who celebrates the accumulation of her years and her wisdom.

Who refuses to use precious energy disguising the changes in her body and life.

MY BODY REMEMBERS

I suffered from chronic back pain as a result of a serious auto accident. I paid as little attention as possible to the pain. I pushed my body mercilessly, and I resented the pain when it slowed me down. My doctor periodically "fixed" my spine which usually helped for a few days or weeks.

In my women's meditation circle, I learned about coming home to my breath, body, and spiritual center. Listening to teachings, I learned that the blessings of the Buddha come through body, speech, and mind.

After a second automobile accident, I was again in tremendous pain. I found an amazing healing partner who paid close attention to the way my body moved. She taught me about my body's own healing resources. I began to see direct evidence of my body's wisdom.

One day, my healing partner directed me to move to the right, which I did easily and gracefully. Yet, when I tried to move on the left side, it felt unnatural. She assured me that my brain was already figuring out the healthy movement, and that I should try it again in a day or two.

When I tried the movement two days later, much to my surprise and delight, I was able to move gracefully to both the right and the left. A few weeks later, I witnessed my body figuring out healthy movements within ten minutes!

My healing partner does not believe my body is defective. She gently points out the consequences of the unhelpful ways I learned to cope with pain. And then she "re-minds" my body of how I moved as a child.

Karen Heide

I am reminded of what I knew in the very beginning of my life.
I trust that my body will remember.
As I walk along the ocean,
> I marvel at the movement of my ribs and the fluidity of my hips.
I feel my pelvis move freely in all four directions.
The stuck places in my ribs and shoulders begin to move more freely.
I celebrate my chest taking up space in the world.
> There is room for my breath.
I lay with my back flat on the ground.
> I feel my shoulder blades make solid contact with the earth.
As I walk to the bathroom, I notice I am stepping from my hip.
Each step is supported by a whole system of muscles
> working synchronously together. No one muscle has to strain.

I now have a different relationship to my pain.
My body is not defective. Pain signals that my body has become disconnected from what it knew in the very beginning of my life. I notice the discomfort at its early stages. I am eager to listen to it and to use the tools I have to work with it. I believe the pain is telling me of an essential disconnection. I breathe deeply and ask: what is it I can learn from you? What basic disconnection is triggering you?

I look forward to the time I spend coming home to my body.
I enjoy moving and stretching and noticing the stuck places. I reconnect with them, and my pain goes away. I don't fear that the pain will get out of control; I trust my body's ability to work with whatever comes up. As I move, I feel my life energy circulate throughout my body. Each movement becomes an occasion for increasing awareness.

I celebrate my body in this moment!

Karen Heide is a Registered Nurse who is committed to the healing of her body-mind. Her passions include walks along the ocean, Buddhist studies, and playing in her fabulous garden. She works in the Biotech industry and lives in California.

MY EARTH DARK WOMAN BODY

I waited politely at the bottom of the porch steps. Our first date was to take place in his kitchen over glasses of cold milk and store-bought chocolate chip cookies. We'd walked home together sharing smiles and catching reflections of ourselves in each other's eyes. He knocked. His mother opened the front door dressed up, high-heeled, and beaming.

In the pivot of a moment, she became possessed and snarling. Foamy-white billowed from the corners of her mouth. It oozed, streaking her make-up. There it dangled before eventually dripping from her chin. Dark wet circles formed on the front of her dress.

Arms flailing, engorged and sweaty she stomped onto the porch. She tossed her head all the way back and screeched her soul-of-a-child curdling discovery: "A ni-i-gger! Joanne's a ni-i-gger!" Then, in slow, measured rhythm she rasped, "Come into the house now, son. Haven't I taught you better than this? You can not love this—this darky." That day, I believed her eyes. I became afraid of myself.

Weeks later, Momma collapsed in a telephone booth. Anguish liquefied and rivered from her face. I'd been sick with a high fever. We'd walked to the corner phone booth to make an appointment for me with a near enough doctor. Momma explained to the receptionist. She answered one too many questions. With the doctor she pleaded, "What do you mean you don't take . . . but you're a doc . . . " The dial-tone failed to harmonize with the moaning silence.

Using the receiver for her shield, Momma tried to prevent me from witnessing the unrelenting flood of grief that this unanticipated Jim Crow storm had released within her. That day, girl-child ears were force-fed her momma's extorted mantra, "She's not colored. She's a little girl." I believed her eyes. I remained afraid of myself.

Joanne K. Coleman

I Reclaim My Darkness

Today, a woman's hands, dark as a Hershey's Kiss, are shaping a doll from clay. Two months ago they wrote another song. Last night, while writing their first book, I watched them move skillfully over the computer keyboard. These are my hands.

Today, I have gathered my years and all of the parts and pieces I was once too afraid to run back and get. I refuse invisibility. I have ceased sipping self-loathing like it was good cognac. I deconstruct the question. I no longer ask, "What's wrong with me?"

Today I do not consider the words dark and beautiful, when used in the same sentence, to be an oxymoron.

Today, lucid, creative, intelligent and touched by Holy Boldness—I believe my own eyes. I live unafraid in my numinous dark.

D. A. R. K. Y. Self-defined—
D. Decent is the natural woman-journey to my spiritual center.
A. Arising, organically, through the lush, dark soil of my creative womb, my life flowers and bears fruit.
R. Resources within me sustain the root, heart, and soul of my woman-life.
K. Keep my vows of faithfulness to my own life.
Y. Yes! I fill my breath, body, and woman-spirit with YES.

Joanne K. Coleman, D. D. is a sculptress of words and clay and the creator of the Living Process Ceremonies, including "Open Her Eyes" and "Enter the Mother." She is the founding minister of the woman-affirming church, The Sacred Gathering. Beyond this, Joanne answered and listens to the Voice Within, inheriting, through her African and Native American Motherline, the gifts of prophetic speech and healing. Mother of songs and Nnalubaale Woman spirit keeper dolls, she is pregnant with her first book.

THE POWER OF THE EROTIC

Born EMBODIED. Every cell moist and alive.
    One with Mother, I glow as I suckle at the breast.
I am whole, complete.

But NO! I hear.
"You are not your body. It is separate and to be loathed!"
"Keep yourself covered!"
"Wear underwear to bed!"

I follow directions perfectly.
And, without ceremony, I become a HEAD.

Without my body I am quiet, obedient.
I have lost my interpreter, my guide, my friend, my protectress.

At 30, I begin my journey back to my body.
Back to wholeness, simple pleasure, and Eros.

A dark goddess emerges from me,
and guides me by her example.
She glories in her sounds, her rhythms,
her natural smells, and her own earthy desires.

In time,
she helps me claim the exquisite gift my body is.
My breasts are temples.
My nipples tingling orbs.
My thighs a sacred path
to the multipetalled velvety rose between them,
Red, ripe, and full.

I AM the dark goddess come to claim her right
to fearless power and pleasure.

I erupt, and matter as I know it shatters
Then rearranges itself in perfect harmony.

Mother and father are equal.
Dark and light are again one.
As it was in the VERY BEGINNING, I am as I should be
EMBODIED.

Colleen West

I Celebrate my Body-Connection in Everyday Life

A Guide in Decision Making. When I need to make a decision, big or small, I center myself and ask my body what I should do, and it faithfully responds: "no" I experience as a closing-down or a tightening sensation in my chest; "yes" I experience as an opening-up or a lightening sensation in my heart. Making a decision is no longer the protracted mental exercise it used to be, and now I make better choices!

Clarity and Connection with Others. When I work with parents and children, I find that if I can relax and be present in my body, I can listen in a deeper way and offer feedback that is deeply intuitive. I try to use my mind as a secondary helper, because I find the mind's analysis and interpretation can easily bring me to a wrong, if tidy, conclusion. The body, however, never strays far from the truth.

Safety in the World. I have always experienced a lot of fear in my everyday life. For instance, when coming home to an empty house at night, I would check behind doors and look in closets, with my heart racing, afraid of someone lurking in the shadows. But as my relationship to my body and my sexuality has grown strong, I have begun to feel deeply safe in a new way. My body is now my ally in all settings, a safe home within me, and consequently, the world has much less power to frighten me.

Colleen West, *founder of Conscious Parenting in Berkeley, California, empowers parents to create respectful and deeply nourishing relationships with their children. She lectures in schools and corporations in the Bay Area, teaches parenting classes, and counsels parents individually. She enjoys unhurried time with her kids, long walk in the woods, and time alone to paint. She lives in Berkeley with her partner and three spirited children.*

Death/Resurrection

Yards and yards
Of heavy black serge
Covered every inch of me
Save face and hands
Not a curve
Not a limb
Not a hint
Of my beautiful
Woman-body
Could be seen.

No wind
Could blow through my hair
Swirl my skirts
Playfully
Around my thighs.
Warm moist earth
Never tickled
My firmly-shod feet.

Thus was I bound
Bride of Christ
For twenty-five youthful years,
The male magisterium
Male theologians
Male spiritual directors
Properly dressed
My body
And my soul.

Then God the Mother
Released me
I
Sensual woman
Earthy woman
Beautiful woman
Am good.

Marcelline Niemann

Golden Moments

Foraging through a box of memoirs recently,
I approached old letters and cards
with messages of love and affirmation
like an unspoiled child who expects
to be acknowledged for her uniqueness.
It felt like skinny-dipping
in a pool of sun.
For a few golden moments
I was released
from the deeply entrenched
fear of pride
and I let the applause
I love so much
fill my hungry heart with gratitude.

Marcelline Niemann is a retired Crone living as fully as health, friends, and awareness encourage. She enjoys writing personal letters, poetry, memoirs, and essays. She is active in efforts to abolish the death penalty and to improve the plight of incarcerated women. She is a member of the Richmond (Virginia) Peace Community, an Ecological Working group, and two women's spirituality groups.

CELEBRATING FEELING

Imagine a woman who has access to the full range of human emotion.

A woman who expresses her feelings clearly and directly.

Who allows them to pass through her as gracefully as the breath.

Imagine a woman who is aware of her own emotional needs.

A woman who takes responsibility for meeting them,

Who enlists the support of respectful friends and chosen family.

Imagine a woman who lives in harmony with her heart.

A woman who trusts her impulses to expand and contract.

Who knows that everything changes in the fullness of time.

A BIG, BIG HEART

I have a big, big heart.

My heart is full of gratitude for who I've been, for who I am, and who I am becoming.

They called me selfish as a child, but I look back and see the little girl who hid her heart because it hurt so easily. She was so moved by her own and others' sorrows that tears flowed all too soon and all too often. Therefore she held tightly to herself, held on and prayed, and hoped for a different future. From the place of the present—that future she dreamed of—I know that she was only waiting to remember where she came from (the time before she was her parents' child) to dare to open up and show her heart, to give in safety, to feel for others in their joys and in their sadness. *Now I know that I have always had a big, big heart.*

My heart contains my partner and our sweet, alive alliance. For many years, I was not ready, did not love myself or know I was enough. I was alone and lonely, or trapped within relationships which did not nurture who I truly am. In time I came to celebrate my life alone, to heal and to forgive my past. As my heart grew in understanding, it opened to the world and to myself and to this man with whom I share my life today. He is kind and good and generous, and honors me as I do him. *We love each other and we trust the good intentions of our great big hearts.*

My heart holds my story, an unfolding tale of pain and joy and learning, always powered by a deep and tender longing to return to God. I love my story. It is that of a life guided by a Deeper Wisdom even when I didn't know or quite believe that this was true. My fifty years of searching has brought me home to where the truth was all along, to my heart, where God was all along. *I love sharing all the stories in my big, wise heart.*

Virginia Logan

I am an astrologer and I bring this heart which holds my story to my work, which is in part the telling and re-telling of a story, uniquely mine yet universal in some fundamental ways. Listening to others with my heart, I learn and understand. Opening and sharing from my heart, I make connections. Finding common truths has helped me see the value of each journey through a human life, and to celebrate with clients the story which is theirs and theirs alone. *We are all together in our vast, great hearts.*

My heart believes in Truth and Beauty. I work at home, and take great pleasure in the sharing of this place in which I live. It is always full of flowers, good food and lovely colors, and lots of bright, clear light. It is like an island of peace and comfort in a busy city and is offered as a haven to my family of friends and clients. *A heart makes room for others. There is always room for others in my home and in my big, big heart.*

This heart has been a source of pain, but over the years the feeling of my sorrow has helped my heart to grow and strengthen, and made room for great, great gladness. It is strong enough to hold my feelings, all of them, the rage and anger, grief and hatred along with kindness and compassion, as well as sympathy and love. I have come to see my pain and longing as the other side of joy. *I've come to know the depths of Being in my big, big heart.*

Virginia Logan is an astrologer, hypnotherapist, and teacher who for the last fifteen years has divided her time between Amsterdam and California. In both places she has a family of friends and clients. Her spiritual journey has included many years of meditation practice, questioning, and Twelve Step work. It is her profound belief and observation that each of us has within and around us everything we need to heal our lives.

NO MORE HIDING

My feelings are important. I feel sorrow. It doesn't just reside in my heart. It's like a wave that washes through all of me. I feel anger. I feel its heat, its force, its determination. I feel joy. I feel light-hearted and am surprised at the ease of every word and gesture.

When very strong feelings or thoughts come up—the ones that almost take my breath away, the painful feelings and self-judging thoughts—I know that they are memories imprinted from the past when I had no healthy way to digest or interpret my experience. I don't fight against these feelings, or take them to mean that something is wrong with me. I welcome them because they remind me to reach out to my child-self with tenderness and compassion. I breathe. I honor the feelings. I have nothing to hide from myself. I will know in time if any words or actions are needed. I trust my intuition. I trust myself. This is my freedom.

I used to be afraid to meet people for the first time because I thought they would look at me and be shocked by my height. Now I know I wasn't hiding my size. I was hiding my true grandeur, my true radiance. I have gone on a detour but have found my way back home. I assume my full stature. My thoughts are big. My feelings are big. I throw my arms open and once again I dance.

Mani Feniger

No more hiding
The nervous child who didn't want her fears to be seen,
The sensitive child who felt her mother's pain.
The grieving child who wasn't told her father was dying.

No more hiding
The vibrant child who was bursting with enthusiasm,
The tall child who danced around the house,
The joyful child who laughed easily and felt everything.

No more hiding
She is a woman who stands in her center.
She is six feet tall and beautiful,
She feels powerful and confident,
Her voice is magnetic and people listen to her.

No more hiding
She is vulnerable and sometimes feels too tender to speak
She needs to lie quietly in her bed,
And watch the treetops swaying in the wind.

And now I am full of myself
Not the one or the other,
But the fullness that embraces them both,
The self that lies at the core,
No more hiding. Full.

Mani Feniger *is a hypnotherapist, speaker, and author. Her recent book,* Journey from Anxiety to Freedom *(Prima Publishing, 1997), tells the story of eight people, including herself, who have faced panic disorder and phobias and renewed trust in themselves. She was consultant on two ground-breaking documentaries* Breaking Silence *and* Stories of Change. *She is the founder of the Anxiety and Phobia Peer Support Network, a telephone support system for people who suffer from panic.*

What We Are Looking For

Feelings have mounted the walls
    and are throwing tears into the moat.
Pudgy little thought guards
and the rigid orifice sentries
soon follow,
drifting and scrabbling over the sides.

Feelings are rampaging
through the cubby holes and floorboards,
tossing beliefs in a pile
and tearing a wild polka
over grandma's warnings
and the neighbors' spyglasses.

Feelings are overturning the appliances
and confounding pet theories,
poking holes in the foundation
and raising more dust over locked windows.

Feelings are searching,
knowing,
sensing the inner pulse.
Feelings are pounding
up and down the stairs,
sniffing through the laundry
for the electric scent.

Feelings finally skitter
into a hushed quiver,
peering over shoulders
and blinking rapidly,
fixed on these mute flashes
like lightning bugs
of the soul.
And they hover over them,
drinking deeply,
murmuring and passing the light.

Kathlyn Hendricks

In Celebration of My Feelings

I have always been full of feelings. As a child I wondered if feelings were an enemy because I used to be told a lot "you're too sensitive." I took this to mean that fewer feelings would be better.

I've been making friends with my feelings for years now and I find that the more I feel, the more creative I am immediately. All kinds of bright possibilities bloom on the heels of a feeling shower.

Feeling fully allows me to step into other people's lives and share their world for a moment. Feelings give me access to the subtleties of life where all is not black and white. And feelings are the best friends of intuition. Both guide my choice to be in harmony with life.

Kathlyn Hendricks, Ph.D., A. D. T. R., is a poet, professor of dance/movement therapy, international consultant, and CEO of the Hendricks Institute. She is the co-author of ten books, including Conscious Loving, At The Speed of Life, *and the new* The Conscious Heart.

CELEBRATING A SELF-DEFINED LIFE

Imagine a woman who authors her own life.

A woman who successfully implements her desires in the world.

Who refuses to surrender except to her truest self and her wisest voice.

Imagine a woman who knows she is powerful and gifted.

A woman who embraces her inner resources and capacities.

Who initiates and moves on her own behalf.

Imagine a woman who has a fully-formed life.

A woman who refuses to set aside her life.

Who remains faithful to herself. Regardless.

LIFE BEYOND MY WILDEST DREAMS

I am BIG. I am no longer available to support the illusion that I am small. In the past I experienced a disconnection from my internal life so I was always reacting. I didn't feel I had any control over my reality or what I experienced. Everything happened to me. There was no stability or groundedness in my life. I felt very small living from the outside/in.

Sitting in circles of women, I shared the truth of my life and healed into the present. I decided to engage in a significant relationship with myself . . . without distraction. I made a commitment to experience myself as whole and complete, to honor my life as sacred, and to create for myself all that I desire.

I experienced new words and images that personalized 'spirit' as present within me. Spirit and I are one. We dance at my core. The lovely life I live today reflects this inside/out perspective. My life is deeply satisfying and in balance. I feel BIG living from the inside/out.

I celebrate my clarity.

Clarity in the use of my time . . . I have become a skillful manager of my time, acknowledging that there are seven days in a week and twenty-four hours in a day. Recognizing limits has supported me to become clear about my priorities. In setting clear limits, I experience more spaciousness in my schedule. There is room now for the unknown and the spontaneous. I am no longer reacting to life. I am participating in it. I breathe slowly and deeply. I am consciously living.

Erin Louise Stewart

Clarity in the use of my energy . . . Today I notice how I feel after every life experience. Today I have the courage to pay attention to whether or not I am nourished by the experience and then to make choices to eliminate anything that depletes my precious life energy. The feeling of exhaustion has become a gift. It lets me know in an instant what works and what doesn't work for me. It is empowering to choose only that which energizes me.

Clarity in the choice of relationships . . . I have spent too much time and energy people-pleasing and caring too damn much about what other people think. Today I consider my feelings, thoughts, and choices most important. I am no longer attracted to relationships of struggle, conflict, and stuckness. I choose to be around people who make me smile, open and creative people who are full of themselves.

Clarity in purpose . . . I offer the gift of clarity to others. I delight in supporting women and men to become skillful managers of their time and energy, to choose relationships that make them smile, and to discover their authentic life purpose and passion. I inspire others to conceive of a life beyond their wildest dreams. I support them to take the next right step to design such a life with simplicity and grace.

Erin Louise Stewart has worked with women of color for 18 years as hairstylist, advocate, supporter, counselor, and creative inspirer. She is the founder of Souls Stirring: A Ministry Among African-American Women in the Greater Bay Area committed to bringing together black women to share the truth of their lives with an awareness of their connected life-line. Erin is also the founder of Clarity Enterprises, providing the benefits of clarity to individuals, churches, and corporations. A resident of Berkeley, Erin is the single mother of two "full of themselves" children, Savoi and Moizeé.

The Living Obituary of Jennifer Anne Biehn

written by Jennifer herself, alive and well at 47 years

Jennifer Anne Biehn (pronounced bean)
Jennifer meaning White Wave in Celtic
Anne meaning Grace in English
Biehn meaning BeeKeeper in German

Daughter of Margaret and Roy, Sister of Kathe and Susan
Daughter of Earth and Sky, Sister of Tree and Mountain

Poet, Storyteller, Gardener
Teacher of Tai Chi, Leadership Skills
Administrator exemplar
    ready to greet each day with beginner's mind

Always a lover of the out-of-doors
Swimming, hiking, camping, canoeing
    ever since she was knee-high to a porcupine
Backpacker and cross-country skier till the day she died

Organizer of the world about her, full of energy
    to make it beautiful and efficient
Double fire sign . . . burning at the edges of new awareness
    generously sharing the heat created

Fearless builder of community
    where students risked and grew
    where teachers shared stories and dreams
    where friends gained nurture and support
    where everyone felt at home

Maker of her own unique politically spiritual path
    learning from Gaia, Tara, Artemis, Buddha, Jesus, Marx, Gandhi,
    understanding that being peace inside is the key to making peace
    in the world

Jennifer Biehn

Kinswoman and lover of Joan Susan
Compañera to beautiful colleagues and friends
Aunt Jen or Great Aunt Jen
      to all who loved her homebaked stories
      to all who wanted their first wilderness adventure

Sometimes . . . she manifested rigid control, unrelenting judgment,
    abounding perfectionism, and alarming lack of boundaries

But overall, Jen, fondly known at City College of San Francisco,
      as Dean Biehn, Queen of the Scene, Lean and Mean
      was a mighty good soul . . . and will be missed by all

Epitaph: White Wave Grace BeeKeeper
"In a life of service for justice and compassion in the world,
the best gift you can give is to take good care of yourself."

Jennifer Biehn is the Dean of Student Development/ Activities at City College of San Francisco. She teaches leadership skills and shares resources enabling students to empower themselves, advocate for their rights, build communities of respect, and participate in the shared governance of the college. Jennifer teaches Tai Chi Chih and coordinates an Educator's Sangha in which teachers come together to share the art of "being peace" in their classrooms and lives. Jennifer enjoys writing poetry, telling stories, gardening, and trekking in the wilderness. She lives with her partner Joan in their home on Whittle Creek in Oakland, California.

MY JOURNEY TO MYSELF

"Your life as you have known it is over!"
Profoundly sobering and overwhelming
words from unknown depths within me.
"But I like my life!" I protest to this inner voice.
"It's safe. It's comfortable. It's predictable."
I'm not ready to let go,
to take a leap of faith!"
"Your life as you have known it is over!"
Repeated the still, quiet, and emphatic
voice of my own inner guidance.
And somewhere within me I know
I am committed to answering this 'call.'

Facing into my deepest fears,
I surrender to my own inner process
and set upon a journey
into the depths of my own being
to discover the source and significance
of this mysterious voice
Descending deeper and deeper within myself
to discover the woundings and internalized messages/beliefs
which kept me stuck
in a life which no longer fit for me,
as well as to recover my deepest wisdom
which would set me free.

Patricia Meadows

Stripping away layer after layer of my former self.
Writhing in excruciating pain.
Feeling as if "I" am disintegrating/dissolving.
Questioning how I will ever be able to function again.
Being re-arranged at my very core.
Following my inner knowing as well as
the strong life force compelling/propelling me
to let go of my outer life.
Dying to my old identity,
dismantling my history,
leaving all that is familiar,
bidding farewell to my 'life' as I have known it.

Moving across country.
Settling into a space of quiet and gentle retreat.
Seeking solitude, simplicity, and sabbatical.
Grieving losses and changes.
Struggling, resisting, letting go.
Nurturing myself and my inner process.
Being present to all that is stirring within me.
Waiting and listening for my deepest truth.
Living out of the formlessness of the void.
Feeling my vulnerability and my fear.
Trusting my intuition, my body and my own inner wisdom
to lead me 'home.'

Journeying into unfamiliar territories.
Exploring, taking risks, surrendering to the unknown.
Noticing, naming, and integrating my experiences.
Stretching into a larger 'container' and cosmology.
Claiming my own inner authority.
Discovering and speaking my truth.
Awakening to the potential of new life emerging.
Acknowledging what is wanting to be born.
Receiving support in the process of birthing.
Being welcomed into the womb of the Great Mother.
Allowing my life to reveal itself to me as it unfolds.
Honoring the sacredness and mystery of life.

Opening to an ancient energy moving within me.
Reconnecting to the power/passion of the divine feminine.
Embracing, expanding and deepening into this energy.
Reclaiming my birthright and responsibility as woman.
Affirming my willingness to live fully and freely.
Connecting with the rhythms of my body and the earth.
Delighting in my sexuality as well as my spirituality.
Discovering the essence of my being.
Committing to my own authentic life process.
Vowing faithfulness to my deepest and truest path.
Celebrating the abundance and joy of being embodied.
Dancing, singing, laughing, crying, living.
Being born anew!

Patricia Meadows, MS, RN is a process therapist/facilitator, educator, and consultant. Her lifework involves supporting individuals and groups as they deepen their process of self-discovery, healing, and psychospiritual transformation. She facilitates women's spirituality process groups, as well as transformational retreats. Patricia draws upon over twenty years experience in nursing, community health education, counseling, and consulting, as well as over a decade of intense psycho-spiritual exploration and a deep commitment to her own healing.

CELEBRATING A SELF-DEFINED SPIRITUALITY

Imagine a woman who names her own gods.

A woman who imagines the divine in her image and likeness.

Who designs her own spirituality and allows it to inform her daily life.

Imagine a woman who refuses to surrender to gods, gurus, and higher powers.

A woman who has descended into her own inner life.

Who asserts her will in harmony with its impulses and instincts.

Imagine a woman who embodies her spirituality.

A woman who honors her body as the sacred temple of the spirit of life.

Who breathes deeply as a prayer of gratitude for life itself.

A Spirituality in the Present

By education and training I am a registered nurse and graduated from nursing school in 1978. I left the profession in August, 1995 to pursue my true interests: spirituality, psychology and writing, and to—at long last—live my authentic life. My first step toward the life I want was to serve as Director of The Wellness Center at my church, Unity of Birmingham. Unity is a wonderful haven of unconditional love that embraces the feminine as well as the masculine aspects of the divine. Recently I received the courage to take the next step. I quit my job at Unity and enrolled in school full-time to pursue a degree in psychology and religion.

Creation of the Goddess
She is the wonder
Of those things hoped for,
The substance of those not seen,
The mystery at the beginning
Of all that comes to be.
In this the women of old
Received the approval of
The Divine Feminine.

She is the desire of union
Before two as one are blest.
She is the centre
Of the unbloomed
Scarlet bud awaiting
Unfolding as only
She can see.

She is the quickening
Flutter in my belly
Before the birth.
She is the butterfly
Before the cocoon.
She is the rain-deluge
Before the multi-coloured bow.
She is the palette
Before the stroke.

Susan Scott

She is the urge
That raises a baby
To its feet.

She is the pucker
Of Cupid's lips
Before the kiss.
She is the clay
Before the smooth
Sculpted stone.

She is the seed
Splitting two yellow halves,
Bursting green through
The black mulch.
She is the gold charge
Before the bolt.

She is the still quiet
Womb out of which all
Creation is Born.
She is the rest
Before the death to come.
She is peace
When the day is done.

She is the Love
From whence I came.
She is me
From Potential to Fulfillment.

Susan Scott was always an avid reader which informed and supported her independent thinking. Her primary passion today is writing. She has completed her first book, Holy Whore. *She is now writing* The Goddess Poems, *a book of poetry in celebration of the Divine Feminine.*

Bonjour Soleil

THESE DAYS I am watching vegetable seedlings beginning to emerge from their dark earthen peat pots. It doesn't matter that I can't tell which will be an eggplant and which will be a pumpkin. Each tiny sprout knows what it will become. It's so simple. It needs the dark to germinate, and a lot of nurturance to bring it into the light. I try to remember, when I sink into the dark that it's a time of beginnings and that I too need love and support so I don't shrivel like an untended seed. That's how we can be for each other, we women who bring our visions into the light. We can stand there with our spray bottles, adding just a little more moisture and a little extra light and warmth, when one of us is in the dark place.

Today I greet the sun in a posture of celebration. *Bonjour Soleil!* Up you rise above the pond and through the trees. A pink light fills the room. The houseplants stretch toward you. I thank God for the abundance of another day, for the female cardinal who joins the chickadees and nuthatches, at breakfast on the ground beneath the feeder, for the mourning dove's coo as I wheel the garbage can to the road. I move and stretch my body—a flow of postures and every cell rejoices. I chant the Atma Gita in the shower. *"Tis only one Self which exists within all. Tis that very Self which you see as the world. God who is love is found only through love."* I sit in full lotus position to daven, chanting the *Shma. Here, Oh Israel, Source of All, All is One.*

I balance my energy centers using *Kabballistic* tones, Sanskrit mantras. Each posture strengthens this vessel. Each breath purifies it. Each prayer aligns it. All tools to purify and strengthen my relationship to the divine. Practice keeps me awake to the divine, awake to who I really am, awake to holding the posture of living rightly.

Amy Weintraub

Then turning to *Torah,* finding moments of nourishment, of challenge, of despair at the messages I receive. I find balance by coming together with other women, gathering as our foremothers did, taking what we know and going deeper, letting the truths emerge. I find balance by welcoming God the Mother into my life, by clearing space for the *Shekhinah,* the feminine in-dwelling presence of God, by resting my mind against *El Shaddai,* God's breast.

Perhaps I risk calling all the curses in the Hebrew Scriptures down on my head, and yet I have to believe I'm not turning away from the religion of my childhood now but widening it, deepening it, not only to include me, but to include the real stories of women in biblical times, to include you, to know as I look in your eyes that you are divine. That we are one. Celebrating me, I celebrate you and I'm filled with gratitude. If you hold this book in your hand, if you read these words, we are celebrating each other in this moment. How, in this moment can we reflect back to one another our own divinity? How can we support each other on this journey? How can we lift each other up? My dear Sister, let's find a new way every day!

Amy Weintraub's spiritual practice includes her writing, yoga, meditation, Kabballistic studies, and a commitment to serve through relationship and community. She teaches yoga and writing classes and authentic spirituality workshops. She recently completed "Confessions of a Temple Dancer", a novel about an American woman's past life as a devadasi in India, and hopes to see it published in this lifetime. She was a national award-winning television writer/producer before simplifying her life.

divine rebellion

reality is a friend
    and my grandmother
who told stories
and welcome

I walk on earth up hills of lifetimes
to my tune of daily yes
no inconsequential grain of sand
or thought
across my path
stretching legs of meaning the muscles of my soul
a child seeking truth

I live questions church will not hear
but universe replies
answers in forbidden fruit
our own wise knowing
my inward Self vibrant
despite the name god-not-mother

in the beginning
ever present
my great-great grandmother
delivered babies ran a store defending
her dark-skinned swami friend
not-a-christian
to neighbors' chagrin

I step over weeds in sidewalk cracks
concrete block society
nature's green resurgence hope
persistence
faith first in ourSelves
guidance
in coincidence
my surgeon's hands
a book

Carroll Begley

my grandmother wise beyond our eyes
not-allowed-to-vote
spoke
stories of injustice counseled passersby
heart a spirit home embracing
everyone one family
authority grandmother love

power abuse culture's underbelly
we work our way to freedom
canes and braces inconvenience
not disability
we bring our hardware with us
visible or unseen
redwood tree wounds become
burl beauty
pain decomposed
in the compost heap
of life

a young flower vendor confides
unlike-her-family dreams
we women dance to equinox skies
singing ancient mother
no woman fallen when we tell our truth
darkness birthing life

the universe is a friend
and my grandmother
whose life I celebrate
with mine

Carroll Begley was born in San Francisco, land of Ohlone people, where she studies, writes, and practices divine rebellion.

Women in Support of Women

I am one of the "core four" in a group we call Windows (Women's Independent Nurturing Discussion with Other Women). We all started in a similar place—yet each one of us is in a vastly different place: Christian, non-Christian, exploring a new faith, or finding sustenance in the old one. The "core four" Kris, Becky, Beverly, and Elizabeth span 28 years in age. We are diverse but equal. We have no organization, no leaders, no agenda. We just are. We have as many as ten in our group flowing in and out of our lives.

Soon after Carlene joined Windows, we gathered one Sunday evening on a green hillside at a cemetery in Bountiful to redo the funeral of her father. The original funeral had been a painful experience because Carlene's mother would not allow her to give her father's eulogy. Carlene had cared for him during a long illness.

After Carlene welcomed us, Becky, radiant in ritual clothing, opened a circle around the grave in a pagan ritual addressing the four directions, our Mother Goddess, and Father God. Elizabeth talked about fathers and Christianity with an emphasis on God's love for us. Carlene asked Beverly to sing. As I listened, I wanted to weep for all the things I have not dared to try.

Carlene presented the eulogy "Avi Met," Hebrew for "My Father Died." She introduced us to her father through memories, photos, and shared grief. Kris burned Indian sweetgrass (cedar and sage) as she banished the negative and thoughtless rejection of Carlene by her mother. After strewing the grave with flower petals and bits of Carlene's red hair, we sang Beautiful Savior after which Becky led us in closing the circle. Blessed be. Homemade snicker-doodles completed the ceremony.

Carlene expressed amazement that we who had spent "all of five hours" with her would offer her such a gift. But I am amazed that after "all of five hours" she asked each of us to participate in a way that expressed so fully her respect for and acceptance of us.

Windows

I believe that God was there that day—God the father of Christ, the Hebrew Yahweh, the pagan Mother Goddess, the Great Spirit. And God saw that it was good. With sadness I acknowledge to myself the half-century in which I thought pagan meant godless, and the decades I thought Indian and savage were synonymous. What ignorance! What arrogance!

Without Kris' tenacity, Windows would have faded away after six months. Now Windows is beginning its third year. Our relationship has deepened to a level of acceptance, respect, and support that I have never before experienced. I thrill to our diversity in beliefs, talents, age, and experience. I thrill to our common values of acceptance (it's so much more than tolerance), respect, caring, and mutual support in all our roles as women. We met as strangers, sitting next to each other at the Mormon Women's Forum. We were looking for a place to be honest about our lives without fear of censure. What we found was acceptance and family—women in support of women.

Windows is an open group that has been meeting monthly since the summer of '92. Although we originally were seeking spiritual sustenance, we have supported each other through life's multi-faceted challenges.

Kris is 41, married, and has three children. She has a degree in Home Economics Education and is currently a full time homemaker. Born and raised in a strict Mormon family, she left Mormonism at age 30 when she realized how much her self-value had been damaged by the male-only priesthood of her church. Today she wears a ring with circles and curves to remind her that since God is also female, she herself is as worthy as the males she once obeyed. She practices Zen meditation and personal rituals using candles and sweet grass.

Becky, the pagan, is 26 years old and owns her own business. Married to an agnostic male feminist, she is the mother of two cats, her fur children upon whom she is practicing motherhood skills. She and her beloved spouse left the Mormon church together to seek God/dess else-where. In a joyous celebration of life, Becky reclaims her female body from the ravages of patriarchy by being a belly dancer in Salt Lake City.

Carlene, *age 44, is the single mother of three daughters, all redheads like herself. She has a master's degree in Organizational Development and is working as a counselor at Job Corps. Her father's unconditional love gave Carlene the grounding and confidence that sustains her. The loss of her father penetrated her soul and caused her to seek deeper spiritual comfort. Carlene is taking cello lessons and desires to further her education.*

Elizabeth Jensen, *age 53 and happily divorced, works in accounting and software implementation. She provides a home for her artist daughter and rock musician son. Although hopelessly Christian, she is still seeking her spiritual home and often feels like a spiritual bag lady. She currently finds spiritual nourishment in her wildflower patch where she finds father God and Mother Earth. A writer, Elizabeth captures memories such as this essay in word pictures.*

Beverly Hyatt, *age 43, has a Masters of Public Health and manages a community clinic for the County Public Health Department. She also manages a family of four children and one spouse. Beverly is a practicing Mormon and enjoys exploring new dimensions of spirituality with the Windows group.*

CELEBRATING WOMEN PRESENT IN THE WORLD

Imagine a woman who has developed her talents and gifts.

A woman who is not waiting for the prince to arrive.

Who has prepared a financially stable future for herself.

Imagine a woman who is taking full responsibility for her life.

A woman who has awakened to the truth about herself.

Who has assumed her rightful place in the human community.

Imagine a woman who has relinquished the desire for safety and approval.

A woman who makes a powerful statement with every action she takes.

Who asserts to herself the right to reorder the world.

MY OWN BUSINESS

While I enjoyed being home raising my three young children, a time came when we could no longer live on only my husband's income. I decided to open my own business: a family daycare in our home. This solution unearthed as many challenges as it solved, including my husband's opposition, my fragile self-confidence, and the reality of my "less than perfect" home but I was determined to make it work.

I drew on my previous office experience to compile contracts and forms. I worked very hard to present myself, my business, and my home in a professional way. Much to my surprise, I discovered a deep sense of pride in myself and the kind of work I did. I began to network with other family daycare providers for support and business tips. Soon I had a thriving business.

With the help of my recovery program, a circle of women, and a new found belief in my capabilities, I learned to use each difficult experience as a learning opportunity. I used my clients as a source of renewal and positive feedback. In response to my tendency to allow the comments and opinions of others to fan the flames of doubt about my choices and capabilities, I devised a questionnaire asking my present and former clients why they chose me as their provider. I also asked them about specific areas of service that I tended to obsess about, areas that weren't, in my eyes, quite good enough.

Most of the questionnaires contained glowing praise for my business and my abilities as a childcare provider. The written responses of my clients continue to provide a reality check whenever I have that "not good enough" feeling. They are a ready-made stack of affirmations that I can pull out and read on those down days. Again, I am reminded that I am good at what I do and parents, as well as their children, like me and appreciate what I have to offer. I also use them to prepare before an interview with a prospective client. Reading them is an easy way to feel instantly confident and strong.

Irene Nicol

In the last year I have had the courage to expand my business. I feel very good about what I do and the way I do it. I am here for my own family and will never go back to working for someone else. My day is my own to structure in a way that is pleasing and gratifying to me. I am in charge of my free time and I am in charge of my work time. I answer only to me.

I experienced a great surge of happiness a few months ago when I read an essay that my 13 year old daughter had written about the person she admired most. The essay was about me and my daycare business. If I ever had any doubts about starting the business and the impact it would have on my own family they vanished as I read her words. "I chose my mom because she inspires me. She inspires me because she went to college and got her degree. I also chose her because she's so smart. My mom owns her own business."

Irene Nicol is a licensed family daycare provider in Berkeley and mother to her own three children, ages 7, 11, and 13. Her daycare program of six children includes a mixture of infants, toddlers, and preschoolers. She continues to strive toward a better understanding of children and to meet the demands of combining parenting with a home-based full time business.

TAPESTRY

"My life has been a tapestry . . . " Carol King

On a rainy August morning in 1995, I stood in a circle of women of all nations, beating a drum, invoking spirit to consecrate the Healing Tent at the Non-Governmental Organizations Women's Forum in China. As a bodyworker, I had come to China to touch and be touched. I had come with a team of twenty six women from North America and seven Latin American countries. Where did the journey to China begin? What are some threads in my personal tapestry that led me to an international gathering of 30,000 women in my 52nd year?

I celebrate six colorful threads that weave through my life, leading to the decision to facilitate the Healing Tent in China. I honor the threads of commitment to women's strength, service, spirit, peace and justice, international consciousness, and healing.

I honor the thread of commitment to women's strength.

I always knew that a woman could do anything. In 1961 at East Bakersfield High School, California, I lettered magic marker posters . . . Vote for the High Woman, Vote for Lohman . . . first girl to run for student body president. I lost the election, but won self-esteem for myself and all my sisters.

In the late fifties, in a classroom jammed with erstwhile boy reporters, I sat clicking out an original story in the San Joaquin Valley Press Association sportswriting contest for high school students. I won first prize . . . three years running.

I honor the thread of service.

This thread was first woven into my tapestry by my parents, Neal and Gertrude Lohman, who devoted their lives to community and world service. She sewed, baked, and tutored. He fixed, built, and kept books. They were pillars of their local Methodist church.

In New York City in the 60's, I met the mothers of six young African-American men from Harlem. Their sons were in prison, convicted of murder. As liaison between the mothers and their sons' lawyers, I donated many hours in an effort to win a new trial. I organized a successful benefit, at which James Baldwin spoke. Years later, five of the young men were freed.

Joan Lohman

I celebrate the thread of spirit in my life.
In a hospital room in Bakersfield my brother and I breathed with my mother during her last hours. As friends came to say good bye and thank her for her presence in their lives, we felt spirit holding her gently. I sang to her,"Tis a gift to be simple."

The day my friend Diane died of cancer, I felt her spirit dancing wildly with me in a ritual circle of women. And my heart opened to spirit in crowded churches in Nicaragua. Despite the hardships of their lives, the poor filled the air with contagious joy as they sang the Misa Campesina, the peasants' mass. I wept and renewed my commitment to the people of Central America.

I celebrate the thread of peace and justice.
On Washington, D.C.'s snowy streets in the late sixties I marched with thousands of women in the Jeanette Ranking Brigade to protest the war in Vietnam. Outside Livermore's National Weapons lab, five hundred women protesters, jailed together for eleven days in old circus tents, created workshops, a gay day parade, and a birthday party for Emma Goldman. From crone elders I heard herstories of the labor and communist movements in the U.S. I marveled at the stamina, commitment and spirit of my senior sisters.

I honor the thread of international consciousness.
On the border between Nicaragua and Guatemala in 1984, a week before the Sandinista election victory, I held hands with Witness for Peace delegates from across the U.S. and Nicaraguan friends. As mortars exploded in the distance, we formed a warm, vulnerable human shield against contra attacks. In a humid classroom in the village of Mateare, Nicaragua, ten years later, I taught Rosen Touch to seamstresses and their children.

I cherish the thread of healing.
In the late eighties, a painful herniated lumbar disc became a powerful teacher. For weeks I lay under giant evergreen trees, resting and healing, unable to drive, work, or open a window. I sought chiropractic, massage, physical therapy, Rosen Bodywork. I stretched, meditated, prayed, swam. Always fiercely independent, I learned to depend upon friends, family, healers, and spirit. Three years later, I backpacked to 10,000 feet meadows in the Sierras.

An Indian woman dressed in a pale yellow sari turned to me in the Healing Tent. We had just completed a circle of Rosen touch. "You have touched me like I have never been touched before. You have touched me as my mother could never touch me." All the strands of my tapestry led to the Healing Tent. As women from every continent poured into the tent for classes, rejuvenation, information, I touched the women of the world and was in turn touched and changed.

Joan Lohman, a Rosen Method Bodywork Practitioner and massage therapist, gardens in Oakland California with her beloved partner, Jennifer Biehn. Joan brings massage and gentle stretching to elders in retirement settings. In 1995 she coordinated the program in the healing tent as co-leader of the bilingual CAPACITAR delegation to the 4th United Nations/NGO Women's Forum in China. Through CAPACITAR, an international network of women exchanging healing arts, she leads women's journeys to Nicaragua and Guatemala. Joan loves wilderness adventures, cross-country skiing, gardening, writing, poetry, singing and sports. For her 52nd birthday, she received a basketball hoop and dreams of starting a woman's masters team.

LOVING WILLFULNESS

To write this Self-Celebration with assurance and pride has meant being in the world fully and unequivocally as myself and accepting the consequences. I celebrate my ability to create a wondrously loving, engaged, and abundant life for myself. I celebrate the abiding faith in myself and the confidence to go after my dreams. I celebrate loving friendships and the respect of many in the larger community. I celebrate my marriage with a man who desires my happiness and contributes to it by loving and kind words and deeds. I celebrate my vision as founder of a nationally respected bookstore and, while working with a staff of dedicated professionals, full engagement in work that brings wisdom, beauty and spiritual dignity to the lives of others. I celebrate my family of origin, who are there in turbulent times to the best of their ability. I am accomplishing my life goals and look forward to possibilities, both imagined and unimagined.

Nothing in my Levittown, Pennsylvania girlhood prepared me for my life's accomplishments—on the surface. Looking deeper I remember the library of biographies my mother quietly created in my bedroom so that whenever I felt the need for a friend (I had four brothers) I could delve into the lives of Joan of Arc, Eleanor Roosevelt, Annie Oakley and Amelia Earhart for inspiration. My grandmother modeled for me a life of adventure and determination. Living in a small mining town she would transform a visit to the woods to pick berries into a sojourn of unimaginable opportunities for excitement. To a large extent who I've become is sculpted from forty five years worth of daily acts of steadfast determination to make my own choices and carve my own niche from the clay of life learned from these women—my real matrilineal heritage and the legacy of great women of the world.

Recently I was awarded Woman of the Year in my community and recognized for my work at GAIA Bookstore. Unlike the numerous awards given to the bookstore, this award was very deliberately an acknowledgement of me. As I stood at the podium looking out at the full audience, I was able to bathe in the pleasure of the honor I was given and to realize how much I enjoy the life I am living. In the front row sat many of my closest friends, women who have lived with dignity and accomplished great deeds that go unacknowledged in the history books yet are the basic soil of culture:

LOVING WILLFULNESS

starting their own business, tending to a dying parent, raising a son, building community, and creating housing for the homeless.

I celebrate my friendships with these women who are genuinely supportive, encouraging me to be fearless, to choose risk and daring over safety and stagnation. These women are intelligent and thoughtful, wickedly playful and striving to live authentic lives. An evening together with this circle of friends is always a gourmet life experience. I celebrate my friendships with women of spirit, grace, and power and I celebrate the passing of old friendships that served my growth in different gardens but needed new soil to grow in other directions.

In the audience among my friends sat my beloved husband. He is a kind and grateful man, without competitive urges towards me and with a sincere desire for my fulfillment and contentment. Our lives are entwined in love and creativity, as we strive together to reach our dreams as individual souls and as co-owners of GAIA. I celebrate the inner wisdom to recognize Eric's innate goodness and to choose a mate who would unequivocally support me in my life work.

On our second date as we stood together in the kitchen, and talked about what we wanted in our lives, I said: "One thing I know is that I don't want children." For years he had been in relationships with women who either desperately wanted a child or were anguishing about whether to have children. A look of delight crossed his face for he had made a similar choice but had never met a woman who felt as he did. My decisiveness opened the door for him to love me fully because he knew I wouldn't be wanting from him something he wasn't capable of giving. In that moment each of us knew that our need to create in the world was liberated to move in another direction. Our child, GAIA, was born out of the marriage of our numerous talents, and from our creation innumerable people have derived great spiritual benefit.

I believe that all acts of great endeavor are manifested and sustained through scores of engaged, attentive angels of detail who dwell within us. Anything worth doing will take all of your being to ride through the stages of despair, discomfort, and devotion required to do it well and to do it with dignity. I celebrate my enormous commitment to my life purpose and the

Patrice Wynne

challenges that have tested me every step of the way. My willfulness, my tenacity, and my capacity to endure difficulties have enabled me to stand at this midpoint of my life and say, I have the power to dream a new world.

When GAIA first opened in 1987 we placed a statue of the Goddess of Compassion, Kuan Yin, on an altar at the entrance to the bookstore. Though the store has been transformed innumerable times over the years, including several relocations, Kuan Yin has always remained close at hand and always by the door. Pouring the waters of compassion, she is a symbolic reminder of the spirit of lovingkindness that permeates all forms. I have found her presence comforting, rejuvenating, and empowering in my quest for enlightened action in the world. Without compassion for oneself, how can I be powerful? Behind her sweet countenance, she is the Goddess of Loving Willfulness, for to love the world one must step bravely into the world. The world awaits the visions of women, full of themselves.

Patrice Wynne is the founder, with her husband Eric Joost, of GAIA Bookstore & Community Center, in Berkeley, California, and the author of The Womanspirit Sourcebook, *published by Harper San Francisco. GAIA Bookstore specializes in resources from an emerging spiritual awareness which is transformative, evolutionary, wholistic, cross-cultural, and gender positive. GAIA hosts nightly author readings, concerts, workshops, community gatherings, and cultural events which reflect a search for meaning and values in contemporary culture. Patrice is on the Board of Directors of Northern California Independent Booksellers, New Alternative Publishing and Retail Alliance, and Educational Beginnings of the International Women's Studies Institute.*

A TRANSFORMED PERSPECTIVE:
FIFTY THINGS TO DO INSTEAD OF READING ANOTHER SELF-IMPROVEMENT BOOK, GOING ON ANOTHER DIET, OR STARTING ANOTHER SELF-HELP PROGRAM.

Imagine what your life will be like without the question "what's wrong with me" as the organizing focus. Here are fifty suggestions for what to do with your newly available time, energy, and resources.

1. *Eat an apple.*
2. Breathe!
3. Tape the stories of your mothers and grandmothers. Compile them into an anthology.
4. Volunteer at a local nursing home.
5. Write an editorial about the care of seniors in your community.
6. Start an after-school care program in your home for the children of single mothers.
7. Find out about America's first woman scientist.
8. Read the biography of a nineteenth century suffragette.
9. Rent "Bagdad Cafe" and invite your friends over for a Girl's Night Out (GNO).
10. ACT UP!

11. *Plant an apple tree.*
12. Go for a long walk and then take a luxurious bath.
13. Read the poems of Phyllis Wheatley.
14. Volunteer as a research-assistant for a feminist scholar in your community.
15. Write a poem about your first best friend.
16. Start a "Be Full of Yourself" Club for the girls in your community.
17. Find out about America's first woman doctor.
18. Read the biography of a nineteenth century woman-abolitionist.
19. Rent "Daughters of the Dust" and invite your friends over for a GNO.
20. *LOOSEN UP!*

21. *Bake an apple pie.*
22. Create a painting-space in your garage and free the images within you.
23. Read the poems of Sappho.
24. Volunteer at a battered women's shelter in your community.
25. Write a short story about your first job.
26. Co-author a children's book with your grandchildren.
27. Find out about America's first abortion-rights advocate.
28. Read the biography of a nineteenth century woman-abolitionist.
29. Rent "Antonia's Line" and invite your friends over for a GNO.
30. SPEAK UP!

31. *Climb an apple tree.*
32. Create a meditation-space in your home and nourish the spirit within you.
33. Read the poems of Ntosake Shange.
34. Volunteer as a research-assistant for a feminist minister in your community.
35. Write a sermon challenging the idolatry of god the father.
36. Start a school for girls.
37. Find out about America's first woman minister.
38. Read *The Woman's Bible.*.
39. Rent "Thelma & Louise" and invite your friends over for a GNO.
40. LIGHTEN UP!

41. *Bob for apples with your women's circle.*
42. Create a dance-space in your home and free the movements within you.
43. Read the essays of Audre Lourde.
44. Volunteer as a research-assistant for a feminist physician in your community.
45. Write a song about wearing your first bra.
46. Plan a rite of passage ritual for the adolescent girls in your community.
47. Find out about America's first woman saxophonist.
48. Read *The Creation of Patriarchy.*
49. Rent "Fried Green Tomatoes" and invite your friends over for a GNO.
50. BITE INTO YOUR LIFE AND THE FULLNESS OF ITS POSSIBILITY!

A TRANSFORMED PERSPECTIVE
"Be Full of Yourself!" Groups
Suggested Format

WELCOME: Welcome to the "Be Full of Yourself" group. I am _____. I will hold the circle this evening.

A CENTERING MEDITATION: (See suggested meditation.)

INTRODUCTIONS: If this is your first time here and you came alone, introduce yourself and share with us something you appreciate about yourself. If you brought a friend to our circle, introduce them and share something you appreciate about them.

EXPLANATION OF SELF-CELEBRATION: Many of us grow up asking, "what's wrong with me." This question regularly punctuates our lives as we search far and wide for someone to give us an answer, for someone to offer us a magical insight, treatment, or cure. We have learned a shame-based way of perceiving ourselves and relating to the world. As a result, our natural tendency is to feel inadequate, that we're never quite good enough no matter what we do. For most of us, it would be easier to compose a list of our flaws and character defects than to compose a list of the life-affirming behaviors that flow from our lives.

In this group, we affirm that all of creation is good; that we are originally blessed, not cursed; and that there is strength, goodness, and creativity within each of us. We have discovered that the good is deeply embedded within us, and that it is broad and generous enough to include our injuries. As we embrace our original goodness, our inner spaces are cleared out and reclaimed as our own. We find rest within our lives and accept all of ourselves as worthy.

READING OF WOMAN-AFFIRMING PERSPECTIVES: Our commitment to self-celebration is based on six woman-affirming perspectives. As they are read, celebrate your inner resources. You have everything you need within the rich resources of your own life. The richness of the universe pulsates through you. Be full of yourself! (See attached list of "Six Woman-Affirming Perspectives.")

OPTION 1: FOR "BE FULL OF YOURSELF!" GROUP FOCUSED ON BOOK THE SPEAKER: At each meeting, we will read and discuss selected portions of the book *Be Full of Yourself!* Tonight we will read Chapter ____, pages ___ - ___. (Read aloud or silently according to group conscience.)

SHARING CIRCLE: Now is the time for our open sharing circle. You are invited to bring the questions, insights, and celebrations triggered by the reading into the circle. These are our guidelines for sharing: Each woman is invited to share her experience, strength, and hope without interruption, judgment, criticism, or argument. This "no cross talk" approach supports us to take responsibility for ourselves and to respect each other's sacred journey. We witness and acknowledge each woman's story in silence across a respectful distance.

OPTION 2: FOR AN ONGOING "BE FULL OF YOURSELF!" GROUP
THE SPEAKER: At each meeting, we will hear from a woman is full of herself and who is embracing self-celebration as a healing resource in her life. Tonight's speaker is _____. Welcome!

SHARING CIRCLE: Now is the time for our open sharing circle. During our time together this evening, you are invited to open to the depths of goodness within you and to practice self-celebration. We invite you to bring your life challenges, your creative potential, and your experiments with self-celebration into the circle. These are our guidelines for sharing: Each woman is invited to share her experience, strength, and hope without interruption, judgment, criticism, or argument. This "no cross talk" approach supports us to take responsibility for ourselves and to respect each other's sacred journey. We witness and acknowledge each woman's story in silence across a respectful distance.

GROUP ANNOUNCEMENTS:

CLOSING CIRCLE: "In The Very Beginning Was The Mother" Movement Blessing

"Be Full of Yourself!" Groups
Suggested Meditation

Come home to your breath. Turn your attention inward by taking a few deep breaths. Savor the breath of life as it flows in and through and around you. As you inhale, gather all of yourself from the far reaches of your life. Bring your energy and attention "home." As you exhale, release the accumulation of your day. Weave an affirmation into each breath: "I come home to my breath. Home is always waiting."

Come home to your body. As you breathe deeply, turn your attention toward your body. Move or stretch it, touch or massage it, or imagine the breath reaching into each part of your body while you affirm: "I come home to my body. Home is always waiting."

Come home to your inner life. Imagine being a leaf let go of by an autumn tree . . . a leaf slowly and gradually descending toward the ground . . . its descent cushioned by the breath of life . . . a leaf touching the ground of your being. Make conscious contact with the ground of your being. Make conscious contact with yourself.

Turn a merciful eye toward yourself. Look upon yourself with loving kindness and notice what it is you delight in and appreciate about yourself today.

"BE FULL OF YOURSELF!" GROUPS
SIX WOMAN-AFFIRMNG PERSPECTIVES

I. Our Original Goodness

WE REJECT the dominance of a creation myth that portrays women as the instigators of evil. We reject the historical, theological, societal, and familial messages that stressed our wrongs, our defects, and our insufficiencies, requiring the relinquishment of our natural capacities.

WE EMBRACE a woman-affirming perspective that reminds us of the original goodness and sanctity of all life, that it is right and good that we are women. In circles of women, we recover ancient beliefs, affirming that all of creation is good; that we are originally blessed, not cursed; and that there is strength, goodness, and creativity within each of us. We reclaim Eve as our champion and join women from every age who have committed the forbidden act of stepping outside of systems of thought and belief that denied their very existence. Women who refuse to ask the question, "What's wrong with me?" Women who make a powerful statement with every thought they share, every feeling they express, and every action they take on their own behalf. Women full of themselves.

II. Our Original Equality

WE REJECT the dominance of cultural and religious myths and rituals that excluded the Mother from the creation of the world and the girl-child from the divine. We reject the hierarchically-based messages that convinced us of our inferiority and secondary status in the "natural order," barring us from full participation in the affairs of family, church, community, and world.

WE EMBRACE a woman-affirming perspective that reminds us of our original equality and that celebrates the Mother's intimate involvement in the origins of life. In circles of women, we learn of ancient women who did not apologize for their fertile wombs, pregnant bellies, and full breasts. Women who celebrated themselves as the embodiment of the Mother of All Living. We learn of ancient times when it was from the mother, the giver of life, that the line of the generations was traced. A time when all children born of the mother were legitimate and respectable, and were given her name and social status. We learn of ancient women who did not apologize for their girl-children. Mothers and daughters, full of themselves!

III. Our Original Reverence

WE REJECT the dominance of cultural and religious myths, stories, rituals, and taboos that assault a woman's body and her natural processes. We reject the shame-based messages that alienated us from the rich natural resources found within our own body's cycles and rhythms, and that deposited within us a dread of the aging process.

WE EMBRACE a woman-affirming perspective that reminds us of the original sacredness and wisdom of our bodies in every season of life and that encourages us to fill up the years of our lives without shame. In circles of women, we read of ancient beliefs that a woman's blood was magic, flowing in harmony with the moon. We recall ancient times when the color of royalty was the dark red wine color of our menstrual blood. We learn of ancient women who did not apologize for their bleeding time. We recall ancient societies that celebrated the accumulation of a woman's years and that respected the menopausal retaining of her wise blood. We learn of ancient post-menopausal women who presided at sacred rituals. Women who did not apologize for the fullness of their years and their wisdom. Women full of themselves!

IV. Our Original Self-Possession

WE REJECT the dominance of cultural and religious myths and theologies that exiled self-possessed women and elevated submissive women who relinquished the ownership of their bodies, the authorship of their lives, and the naming of their experience. We reject the dependency-based messages that emphasized our inability to control our own destinies and to function independently in our own lives.

WE EMBRACE a woman-affirming perspective that reminds us of our original self-possession. In circles of women, we recall ancient times when virginity meant a woman who was "one in herself," owned by no man, author of her own life, and creator of her own destiny. We learn of ancient women who did not apologize for their self-possession. Women who refused to surrender the ownership of their bodies except to their natural rhythms and cycles. Women who refused to surrender the authorship of their lives except to their deepest wisdom. Women who refused to surrender the naming of their experience except to their inner truth. Women full of themselves!

V. Our Original Willfulness

WE REJECT the dominance of cultural and religious myths and theologies that exiled willful women, portraying us as powerless victims incapable of independent thought and action, of self-determining choice, and of the successful implementation of our desires in the world. We reject the passivity-based messages that required the surrender of our wills to the dictates of others.

WE EMBRACE a woman-affirming perspective that reminds us of our original willfulness. In circles of women, we remember ancient women who valued their willfulness and who encouraged their daughters to know their own will and to believe it was valid and achievable in the world. We remember ancient ways that taught women to refuse submission and subordination and applauded women for their assertiveness. Women who exerted, initiated, and moved in their own behalf without shame or guilt and in harmony with their own deep wisdom. Women full of themselves!

VI. Our Original Connection

WE REJECT the dominance of cultural and religious attitudes that foster rivalry and suspicion among women. We reject the competition-based attitudes that set women up to compete with each other for the attention of men. We reject the homophobic messages that alienate us from each other and from the organic resources available in women-centered relationships. We refuse to give credence to attitudes and fears designed to keep us separate.

WE EMBRACE a woman-affirming perspective, reminding us of our original connection and solidarity with all women past, present, and future. In circles of women, we recall ancient times when daughters celebrated their essential connection to the mother from whom they came and to whom they return. We remember ancient women who valued each other and sat in circles together to tell their stories and to remind each other of the truth. We remember women who did not apologize for their love of women. Women full of themselves . . . and each other!

"BE FULL OF YOURSELF!" GROUPS
SUGGESTED TOPICS FOR ONE YEAR OF MEETINGS

Group 1   *Introductory Meeting*
Use suggested format as the focus of the meeting.
Acquaint group with each aspect of format.

Group 2 - 10   Outrageous Words: Assuming Intellectual Equality
Week 2   Read and discuss Chapter 2.
Week 3   Read & discuss Wollstonecraft.(Refer to Rousseau in Ch 1)
Week 4   Read & discuss Stanton.(Refer to Paul/Luther/Barth)
Week 5   Read and discuss De Beauvoir.(Refer to Freud in Chap.1)
Week 6   Read and discuss Lerner.(Refer to Rousseau in Chapter 1)
Week 7   Read and discuss Horowitz.(Refer to Aristotle/Aquinas)
Week 8   Read and discuss Lorde.(Refer to Freud in Chapter 1)
Week 9   Read and discuss Gadon.(Refer to Philo in Chapter 1)
Week 10 *Exercise: A Woman-Affirming Immersion*

Groups 10 - 15   Forbidden Acts: Assuming Theological Equality
Week 10   Read and Discuss "An Encounter With Eve.
Week 11   Read and Discuss "Re-Imagine Your Beginnings."
Week 12   Read and Discuss "Re-claim the Divine Feminine."
Week 13   Read and Discuss "Re-define Sin."
Week 14   Read and Discuss "Re-write the Scripture."
Week 15 *Ritual: In Celebration of Eve's Forbidden Act*

Groups 16 - 24 Healing Tasks: Assuming Personal Responsibility
Week 16   Love Your Body
Week 17   Befriend Your Organic Needs
Week 18   Embrace Your Sexual Autonomy
Week 19   Express the Full Range of Human Emotion
Week 20   Assume Intellectual Equality
Week 21   Own Your Original Creativity
Week 22   Honor Your Separate-Self
Week 23   Be Full of Yourself!
Week 24 *Ritual: A Vow of Faithfulness To One's Own Life*

Groups 24 - 30   *The Language of Self-Celebration*

Week 24   The Vocabulary of Goodness
Week 25   The Vocabulary of Equality
Week 26   The Vocabulary of Reverence
Week 27   The Vocabulary of Self-Possession
Week 28   The Vocabulary of Willfulness
Week 29   The Vocabulary of Connection
Week 30   *Exercise: Transforming Your Inner Dialog*

Groups 31 - 38   *Practicing Self-Celebration*

Week 31   Celebrating Women
Week 32   Celebrating Creativity
Week 33   Celebrating Ordinary Life
Week 34   Celebrating Woman-Body
Week 35   Celebrating Feelings
Week 36   Celebrating a Self-Defined Life
Week 37   Celebrating a Self-Defined Spirituality
Week 38   Celebrating Women Present in the World

Woman-Affirming Movies

Every third meeting during your first year, alter the format and watch a woman-affirming movie. Discuss it afterwards from the perspective of self-celebration.

Antonia's Line
A Trip to Bountiful
Bagdad Cafe
Beaches
Boys on the Side
Daughters of the Dust
First Wives' Club
Fly Away Home
Fried Green Tomatoes
Julia
The Associate
The Secret of Roan Inish
Thelma & Louise
The Turning Point

NOTES

Introduction

1. My three primary concerns about the principles of the Twelve Step movement were addressed in *A God Who Looks Like Me* (Ballantine, 1995): the extensive use of male god-language (pp.93-96); the emphasis on ego-deflation (pp.136 - 138); and the requirement of surrender to a power greater than oneself (pp.187-190). A more extensive treatment of each of the Twelve Steps will be available in the upcoming *A Deeper Wisdom: The Twelve Steps From a Woman's Perspective* (Open Window Creations, 1999).

Chapter 1

2. In addition, they were all men of privilege whose writings include race and class biases.
3. Sigmund Freud, "Femininity," in *Freud on Women*, ed. Elisabeth Young-Bruehl (New York: W. W. Norton and Co., 1990), p. 342.
4. Mary Pipher, *Reviving Ophelia: Saving The Selves of Adolescent Girls* (New York: Ballantine Books, 1994), p. 44.
5. I have adapted Aristotle's opening remarks from his writings. As the dispassionate narrator of the symposium, I have taken literary licence over the years and "put words in the mouths" of the participants based on an overall understanding of their worldview.
6. Semen fascinated Aristotle. He considered male semen to be the primary source of life. According to him, women were weaker than men because they didn't produce it. The words seminal, seminar, disseminate, etc. hold within them the assumption of male superiority. One dictionary defines seminal as: "derived of, containing, or consisting of seed or semen; having the character of an original principle or source; contributing the seeds of later deeds."
7. Aristotle, *Historia Animalium*, Book IX, Chapter 1, tr. A. L. Peck (Cambridge: Harvard University Press, 1965), p. 219.
8. Aristotle, *Economics*, Book I, Chapter 3, tr. Edward Walford (London: Hhenry G. Bohn, 1853), p. 292.
9. Putting words in Philo's mouth based on an understanding of his worldview and the historical context within which he lived.
10. Philo, *Questions and Answers on Genesis*, Book I, in Philo Supplement II, tr. Ralph Marcus (Cambridge, Harvard University Press, 1953), p. 16.
11. Ibid., p. 20.
12. Ibid., p. 22.
13. See Gerda Lerner, *The Creation of Feminist Consciousness*, p. 140 (". . . most of the comments pertaining to women attributed to Paul were not written or spoken by him but by post-apostolic writers who ascribed the texts to him for greater authority." So it seems I join a group of infamous writers by putting more words in Paul's mouth!
14. Tertullian, "On the Apparel of Women," in *The Ante-Nicene Fathers*, vol. 4 (Buffalo: The Christian Literature Publishing Company), p. 14.
15. Tertullian, "The Veiling of Virgins," in *The Ante-Nicene Fathers*, p. 37.

16. Ibid, p. 37.
17. Augustine, *Confessions*, Tr. Vernon J. Bourke (New York: Fathers of The Church, Inc., 1953), p. 452.
18. Putting words in Augustine's mouth based on an understanding of his world-view and the theological context within which he wrote.
19. Augustine, *De Trinitate* 7.7.10, in *Sexism and God Talk*, Rosemary Radford Reuther (Boston: Beacon Press, 1983), page 95.
20. Putting words in Aquinas' mouth based on the ongoing nature of the good old boys' club and its reverence for Aristotle.
21. Thomas Aquinas, *Summa Theologica*, Part I, Question 92, In *Thomas Aquinas*, Vol. 4, Tr. by the Fathers of the English Dominican Province (London: Burn Oates Washborourns LTD, 1912).
22. Putting words in Luther's mouth. Italicized words are a direct quote from his *Lectures on Genesis*, Volume 1, found in *Luther's Works*, ed. Jaroslav Pelikan (St. Louis: Concordia Publishing House, 1958).
23. See *What Luther Says: An Anthology*, Ed. Ewald M. Plass (St. Louis: Concordia Publishing House, 1959), p. 1457.
24. Putting words in Kramer and Sprenger's mouths based on an understanding of the historical context within which they carried out their horrific task. Italicized words are a direct quote from *The Malleus Maleficarum*.
25. Heinrich Kramer and James Sprenger, *The Malleus Maleficarum*, Tr. Montague Summers (New York: Dover Publishers, 1971), p. 43.
26. Putting words in Rousseau's mouth based on an understanding of his educational philosophy and the historical context within which he wrote.
27. Jean Jacques Rousseau, *Emile*, Tr. Barbara Foxley (London: J. M. Dent, 1955), p. 321f.
28. Putting words in Freud's mouth based on his radical redefinition of female sexuality which would have seemed farfetched to his Symposium colleagues.
29. Sigmund Freud, "On the Sexual Theories of Children" in *Freud on Women*, p. 158.
30. Sigmund Freud, "Femininity" in *Freud on Women*, p. 353.
31. Karl Barth, *Church Dogmatics*, Vol. III, 4 (Edinburgh: T. & T. Clarke, 1961), p. 170-172.
32. Charles Radding, *A World Made By Men: Cognition and Society* (Chapel Hill: University of North Carolina Press, 1985), Introduction. Note that only two women are listed in the index of Radding's book.
33. Mary Pipher, *Reviving Ophelia*, p. 39.
34. Ibid. p. 41.
35. See *What Luther Says: An Anthology*, p. 1457.
36. See Karl Barth, *Church Dogmatics*, p. 170-172.
37. In Freud's words: "Shame, which is considered to be a feminine characteristic par excellence but is a far more a matter of convention than might be supposed, has as its purpose, we believe, concealment of genital deficiency. We are not forgetting that at a later time shame takes on other functions. It seems that women have made few contributions to the discoveries and inventions in the history of civilization . . ." (in "Femininity," found in *Freud on Women*, p. 360)
38. Epiphanius, *Medicine Box*, in *When Women Were Priests*, Karen Jo Torjesen (San Francisco: Harper and Row, 1993), p.43.

39. See *When Women Were Priests*, Karen Jo Torjesen.

Chapter 2

40. Philo, *Questions and Answers on Exodus*, in Philo Supplement, tr. Ralph Marcus (Cambridge, Harvard University Press, 1953), p. 15.
41. *Gospel of Thomas* 51:19-26, Nag Hammadi Library (New York, 1977), p. 130.
42. See Gillian Cloke, *This Female Man of God* (London; New York: Routledge), 1995.
43. Palladius, *The Lausiac History*, tr. Robert T. Meyer (Maryland: The Newman Press, 1965), pp. 36-37.
44. Mary Wollstonecraft, *A Vindication of the Rights of Woman*, (New York: W. W. Norton, 1967), p. 58.
45. Ibid, p. 59.
46. Elizabeth Cady Stanton, *The Woman's Bible*, 1898 (Seattle: Coalition Task Force on Women and Religion, 1974), Introduction.
47. Simone de Beauvoir, *The Second Sex* (New York: Alfred A. Knopf, Inc., 1953).
48. Gerda Lerner, *The Majority Finds Its Past* (New York: Oxford University Press, 1986), p. 228.
49. Ibid., 180.
50. Maryanne Cline Horowitrz, "Aristole and Woman," *Journal of the History of Biology*, vol. 9, no. 2 (Fall, 1970), p. 197.
51. Audre Lorde, "Uses of the Erotic: The Erotic as Power" in *Sister Outsider* (The Crossing Press, New York 1984), p.53f.
52. Elinor W. Gadon, *The Once and Future Goddess* (San Francisco: Harper & Røw, 1989), p. xii-xiii.
53. Due to copywrite complications I did not include the poetry of these women. Find their poems and read them along with their partner-writings outside the symposium: ". . . refusing dissection/they are women and poets and theorists/who gather our brokenness/into their words . . ."

> Biting into biology with Mary Ann Cline: "The Anatomy Lesson" by Susan Griffin in *Made From the Earth* (New York: Harper & Row, 1982) pp. 101-102.

> Biting into history with Gerda Lerner: "Shakespeare's Sister" by Virginia Wolf in *A Room of One's Own* (New York: Harcourt Brace Jovanovich, 1929), pp. 117-118.

> Biting into philosophy with Simone de Beauvoir: "In the men's room" by Marge Piercy in *Circles on the Water: Selected Poems* (New York: Alfred A. Knopf, 1985).

> Biting into theology with Elizabeth Cady Stanton: "Everywoman Her Own Theology" by Alicia Ostriker in *The Imaginary Lover* (Pittsburg: University of Pittsburg Press, 1986).

> Biting into god with Elinor Gadon: "We need a God Who Bleeds Now" by Ntozake Shange in *A Daughter's Geography*.

54. Gerda Lerner, *The Creation of Patriarchy* (New York: Oxford University Press, 1986), p. 228.

Chapter 3

55. *Key of Heaven: A Manual of Catholic Devotions*, Ed. J. M. Lelen (Catholic Book Publishing Co., 1947), pp. 39-40.
56. *Key of Heaven*, p. 187.

Chapter 4

57. An Encounter With Eve. Resources for further exploration:

   Elaine Pagels, *The Gnostic Gospels*, (New York: Vintage Books, 1979), pp. 53, 57-58.

   J. Phillips, *Eve: The History of an Idea*, (San Francisco: Harper and Row, 1984), p. 3.

   Barbara Walker, *The Woman's Encyclopedia of Myths and Secrets*, (San Francisco: Harper and Row, 1983), p. 288-291.

   Ecclesiasticus 25:24; I Kings 11:5; II Kings 21:7

   Robert Graves and Raphael Patai, *Hebrew Myths: The Book of Genesis* (N.Y.: Doubleday & Co., 1964), pp. 26-27.

   Patricia Monaghan, *The Book of Goddesses and Heroines* (Minnesota: Llewellyn Publications, 1990), pp.118-119.

   Merlin Stone, *When God Was a Woman*, (New York: Harcourt Brace Jovanovich, 1976), p. 199-214, 214-218.

58. Letter from Elizabeth Cady Stanton to Matilda J. Gage, reprinted in The Liberal Thinker (Syracuse, N. Y., 1890) as cited in Gerda Lerner, *The Creation of Feminist Consciousness*, p. 164.
59. Ibid.
60. Program of Women's National Liberal Union Convention, Feb. 24-25, 1890, Washington, C. C. as cited ibid.
61. Available in greeting card form from Open Window Creations.
62. See Gerda Lerner, *The Creation of Patriarchy*.
63. See *A God Who Looks Like Me: Discovering a Woman-Affirming Spirituality* (New York: Ballantine Books, 1995).
64. Their stories are found in *A God Who Looks Like Me*.
65. Available in booklet form from Open Window Creations. See appendix.
66. Adaptation of infancy narrative found in Theodore W. Kraus, "Jesus: The Divine Child of The West," Creation, Jan.- Feb. 1989, p. 17.
67. Adapted from the Baptist Hymnal, "There's Power in the Blood," p. 193.

Chapter 5

68. Masters & Johnson, *Human Sexual Response* (Boston: Little, Brown and Company, 1966), p. 45: "Unfortunately, the specific roles previously assigned clitoral function in female sexual response were designated by objective male consideration uninfluenced by and even uninformed by female subjective expression."
69. Mary Pipher, *Reviving Ophelia* (New York: Ballantine Books, 1996), p. 44.

Chapter 6

70. There are many forms of fundamentalism. For some women, feminism functioned in the same way religious fundamentalism did in my life. They got *caught in the swirl* of feminism and lost their balance. A "swirl" is any relationship or person; religion, cause, or dogma; food or drug; activity or project outside of yourself that becomes the controlling or organizing focus of your time, energy, and attention. A "swirl" requires you to move away from your inner life of feelings, needs, and inner wisdom. In the process, you lose touch with your body by ignoring its organic needs; your breath by tightening the abdomen; and your inner life by neglecting to check-in with your inner wisdom and resources.
71. Apart from the retreat context, I work with individual women and smaller groups to create commitment ceremonies, reflecting their personal or group intentions.
72. The "Home is Always Waiting" meditation tape is available from OWC.
73. Patricia Lynn Reilly offers "Vowing Faithfulness To Your Own Life" retreats throughout the country. Contact Open Window Creations for a schedule of upcoming retreats. The Commitment Ceremony is available in booklet form from OWC.

Chapter 7

74. Walt Whitman, *Leaves of Grass* (New York: Grosset and Dunlap, 1931).
75. Review Simone de Beauvoir's writings in Chapter 2.

About The Author

PATRICIA LYNN REILLY holds a Master of Divinity degree from Princeton Theological Seminary and post-graduate certification from the Women's Theological Center in Women's Spirituality and Feminist Theology. As the founder of Open Window Creations, she conducts women's spirituality and creativity retreats; publishes inspirational resources; and provides project-development, publicity-consultation, and event-coordination services to artists, authors, and small businesses. Her first book *A God Who Looks Like Me: Discovering A Woman-Affirming Spirituality* (Ballantine, 1995) took her to over sixty cities. Patricia lives on Northern California's Sonoma Coast, where the forest meets the ocean.

Companion Resources

PATRICIA LYNN REILLY offers a variety of workshops, retreats, and presentations based on the material in this book. She has also developed woman-affirming resources to enhance the reader's experience of the book, including:

"In The Very Beginning Was The Mother"greeting card and postcard. (Chapters 4 and 6)

"Home is Always Waiting Meditation"cassette. (Chapter 6)

"Breathe" greeting card. (Chapter 6)

Commitment Ceremony booklet. (Chapter 6)

"Imagine A Woman" postcard. (Chapter 8)

"Be Full of Yourself!" greeting card, poster, and group format booklet.

If you would like a schedule of upcoming events and a brochure of companion resources, write, call, fax, or e-mail:

Open Window Creations
P.O. Box 493
Gualala, California 95445
Phone/Fax: 707-785-1902
E-Mail: openwin@mcn.org

Upcoming Projects

OPEN WINDOW CREATIONS invites you to submit your self-celebratory poetry and prose for use in a future anthology. Use the capacities in Chapter 6 and the categories in Chapter 8 as your guide. Please send them to OWC at the above address.